T. Kitahara Collection

WIND-UPS

Tin Toy Dreams

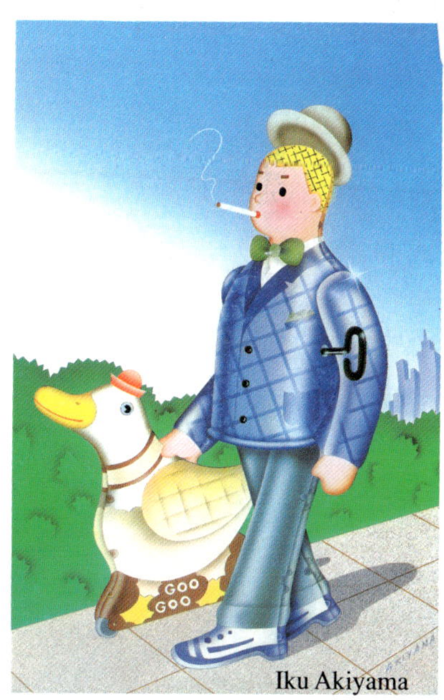

By Teruhisa Kitahara

Chronicle Books · San Francisco

Illustlation by Iku Akiyama

First published in the United States
1985 by Chronicle Books.

First published in Japan by Shinko Music Publishing Co., Ltd. Printed in Japan by Dai Nippon Printing Co., Ltd., Tokyo.

Library of Congress Cataloging in Publication Data

Kitahara, Teruhisa, 1948–
Wind-ups: tin toy dreams.

(Wonderland of toys)
Previously published as: Japanese tin toys. Tokyo: Shinko Music, 1983. With text in Japanese.
1. Tin toys–Collectors and collecting–Japan.
I. Title II. Series: Kitahara, Teruhisa. Wonderland of toys.
TS2301.T7K48 1985 688.7
85-12811 ISBN 0-87701-367-5

10 9 8 7 6 5 4 3 2 1

Editor: Isao Kusano
Art Director: Takuya Ohno
Photography: Yakio Shimizu
Illustration: Iku Akiyama

Chronicle Books
One Hallidie Plaza
San Francisco, CA 94102

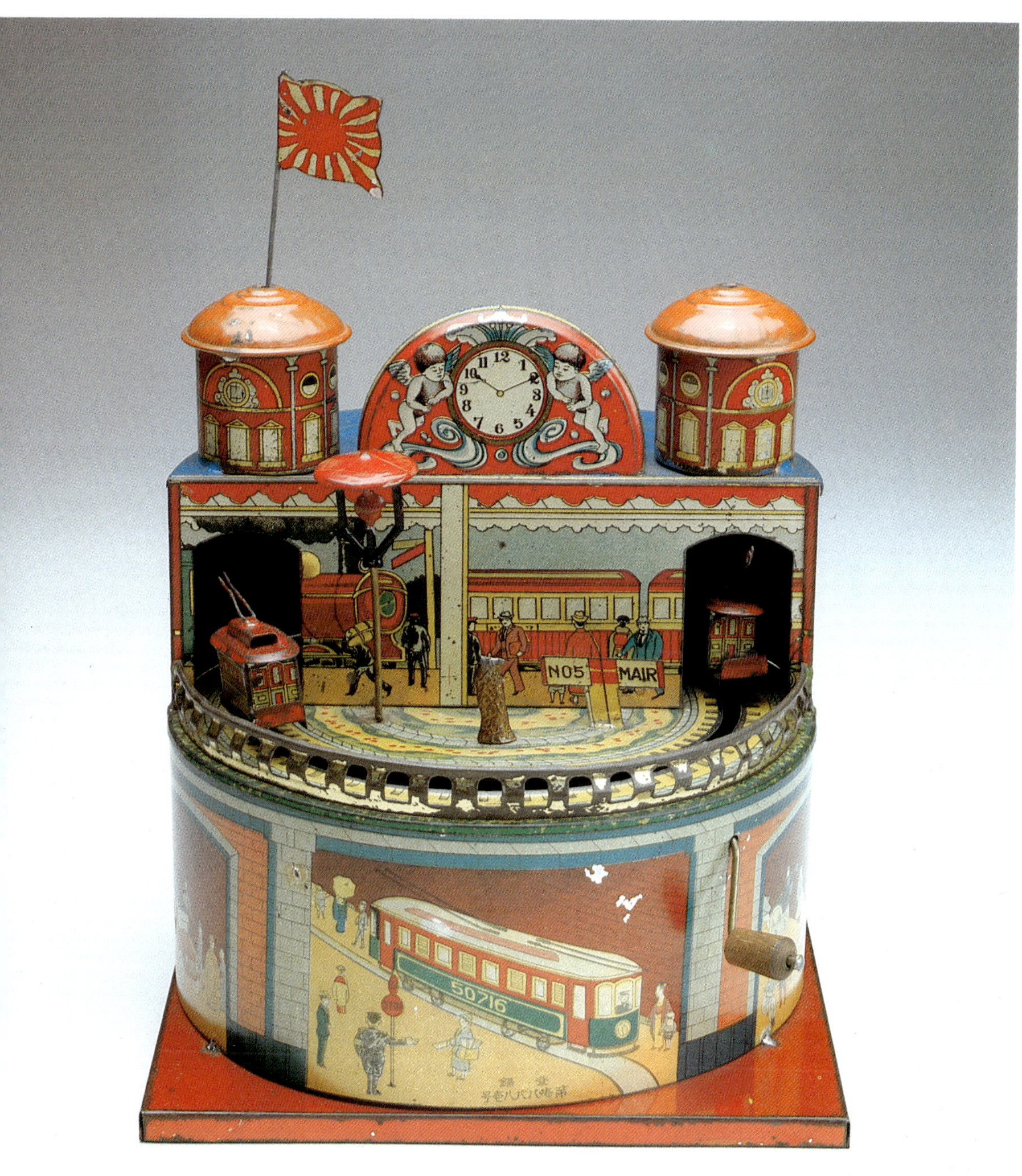

1910'S／STREET CAR／UNKNOWN／150×150×160

MBER／DECADE／NAME／MAKER／SIZE: depth×width×height(mm)

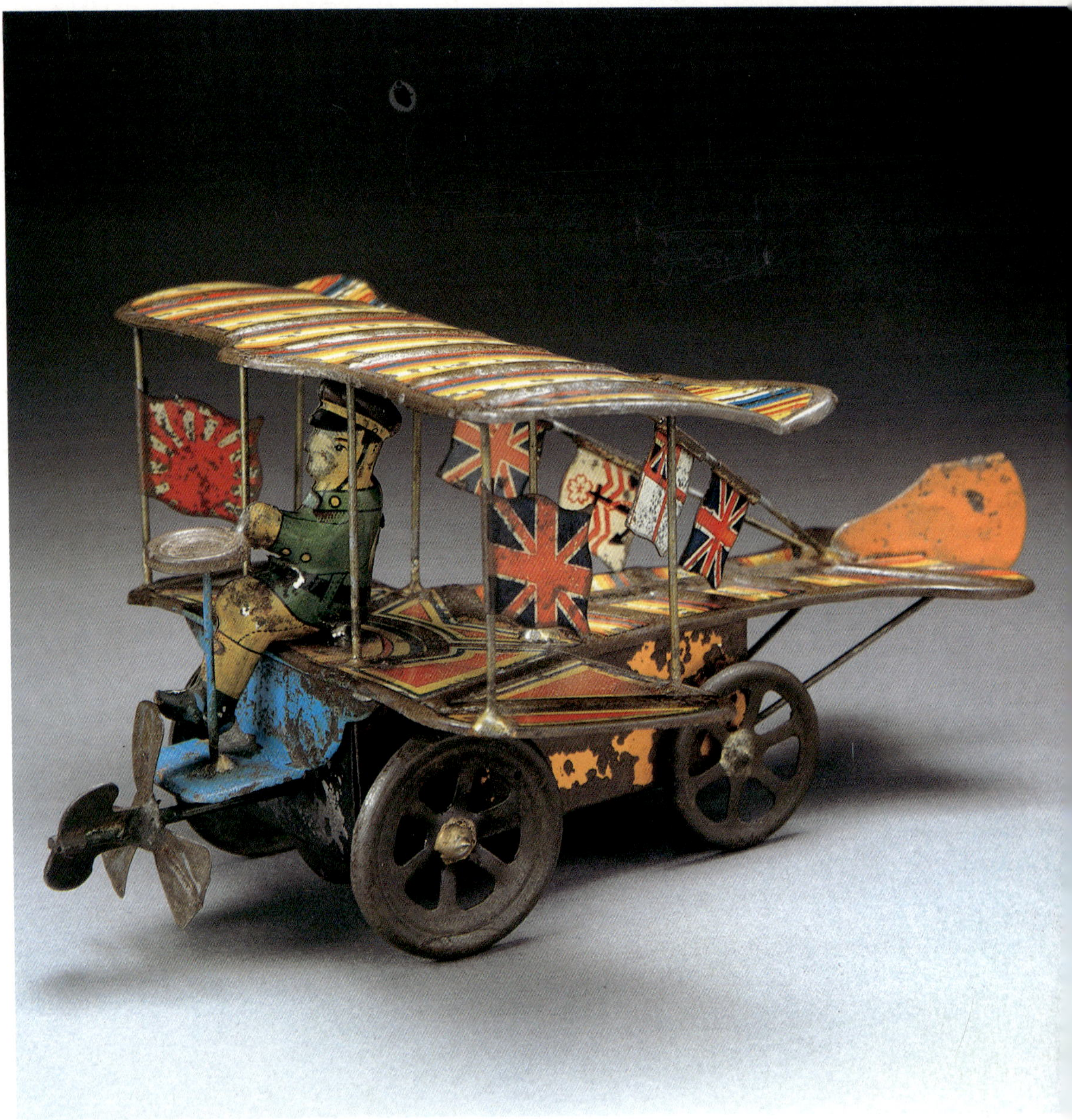

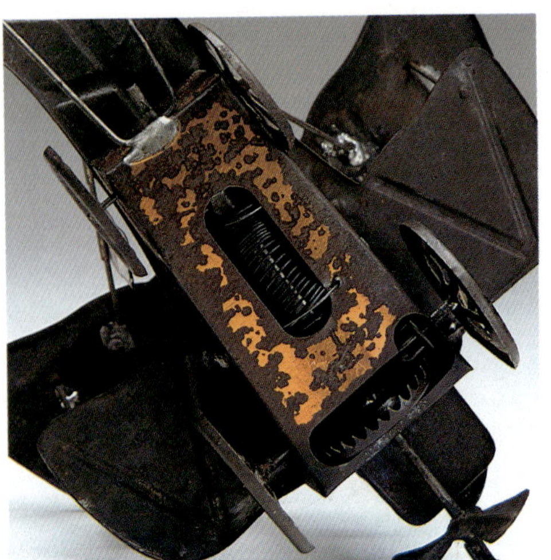

②1900'S/BIPLANE/UNKNOWN/180×140×90

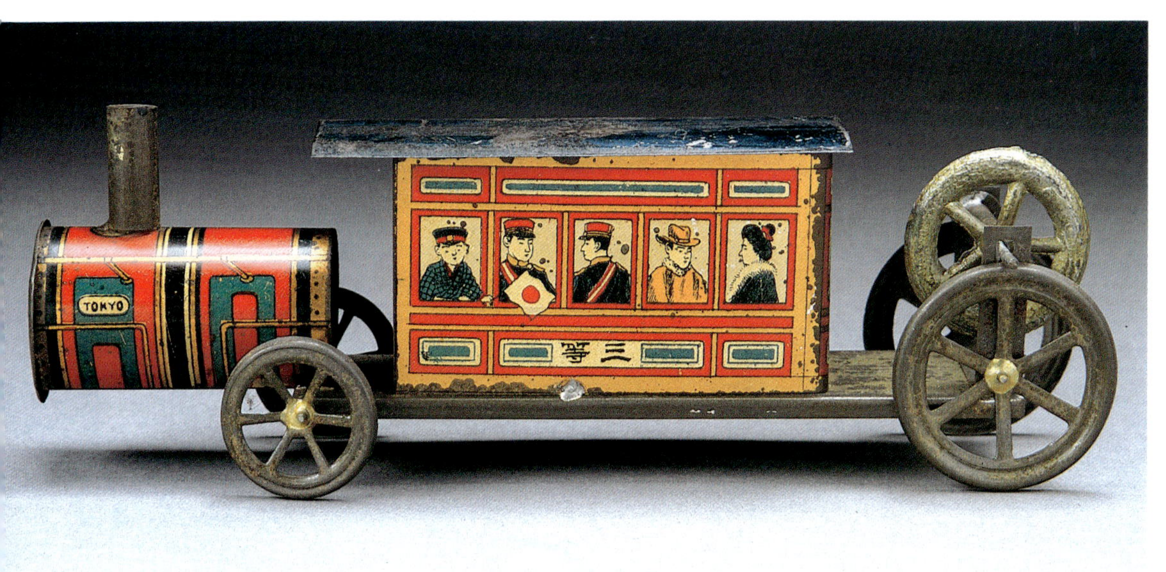

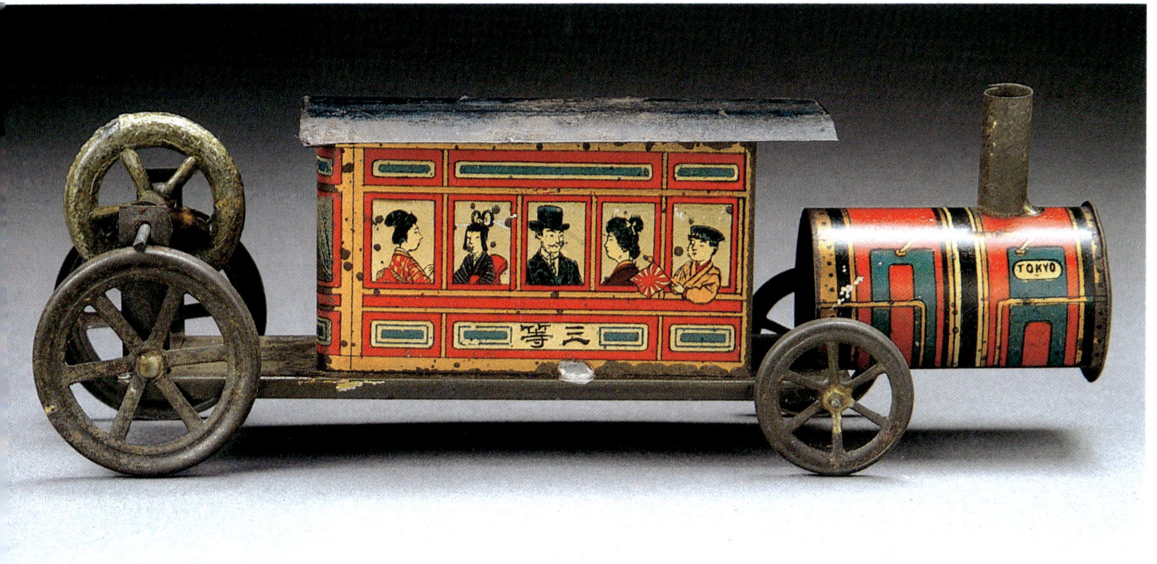

③1880'S／LOCOMOTIVE／UNKNOWN／162×36×50

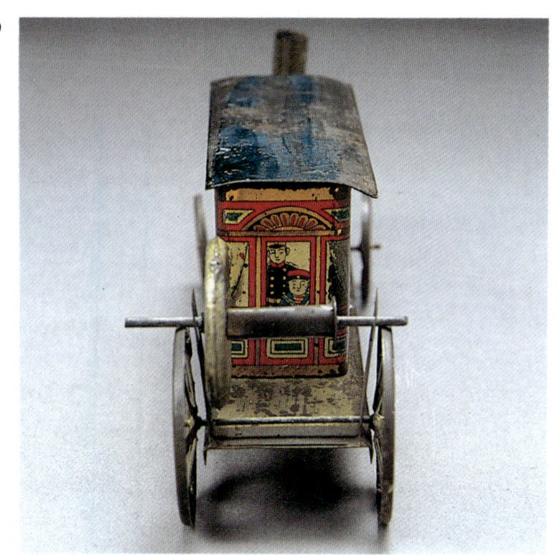

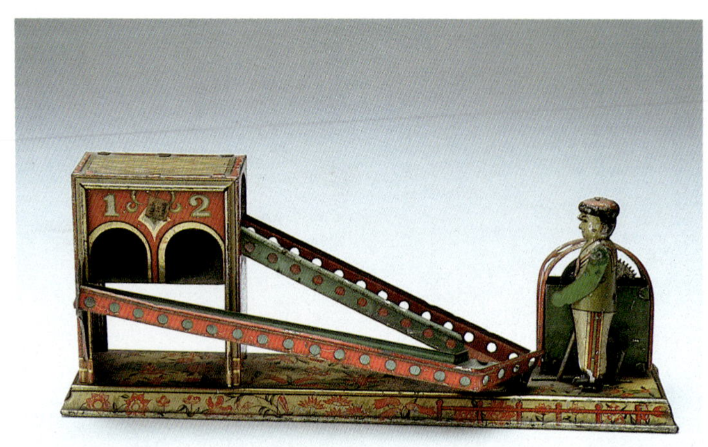

④1920'S／BALL KICKER／UNKNOWN／230×70×90

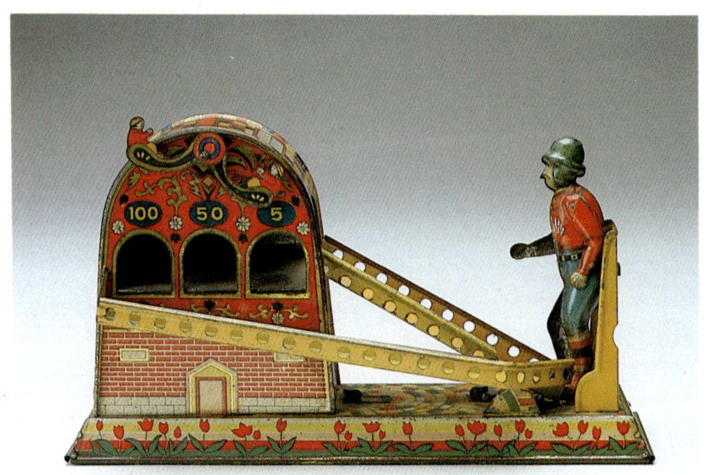

⑤1920'S／BALL KICKER／KURAMOCHI／220×60×140

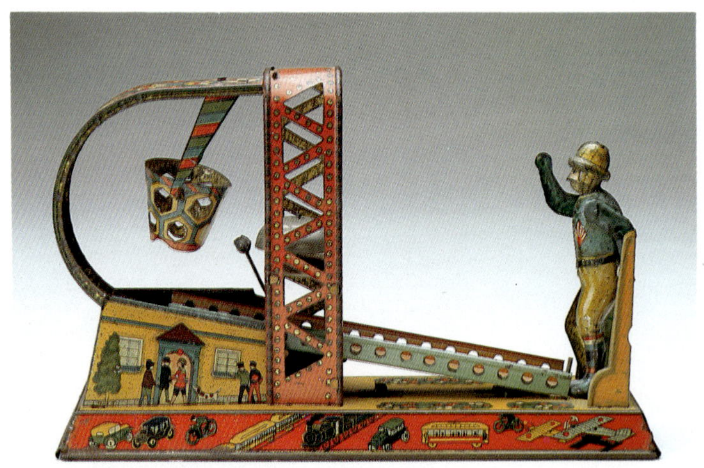

⑥1920'S／BALL KICKER／KURAMOCHI／210×65×115

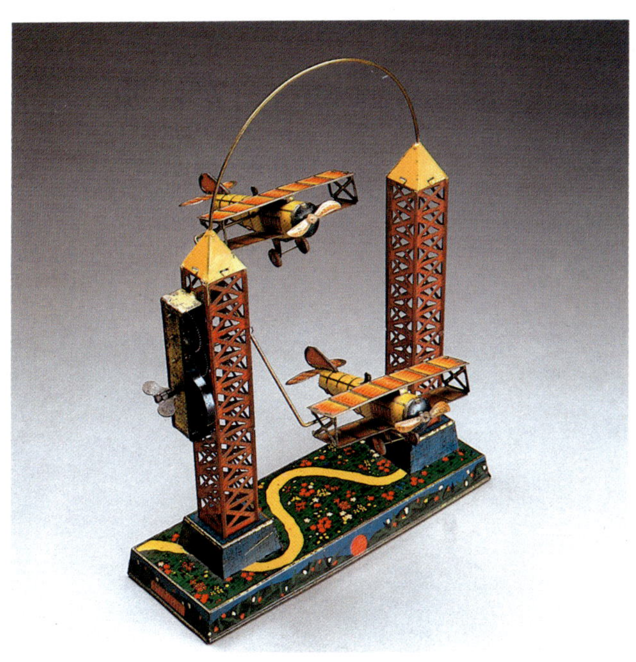

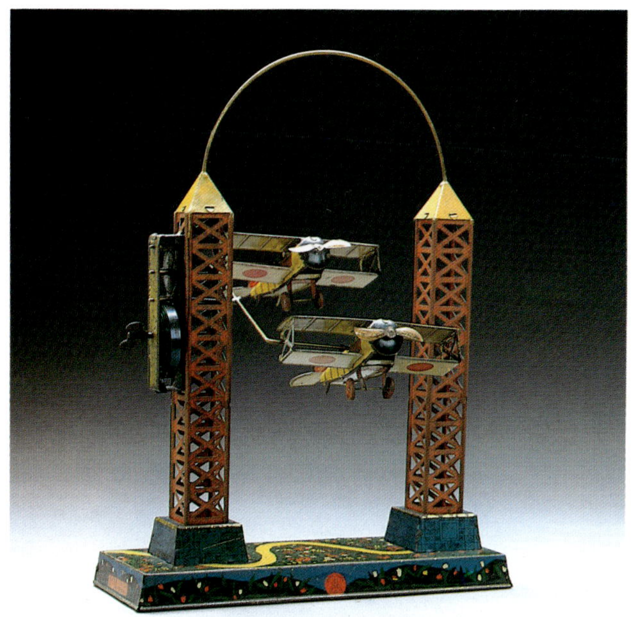

⑦ 1920'S／BIPLANES IN CIRCULAR MOTION／UNKNOWN／
85×240×310

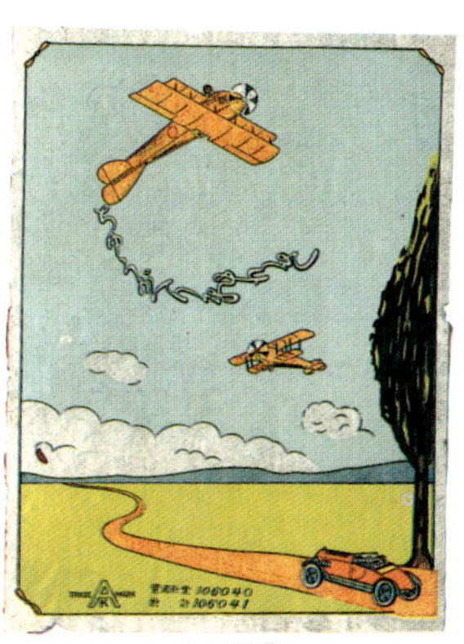

CASE ATTACHED

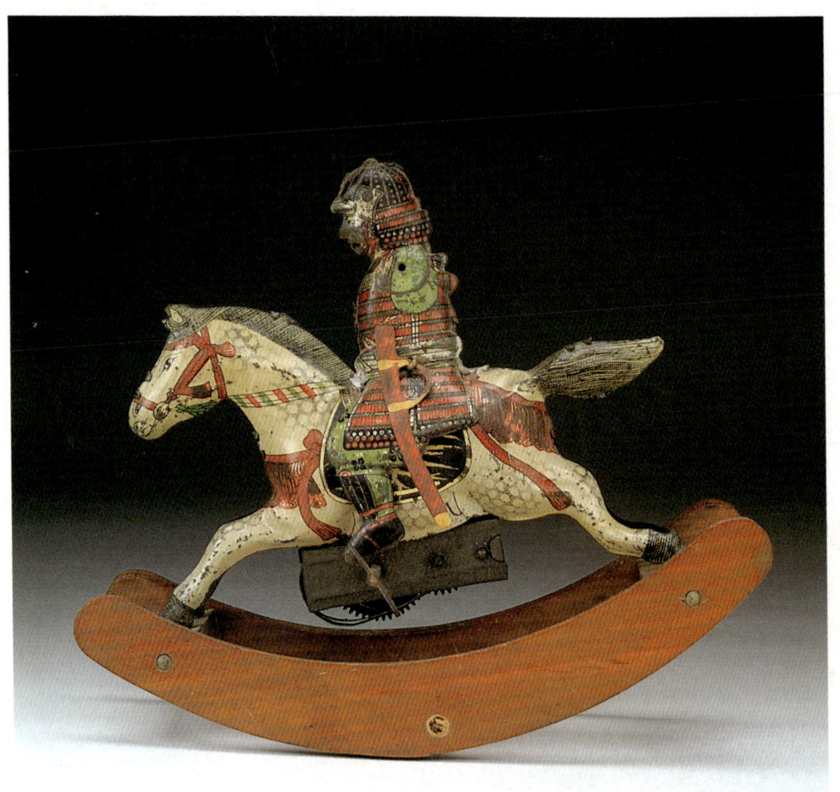

⑧1920'S／WARRIOR RIDING HORSE／ITO／180×55×14

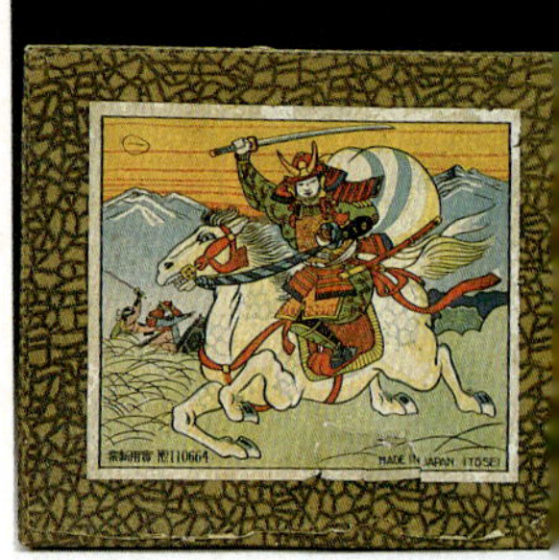

CASE ATTACHED

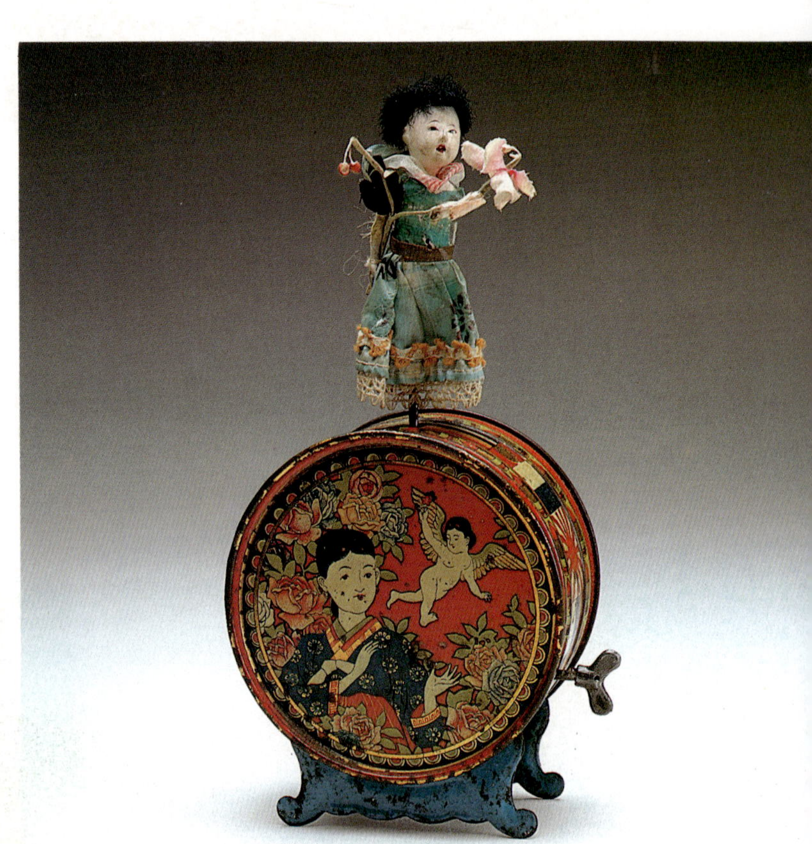

⑨1910'S／DOLL UPON DRUM／NAMIKI／120×60×220

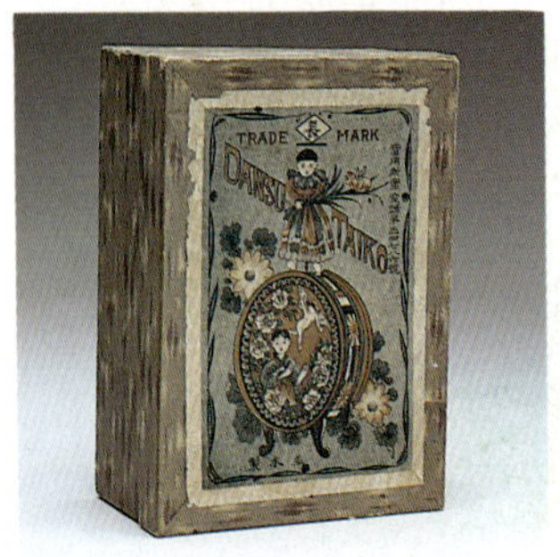

CASE ATTACHED

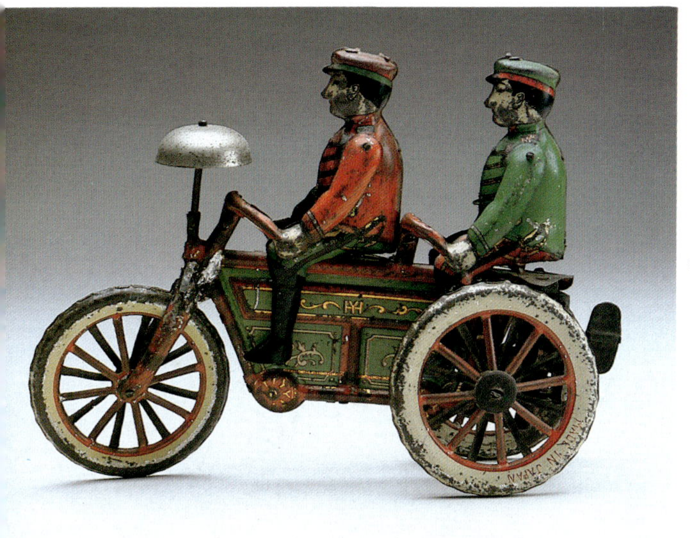

⑩1910'S／AUTO TRICYCLE／H.YAMADA／
190×70×125

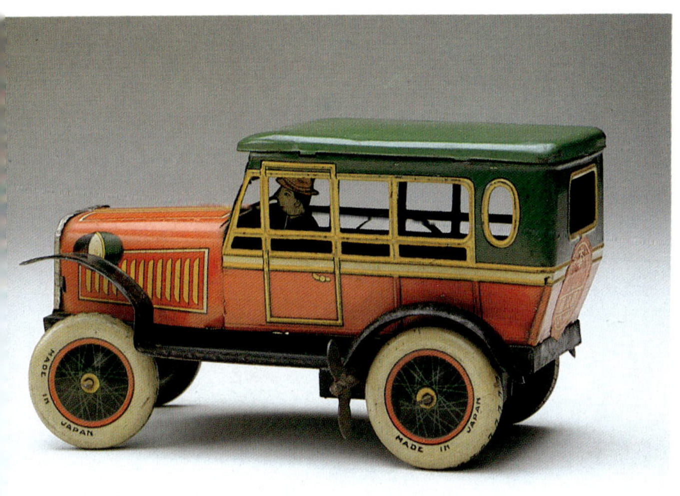

⑪1920'S／CLASSIC AUTO／UNKNOWN／
150×70×82

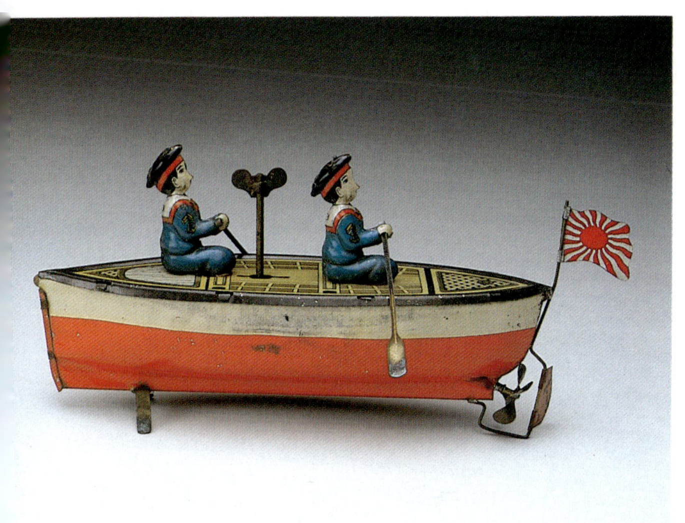

⑫1920'S／BOAT／UNKNOWN／
230×55×100

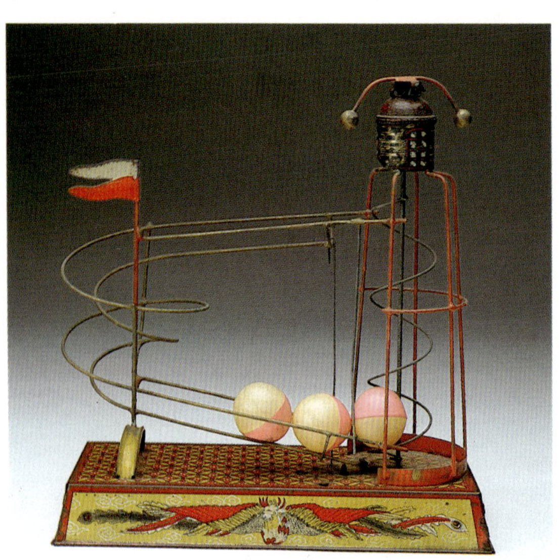

⑬1920'S／BALL ESCALATOR／UNKNOWN／200×85×210

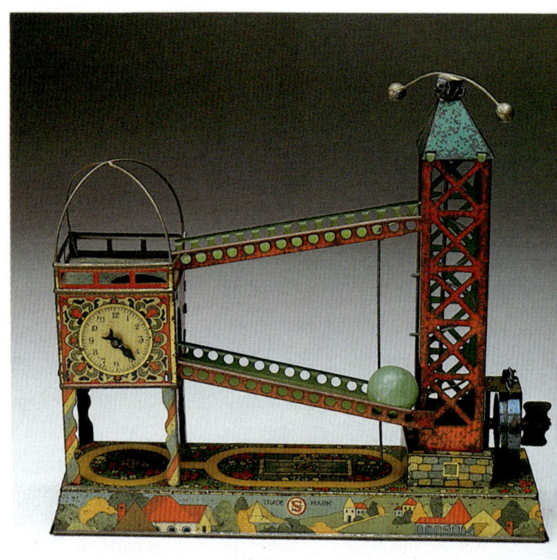

⑭1920'S／BALL ESCALATOR ／UNKNOWN／240×65×

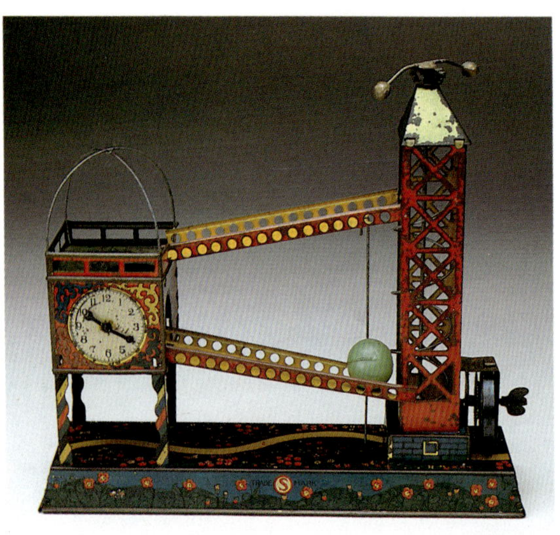

⑮1920'S／BALL ESCALATOR／UNKNOWN／240×65×210

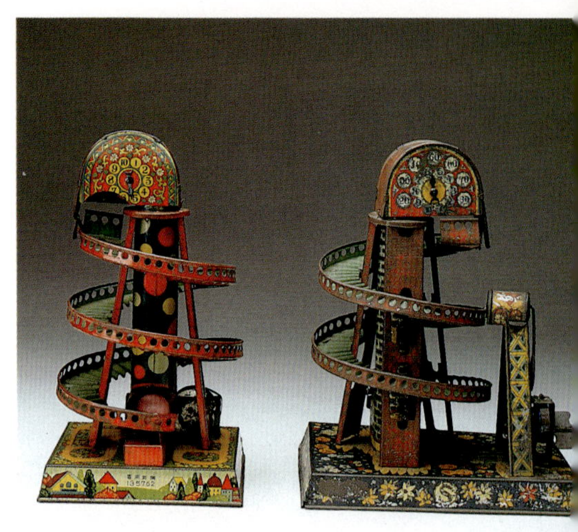

⑯⑰1920'S／BALL ESCALATOR／UNKNOWN／
190×130×220，135×135×230

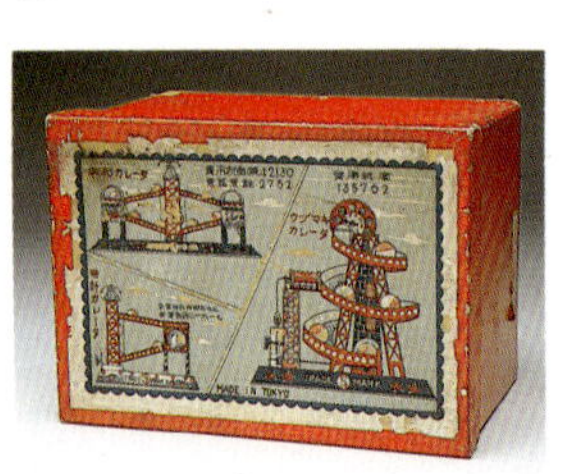

CASE ATTACHED

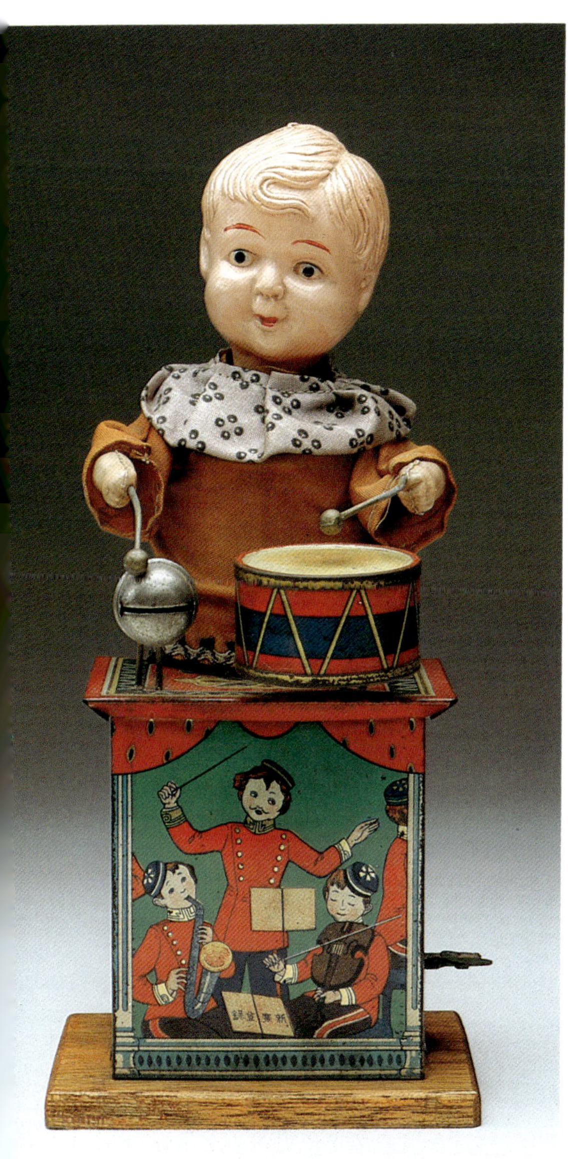

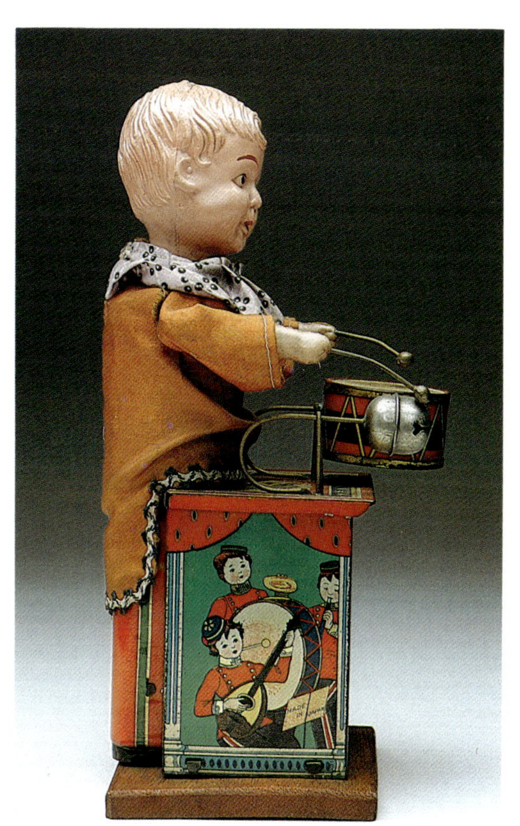

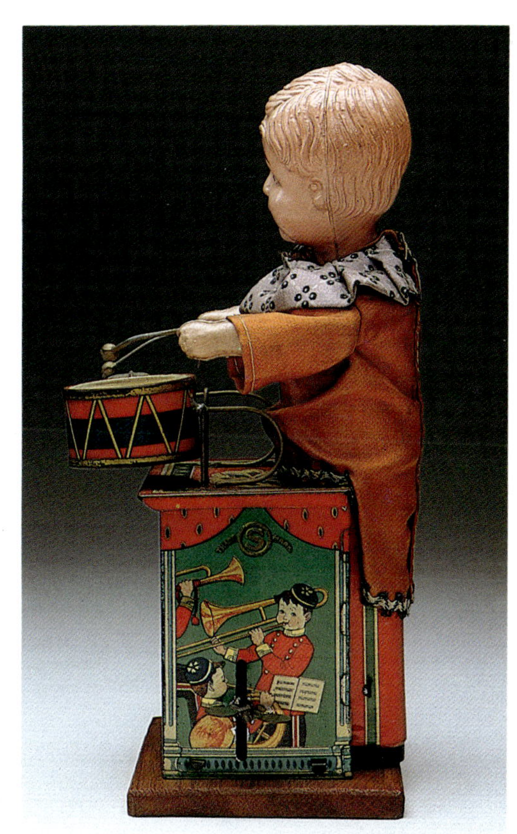

⑱1920'S／DRUMMER／UNKNOWN／90×105×230

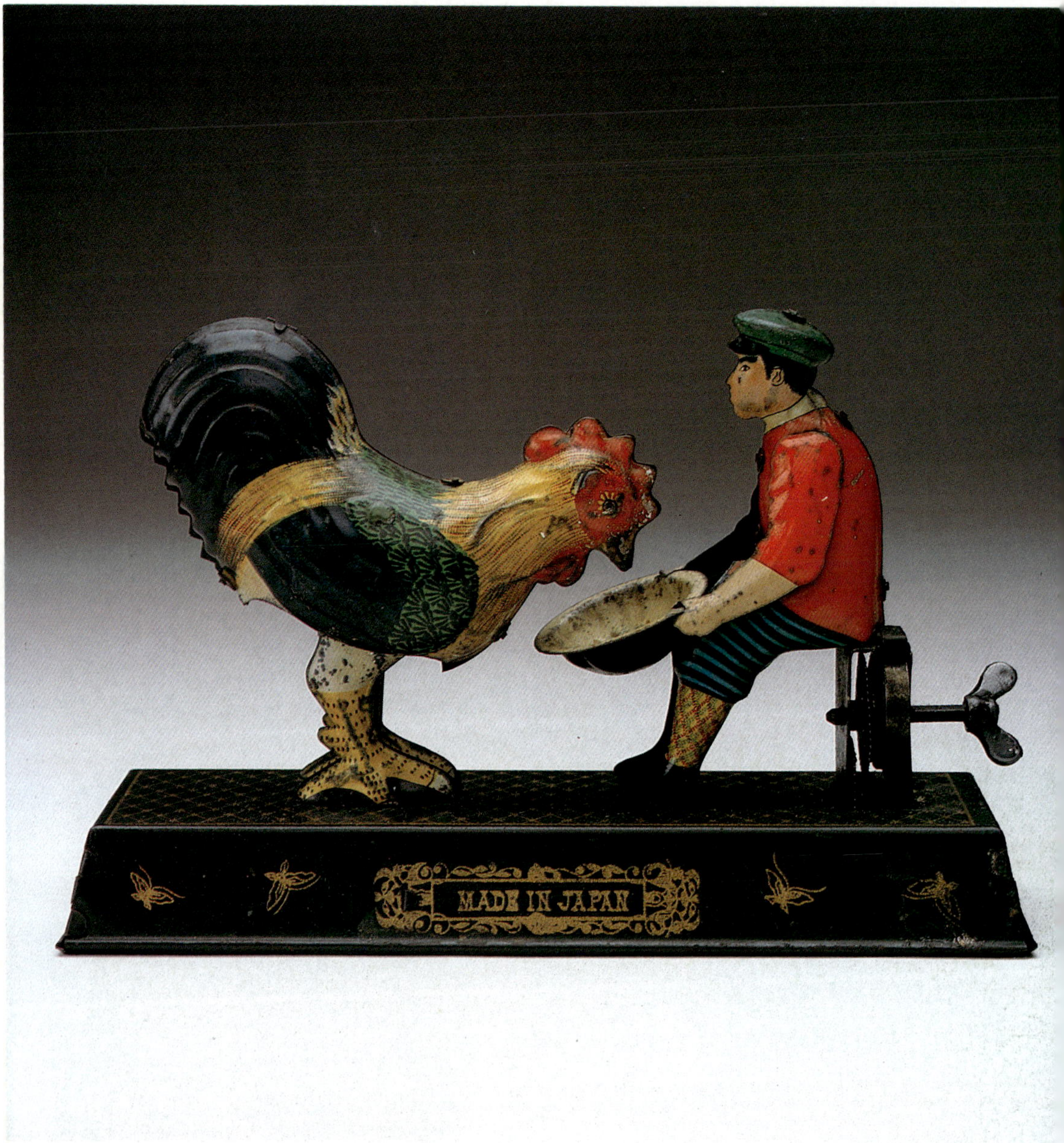

⑲1920'S／HEN HAVING A MEAL／TOYODO／180×60×115

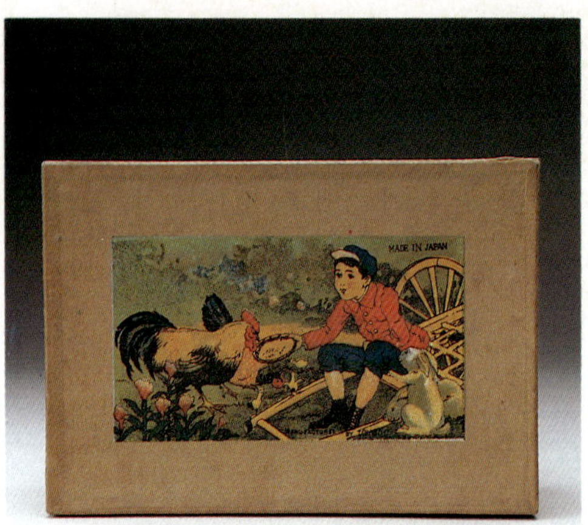

CASE ATTACHED

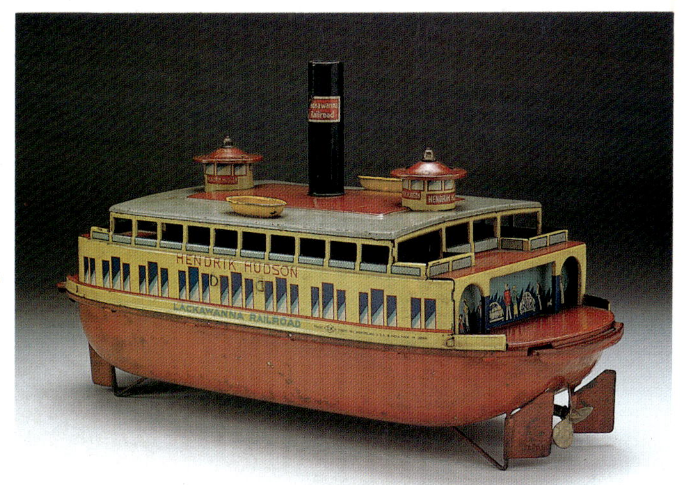

0)1930'S／FERRY／KURAMOCHI／260×110×150

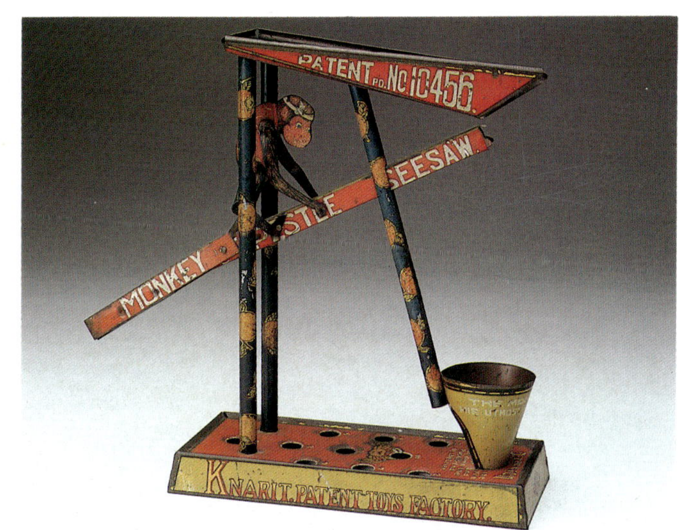

20'S／MONKEY AND CRAB／NPK／
5×80×225

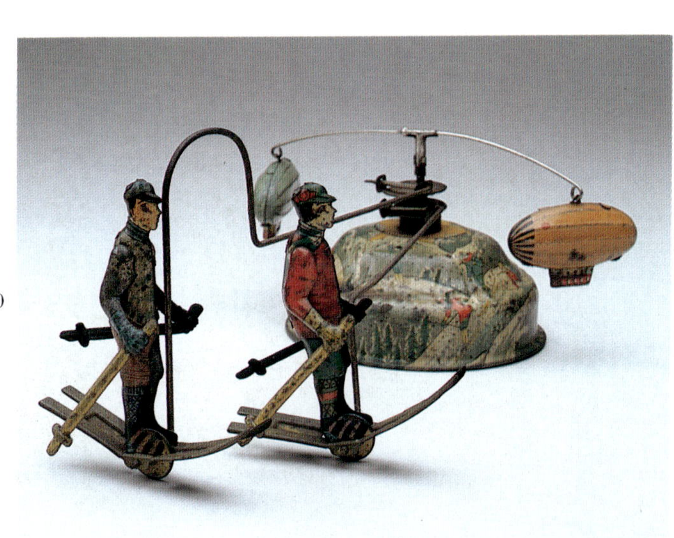

㉒1920'S／SKIERS／UNKNOWN／260×150×100

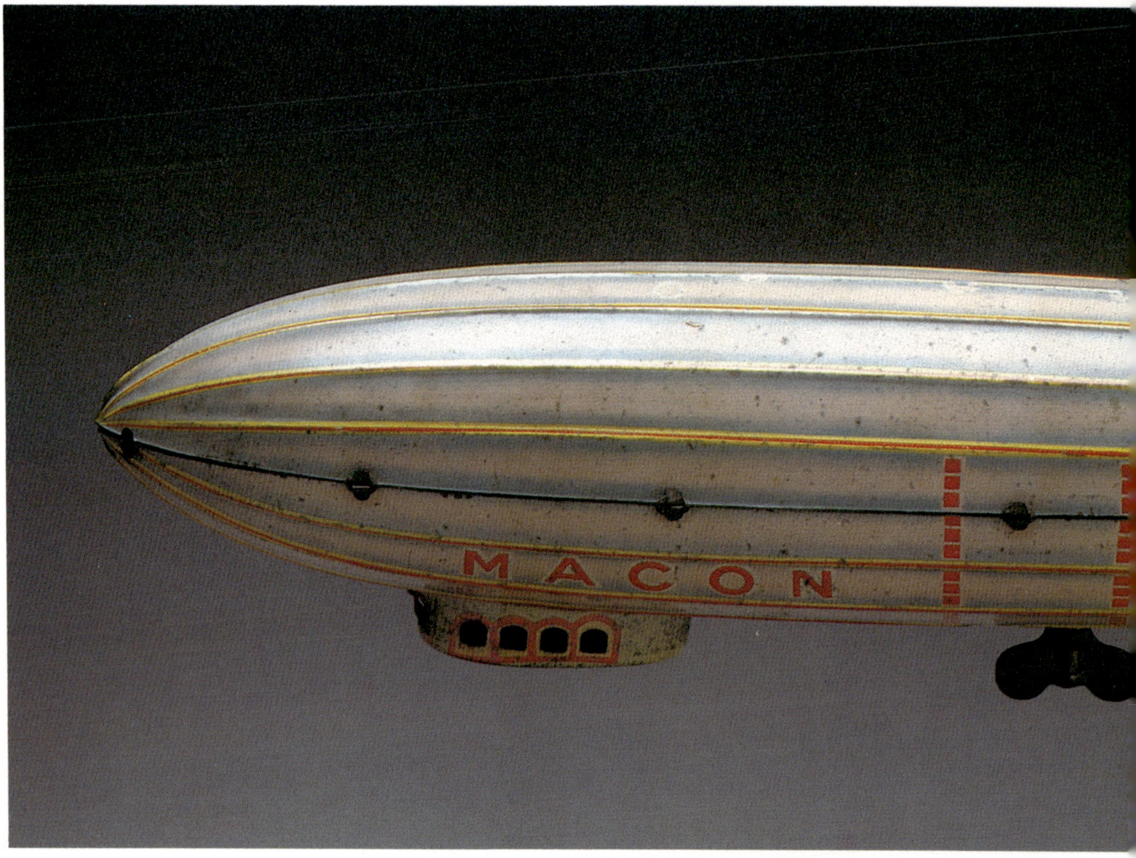

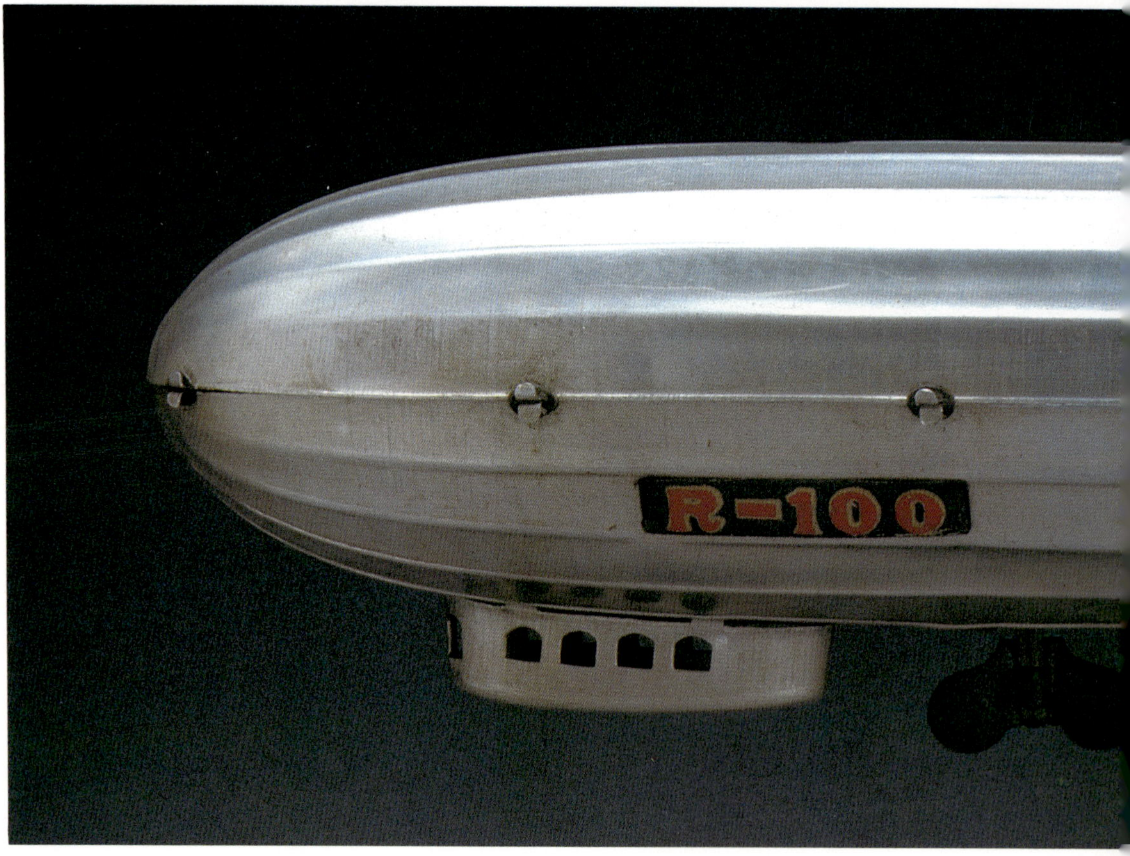

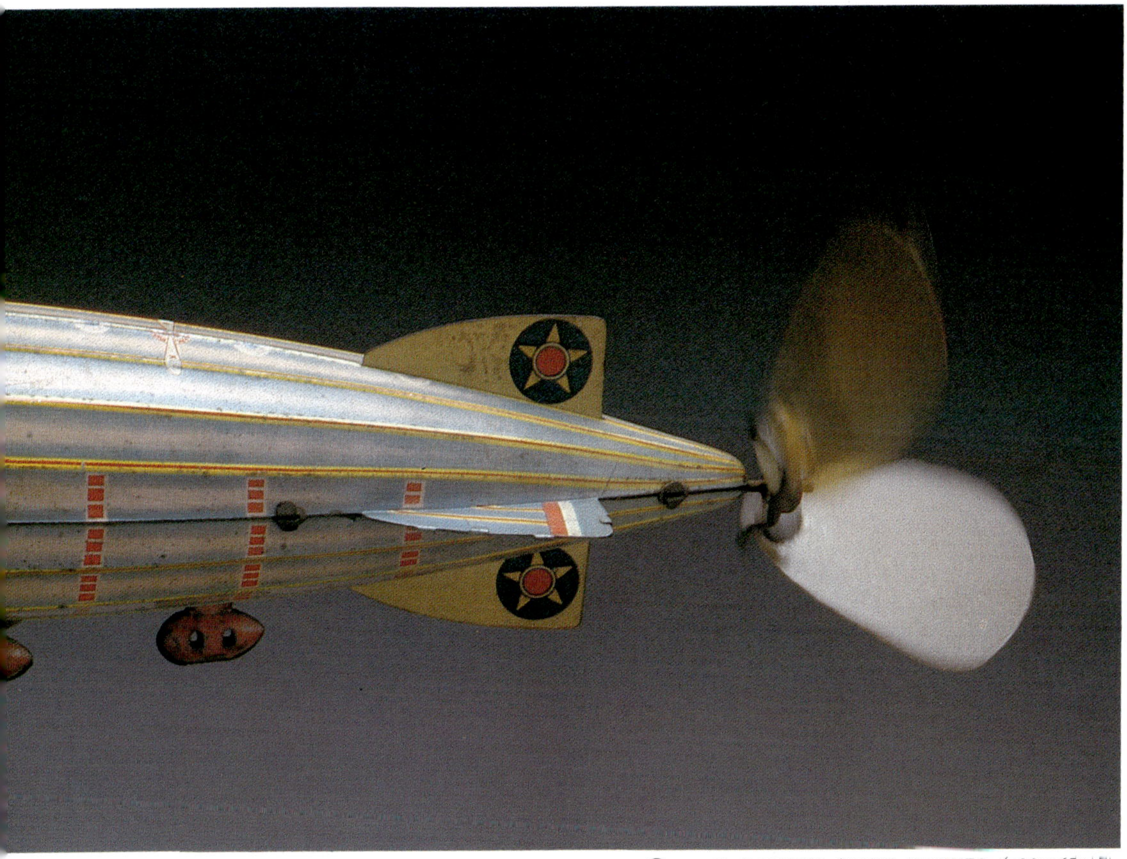

㉓1920'S／AIRSHIP／KONO KAKUZO／430×65×75

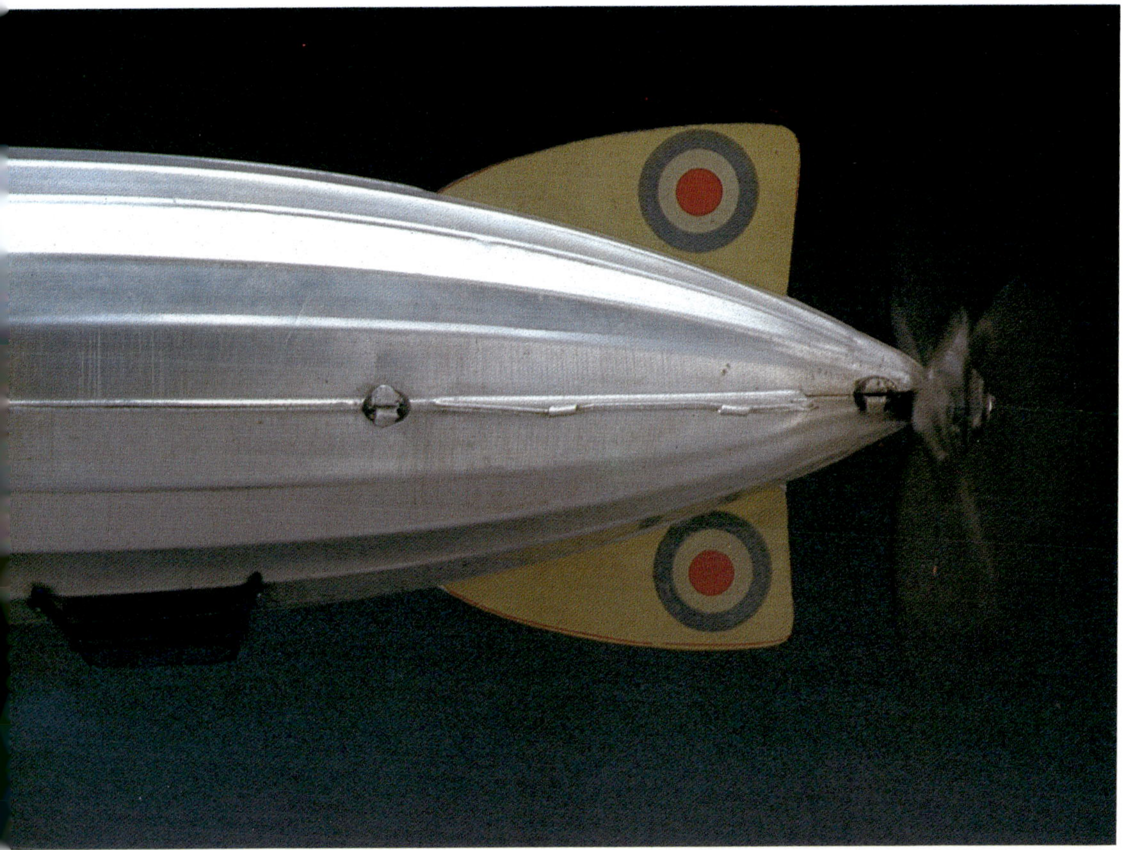

㉔1920'S／AIRSHIP／KONO KAKUZO／315×70×77

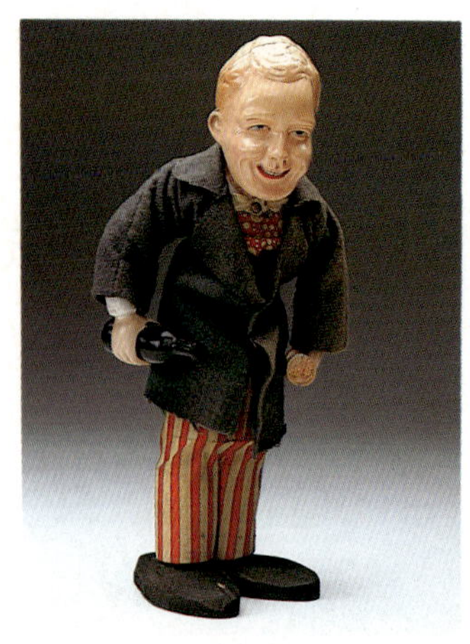

㉕1930'S／DRUNKARD／UNKNOWN／100×140×280

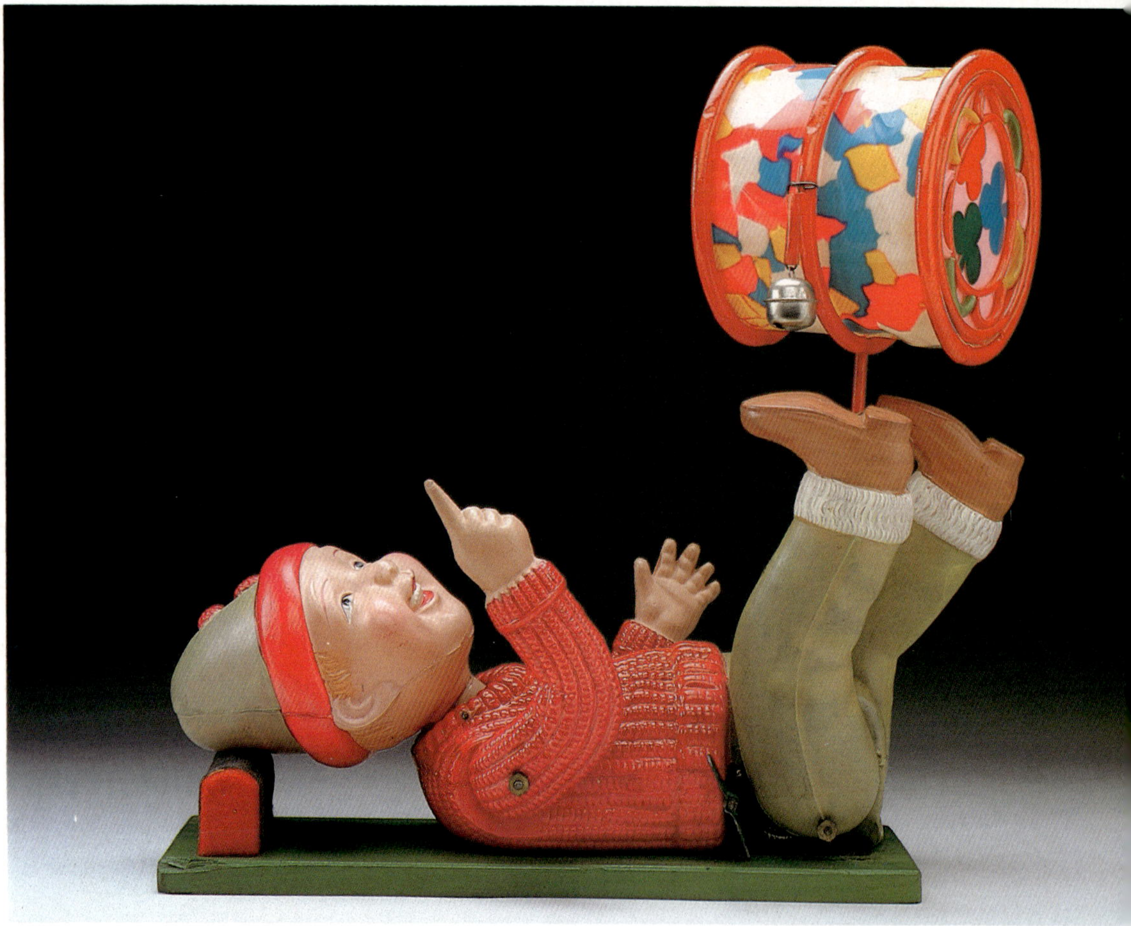

㉖1930'S／CHILD OF THE '30S／MASUDAYA／240 × 85 × 225

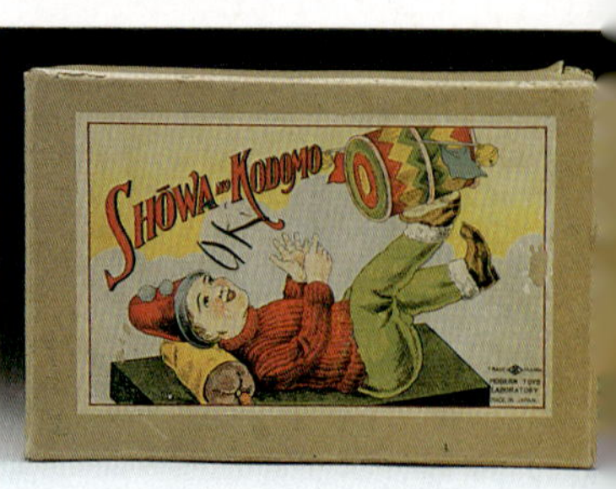

CASE ATTACHED

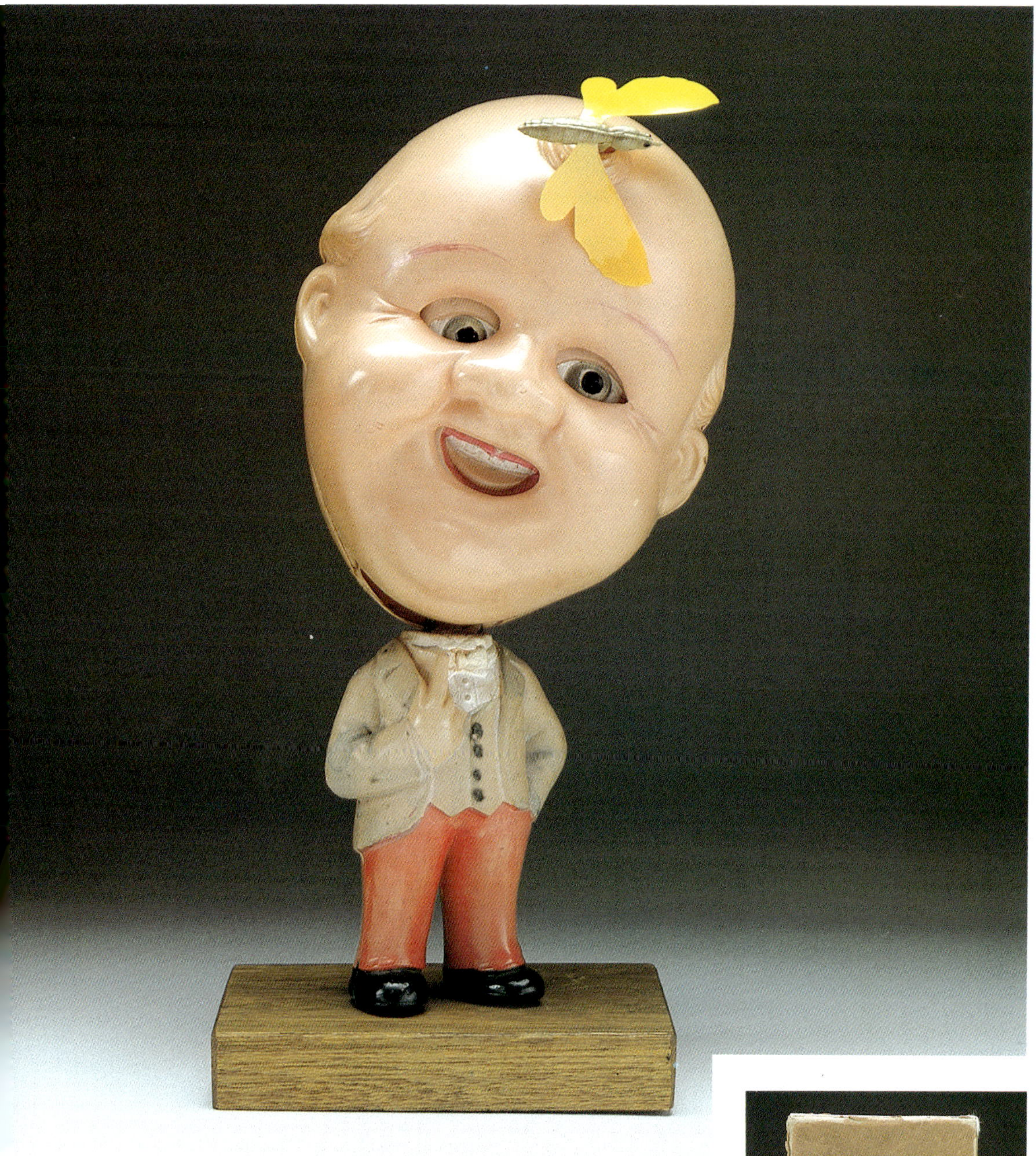

㉗1930'S／MISTER NICE GUY／
MASUDAYA／75 × 105 × 220

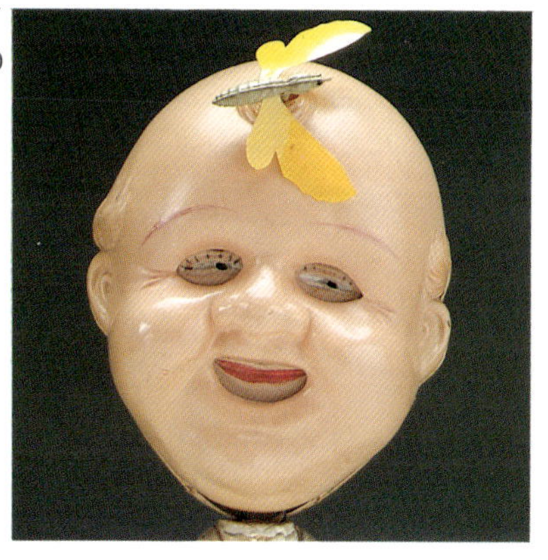

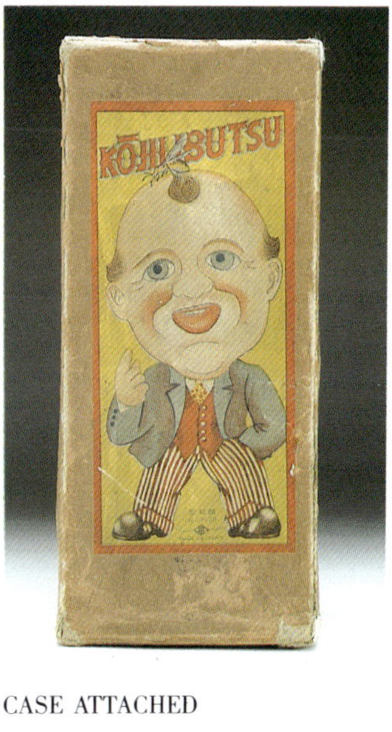

CASE ATTACHED

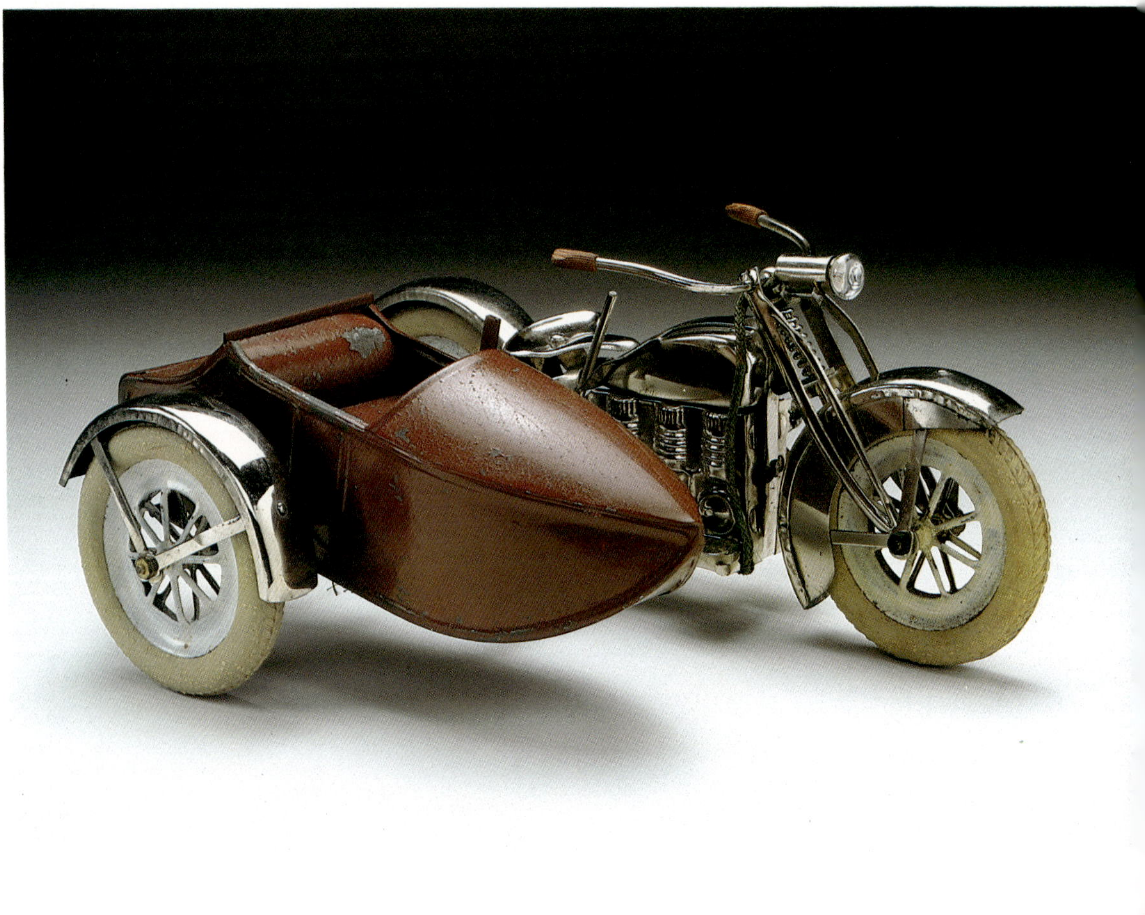

㉘1930'S／MOTORCYCLE WITH SIDECAR／MASUDAYA／230 × 19

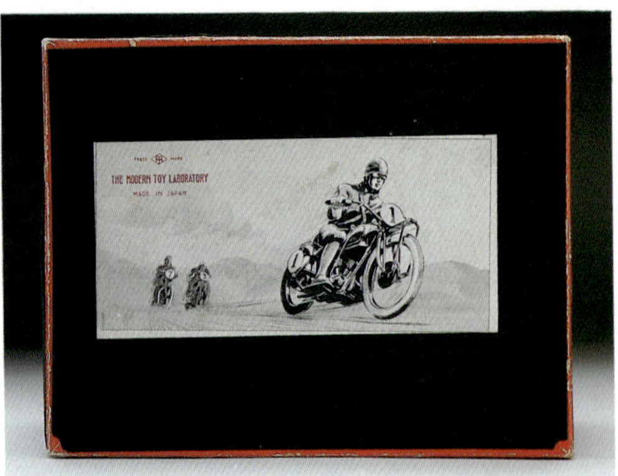

CASE ATTACHED

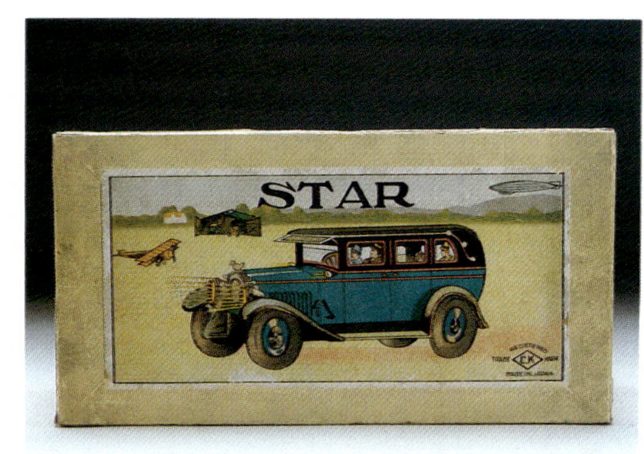

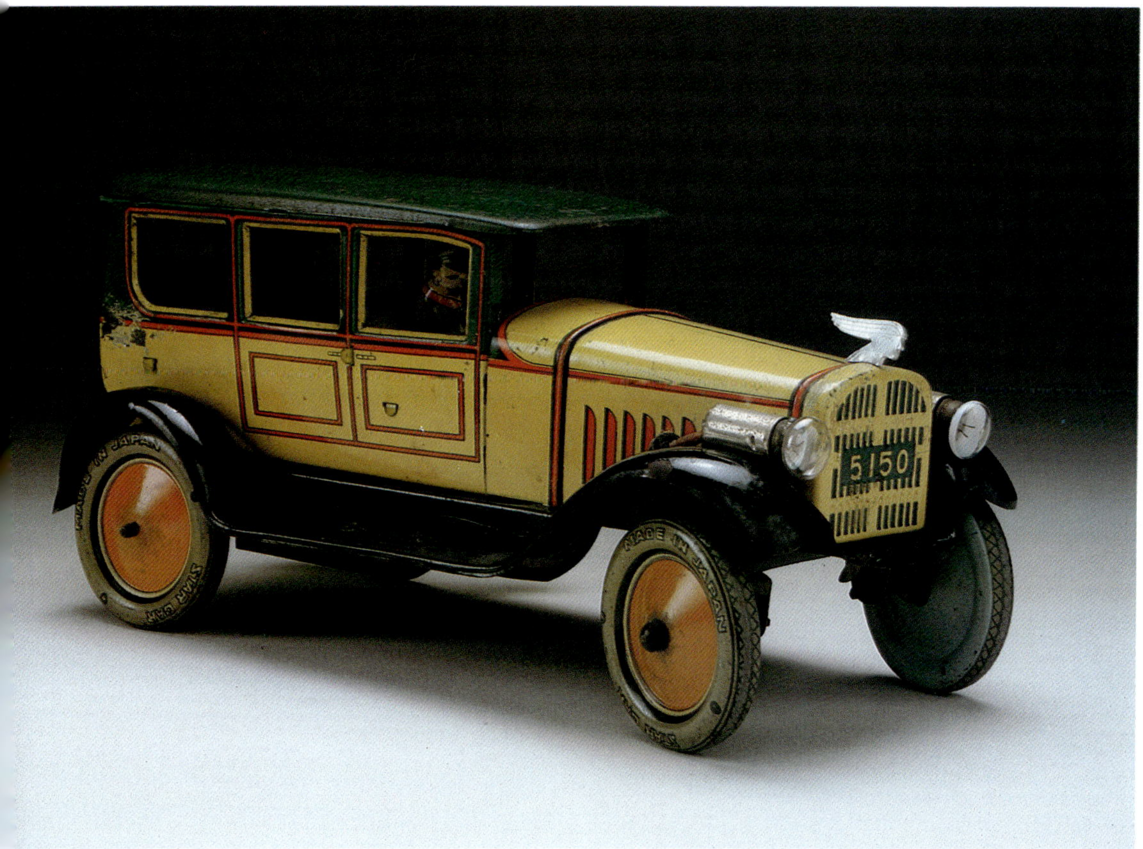

㉙ 1930'S／AUTO MODEL:STAR／KONO KAKUZO／210×110×100

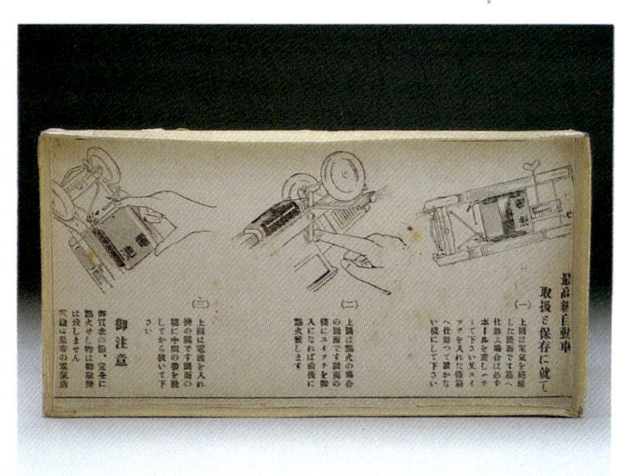

CASE ATTACHED

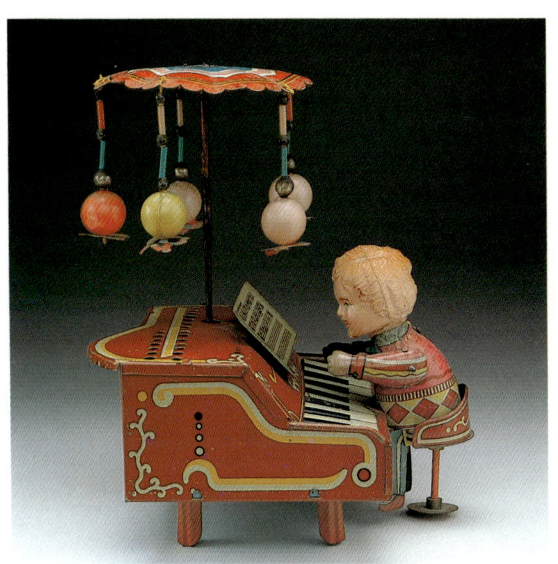

㉚1930'S／PIANIST／YOSHIYA／140×120×170

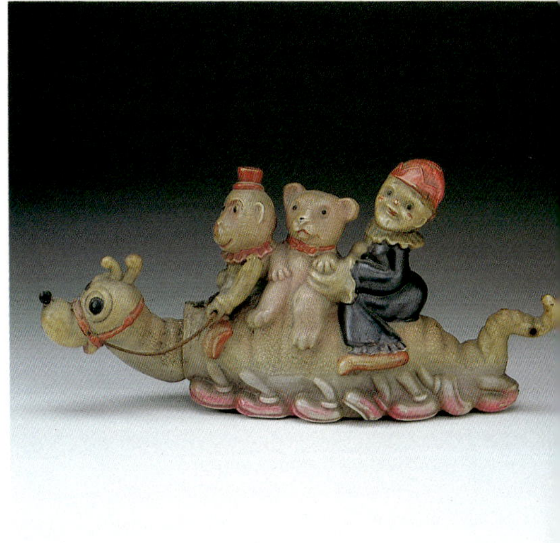

㉛1930'S／DRAGON AND FRIENDS／UNKNOWN
190×55×90

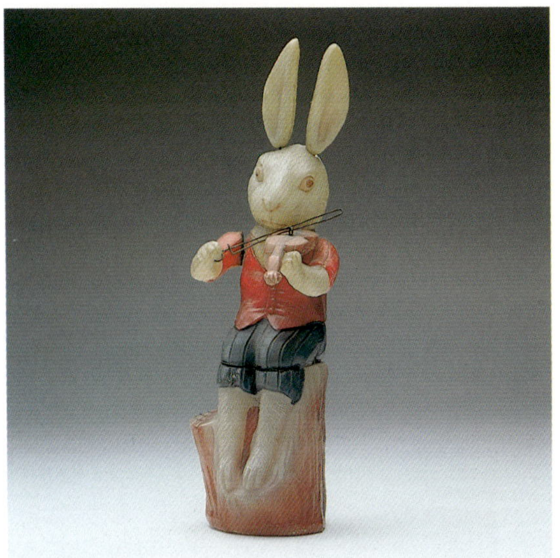

㉜1930'S／RABBIT VIOLINIST／KURAMOCHI／100×70×230

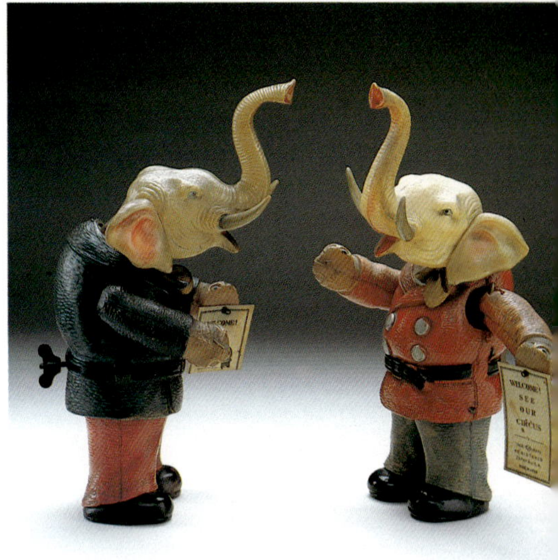

㉝㉞1930'S／TWO ELEPHANTS／KURAMOCH
145×110×230

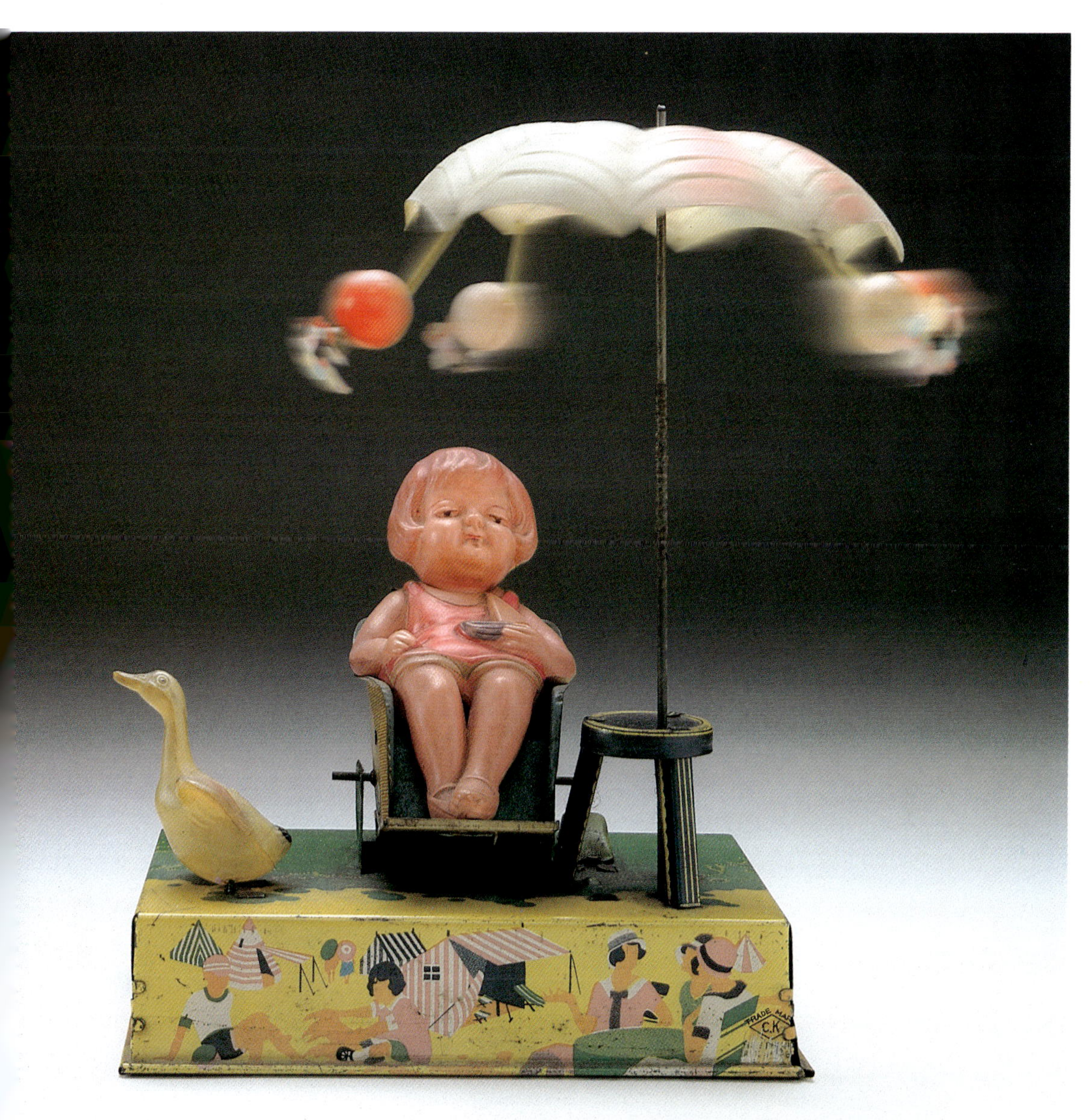

㉟1930'S／HAPPY TIMES／KURAMOCHI／120×170×225

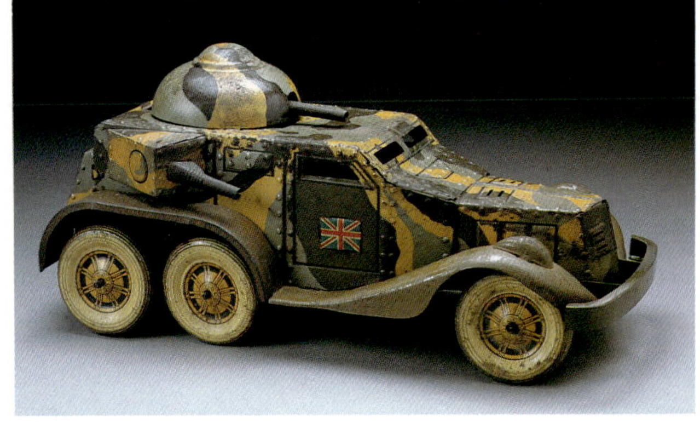

㊱1930'S／TANK／TOMIYAMA／350×145×155

㊲1930'S／TANK／UNKNOWN／255×110×130

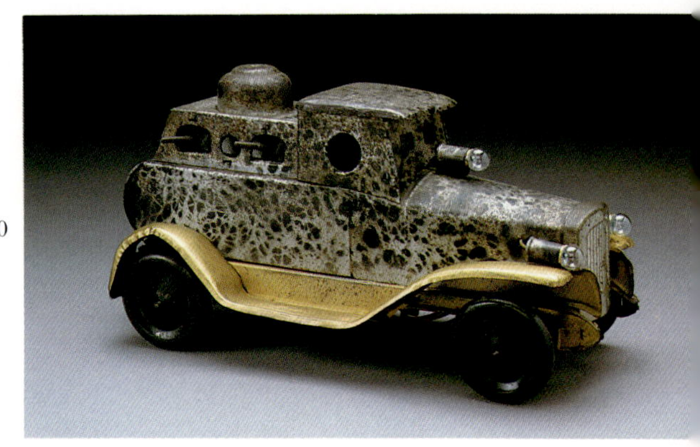

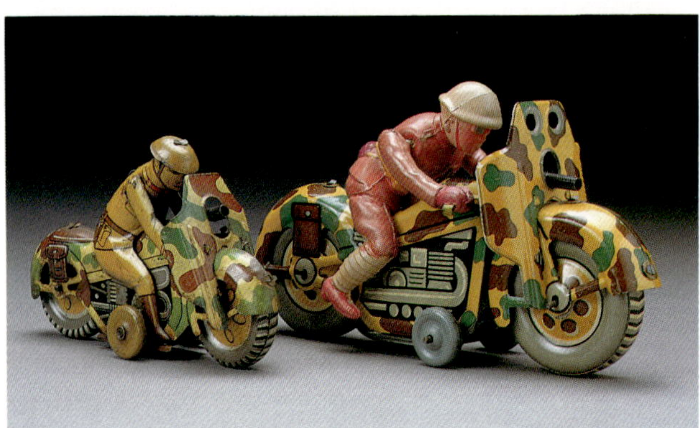

㊳㊴1930'S／ARMY MOTORBIKE／T. Y. D. Y, UNKN
160×55×95, 120×35×75

㊵1930'S／TANK／UNKNOWN／170×80×75

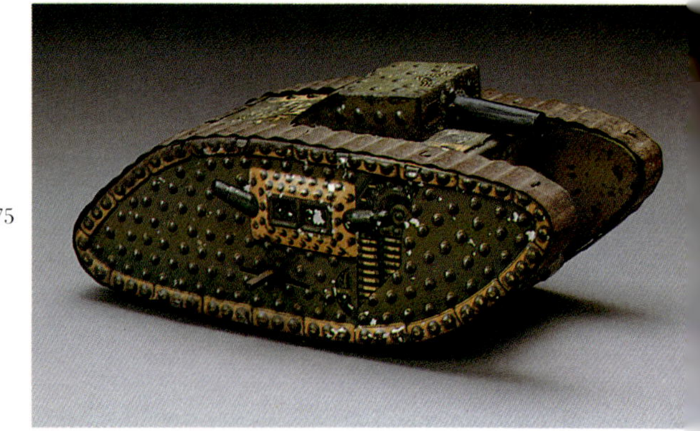

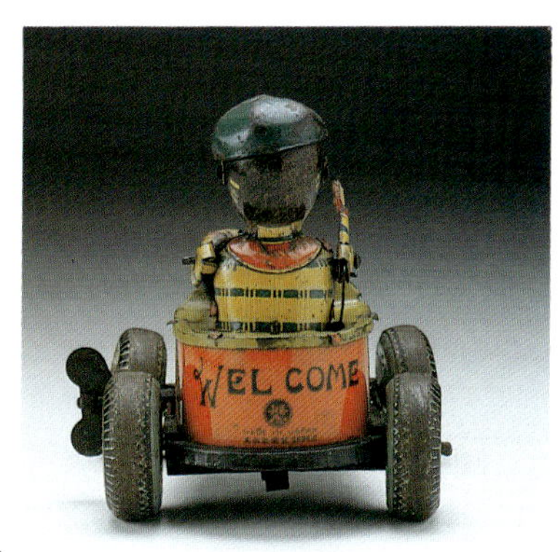

㊶1930'S／RACING CAR／TOMIYAMA／120×95×105

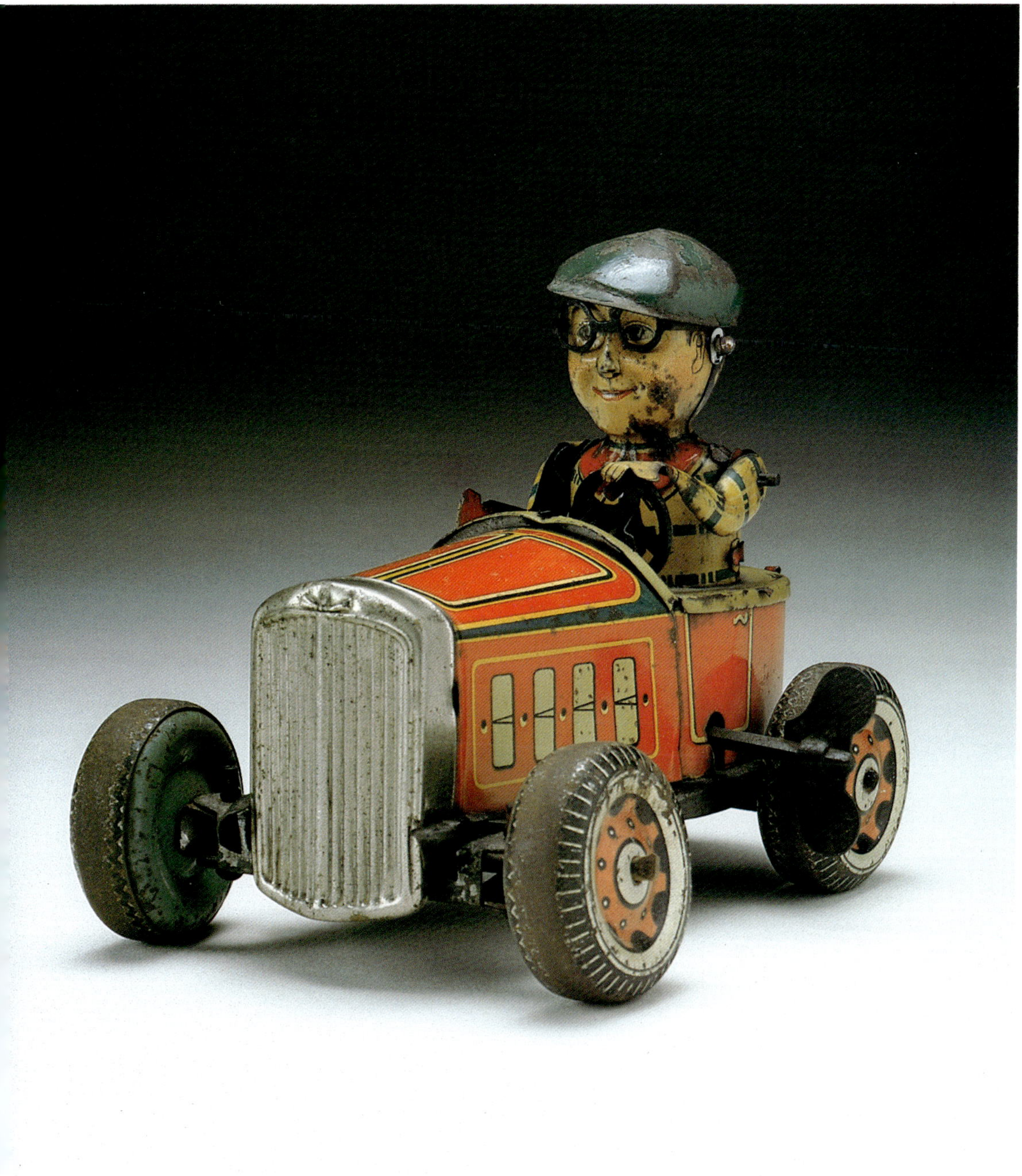

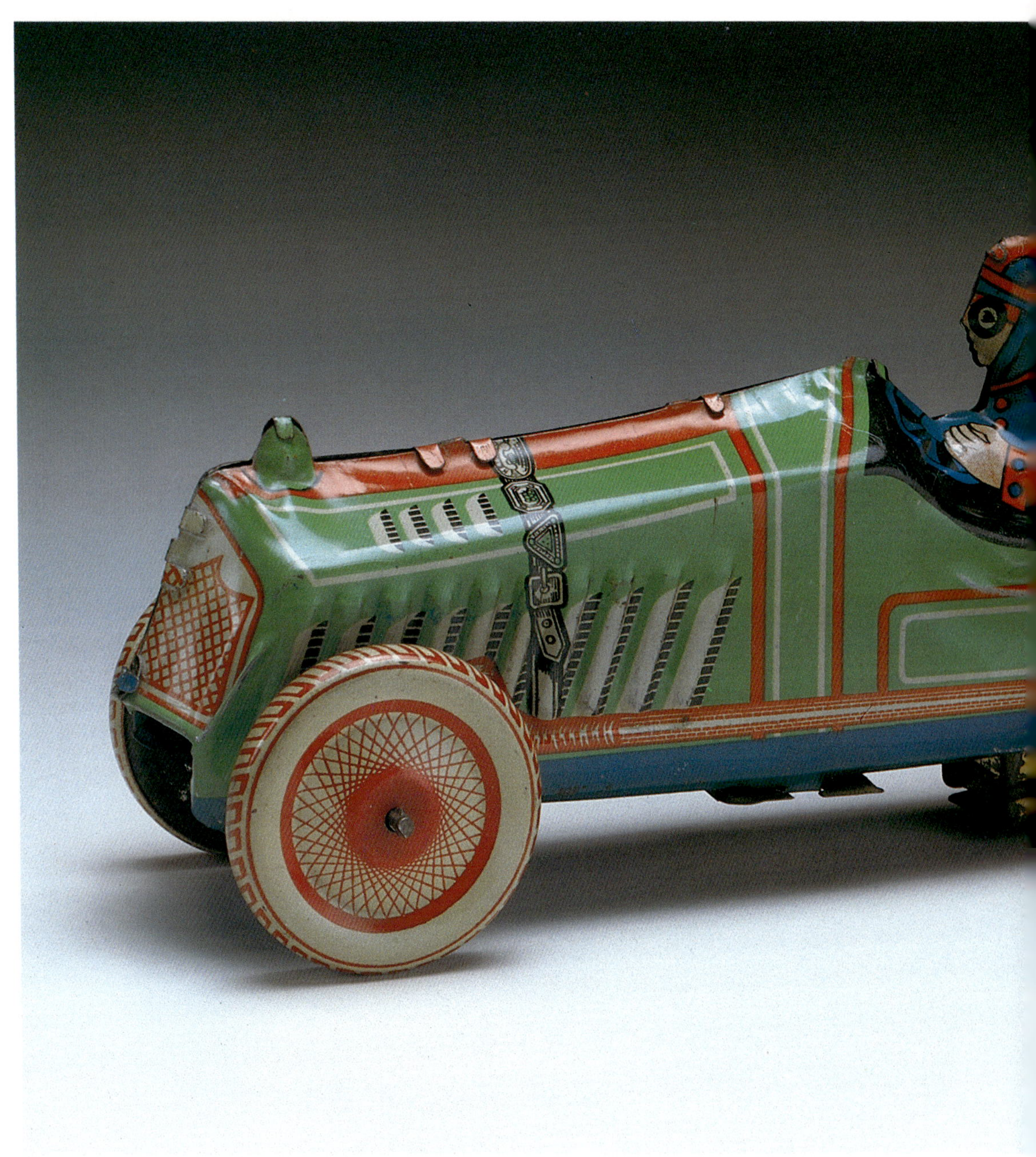

(42) 1930'S／RACING CAR／UNKNOWN／190×80×85

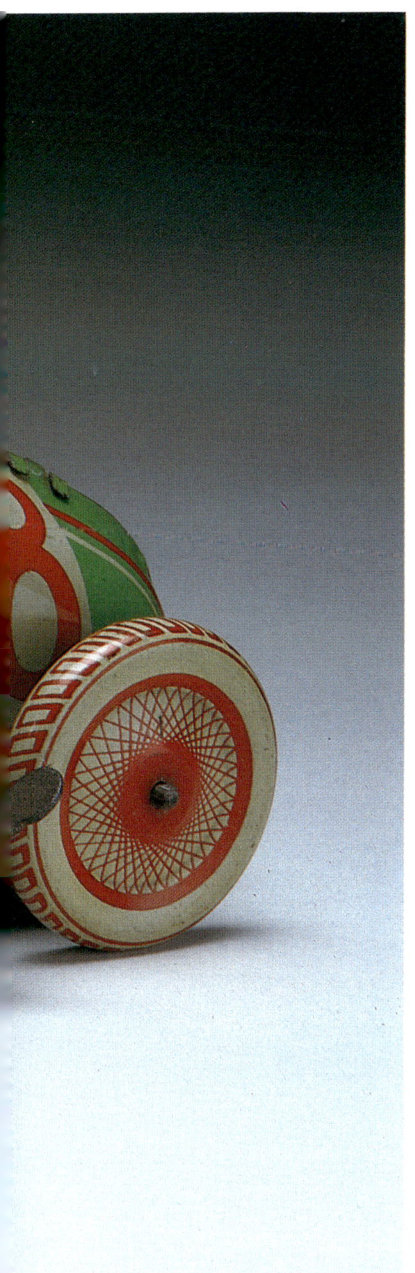

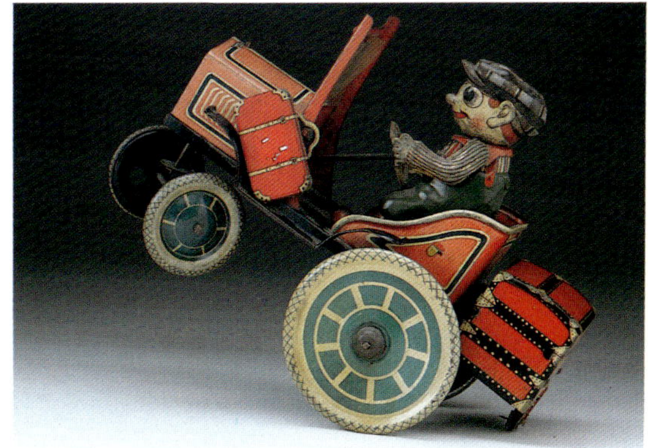

㊸1930'S／CLASSIC AUTO／KURAMOCHI／190×75×150

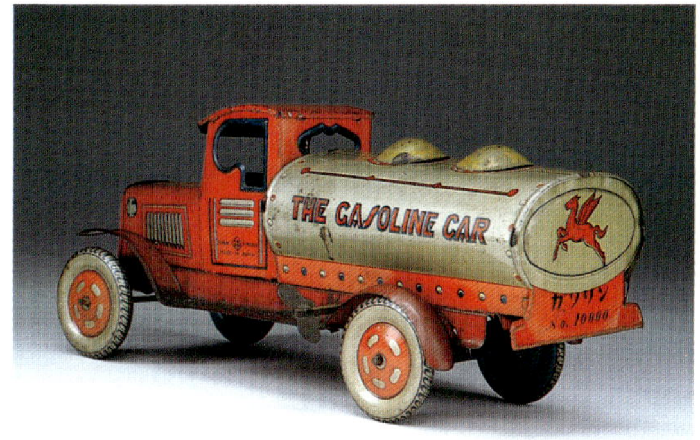

㊹1930'S／TANK TRUCK／MASUDAYA／220×80×100

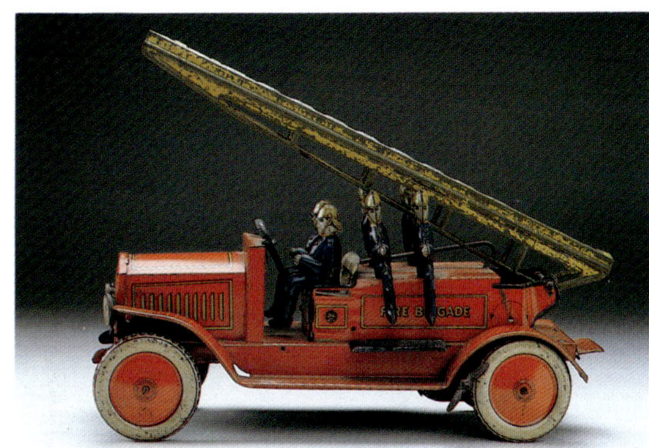

㊺1930'S／FIRE ENGINE／TOMIYAMA／250×90×180

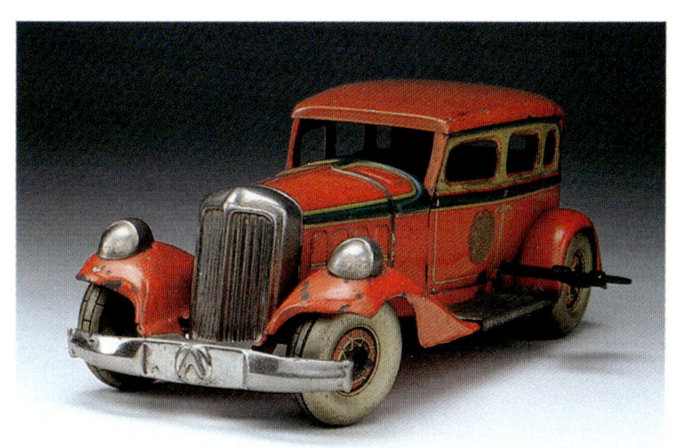

㊻1930'S／CLASSIC AUTO／TOMIYAMA／190×80×70

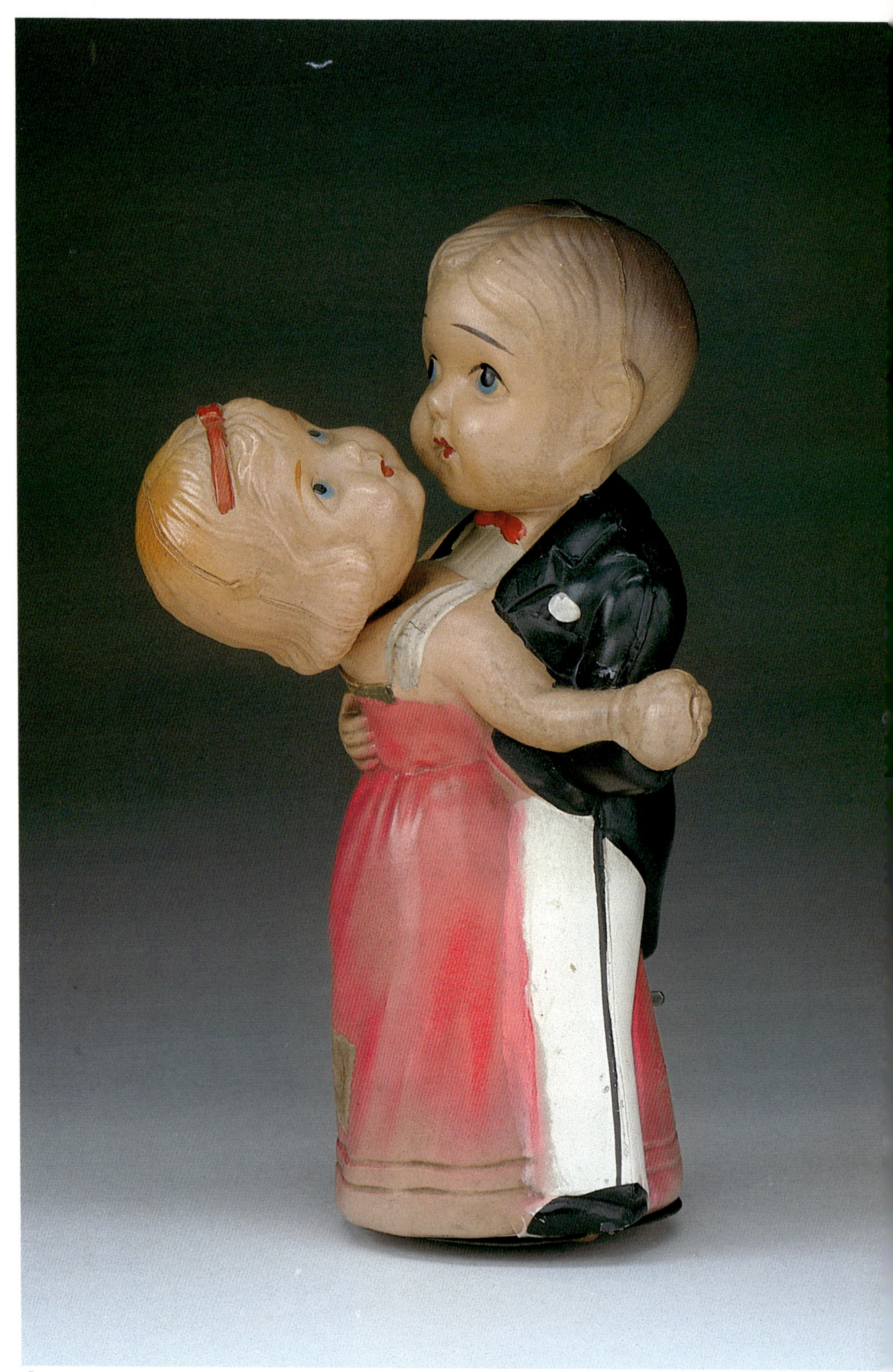

(47) 1930'S／DANCING COUPLE／UNKNOWN／60×55×150

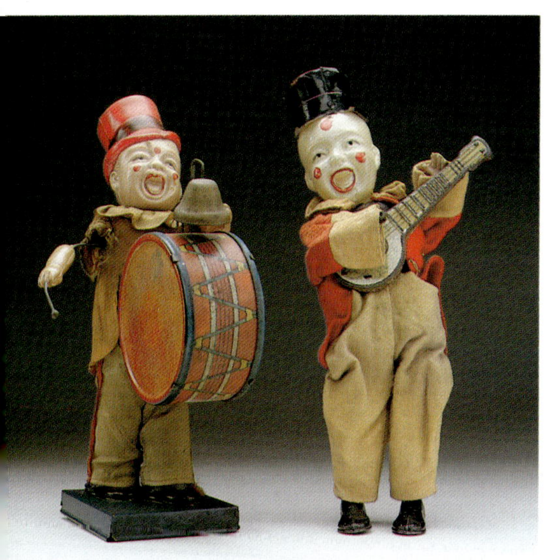

⑱ 1930'S／DRUMMER／UNKNOWN／155×120×240
⑲ 1930'S／BANJO PLAYER／UNKNOWN／100×100×260

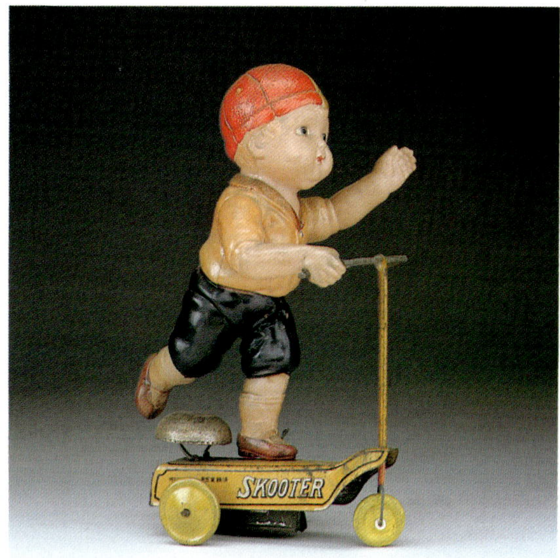

⑳ 1930'S／BOY PLAYING WITH SCOOTER
／KURAMOCHI／120×70×185

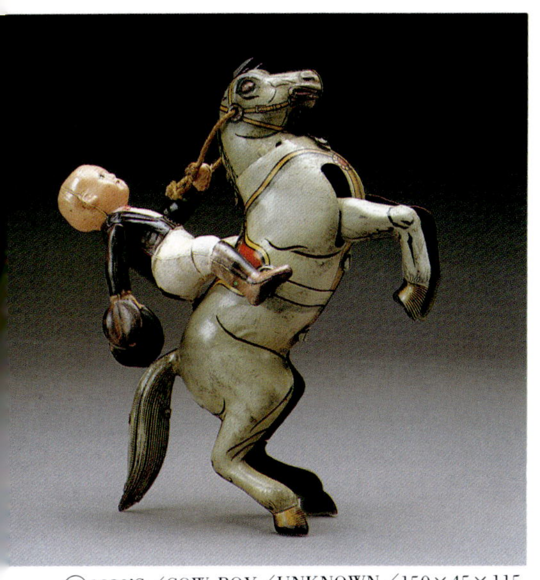

51 1930'S／COW BOY／UNKNOWN／150×45×115

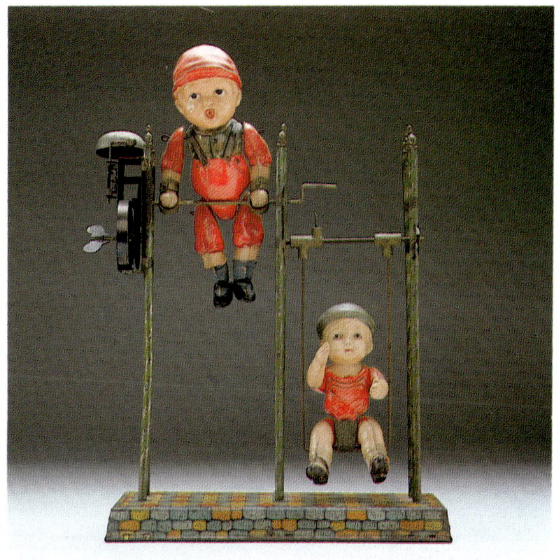

52 1930'S／CHILDREN ON SWING／UNKNOWN／
80×205×250

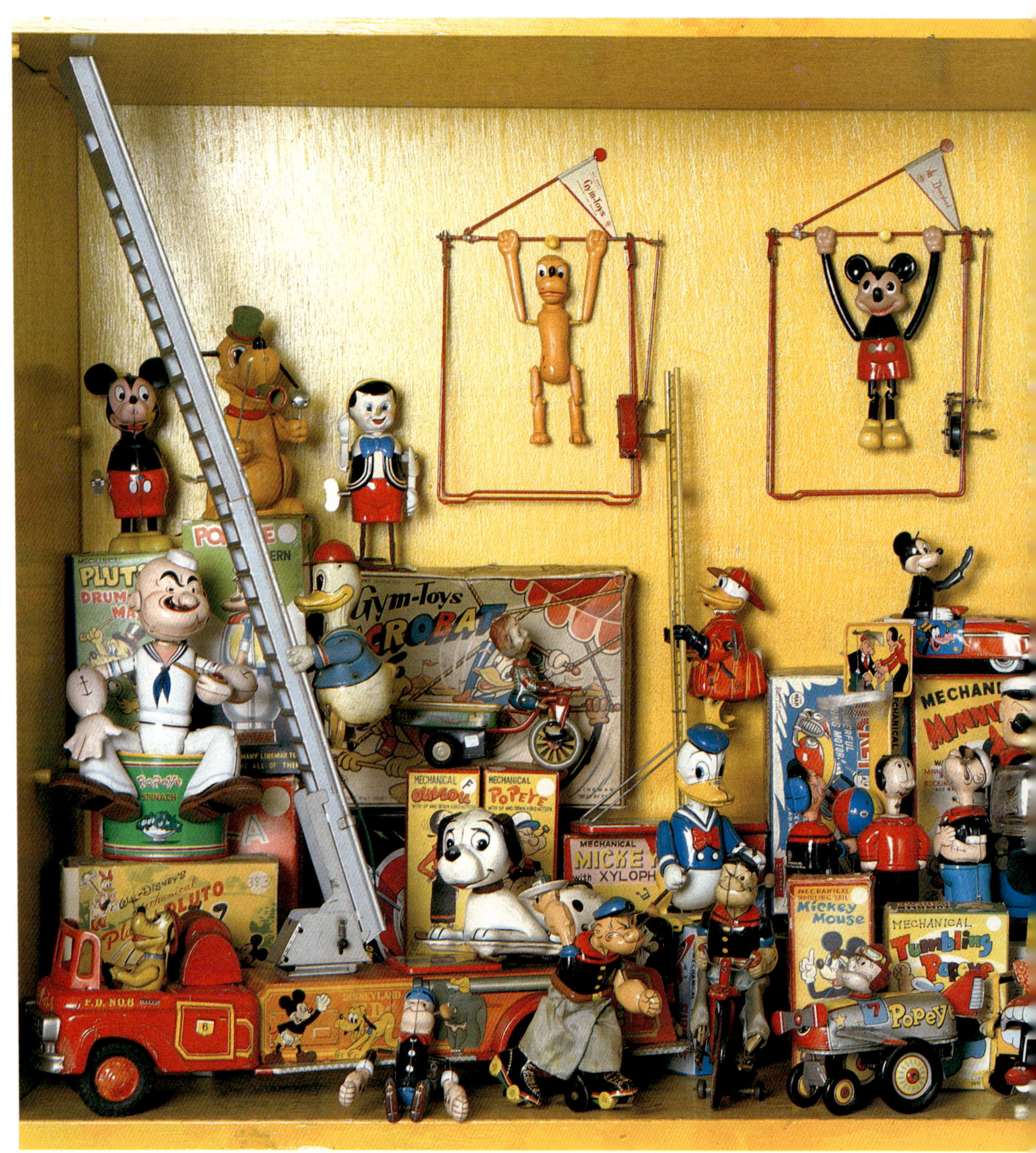

(53) CHARACTER TOYS

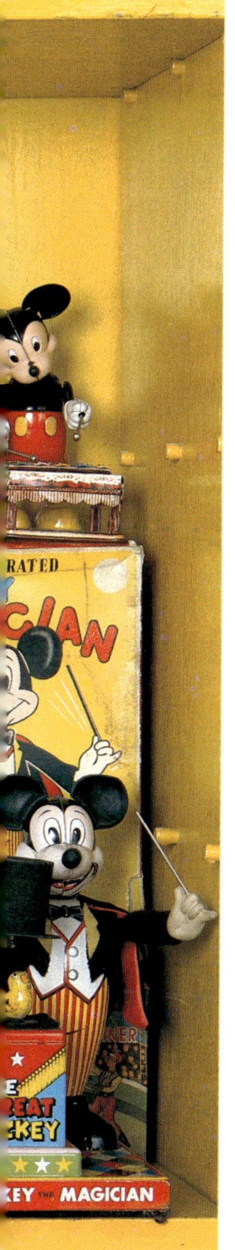

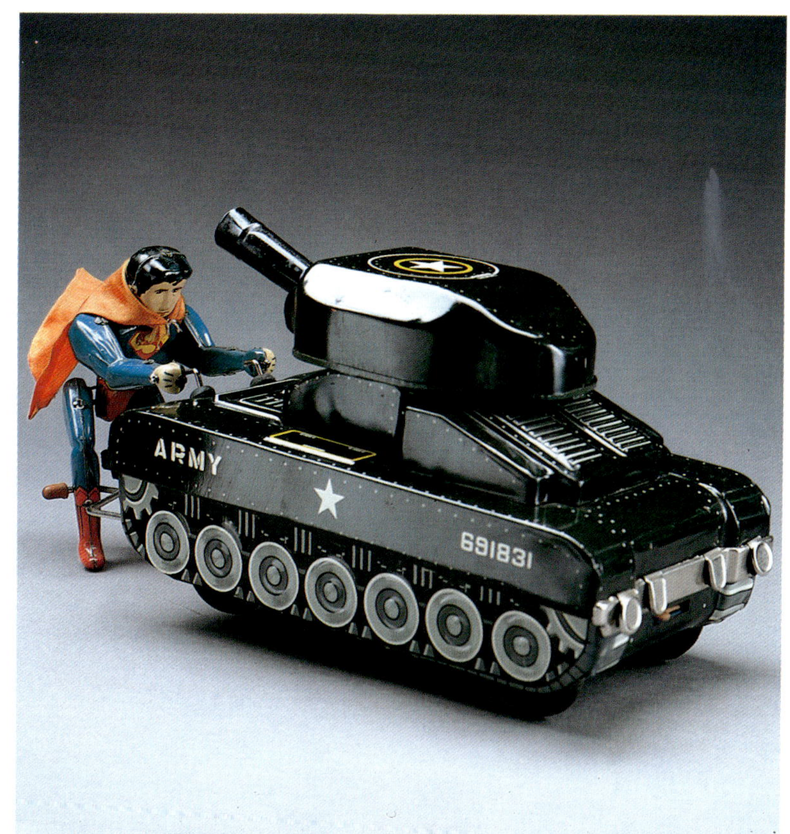

(54) 1950'S／SUPERMAN AND TANK／LINE MAR／270×105×125

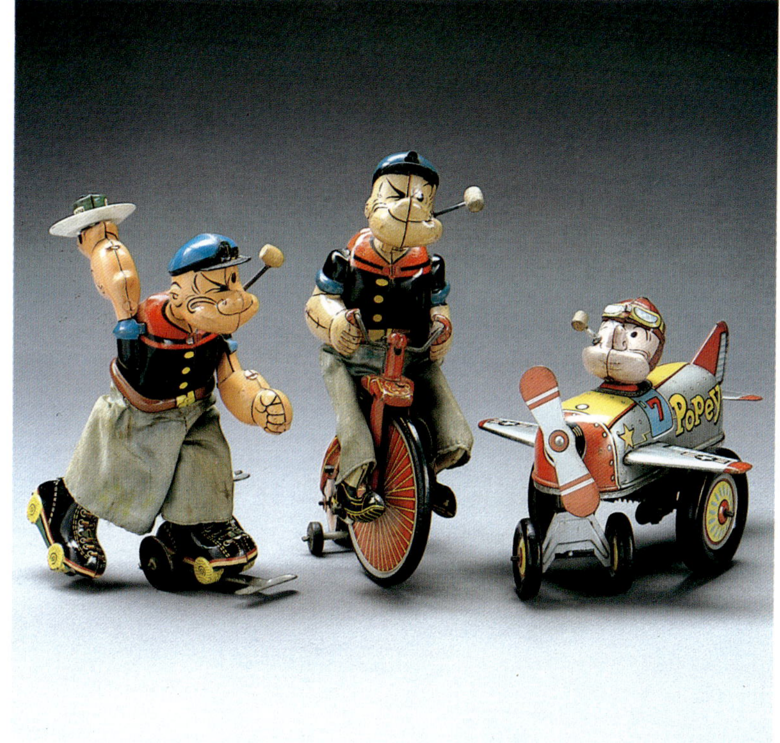

(55) 1950'S／POPEYE THE ROLLER SKATER／LINE MAR／130×75×160
(56) 1950'S／POPEYE AND BICYCLE／LINE MAR／120×70×170
(57) 1950'S／POPEYE THE PILOT／LINE MAR／150×130×110

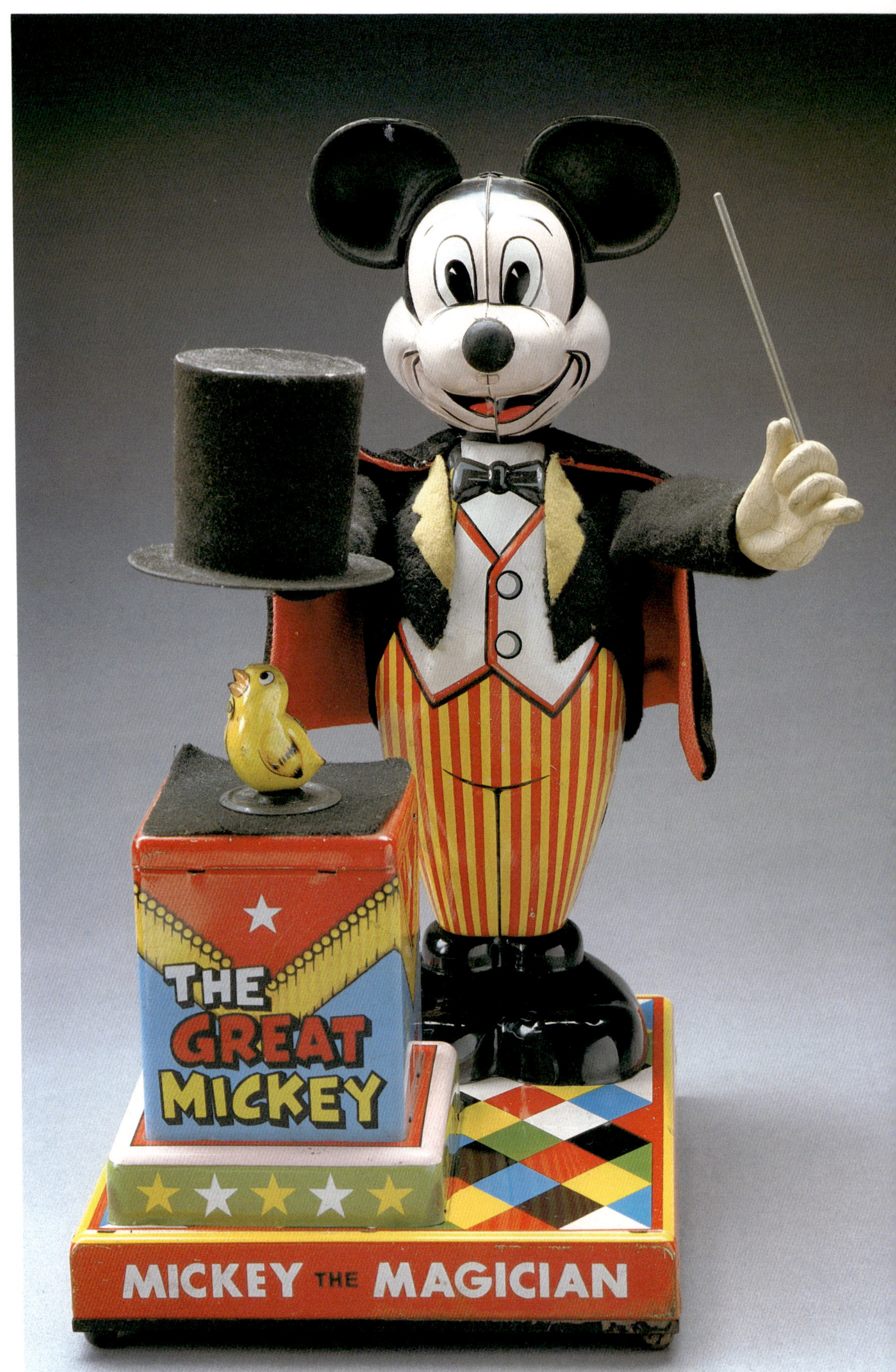

58 1950'S/MICKEY MOUSE THE MAGICIAN/LINE MAR/173 × 135 × 265

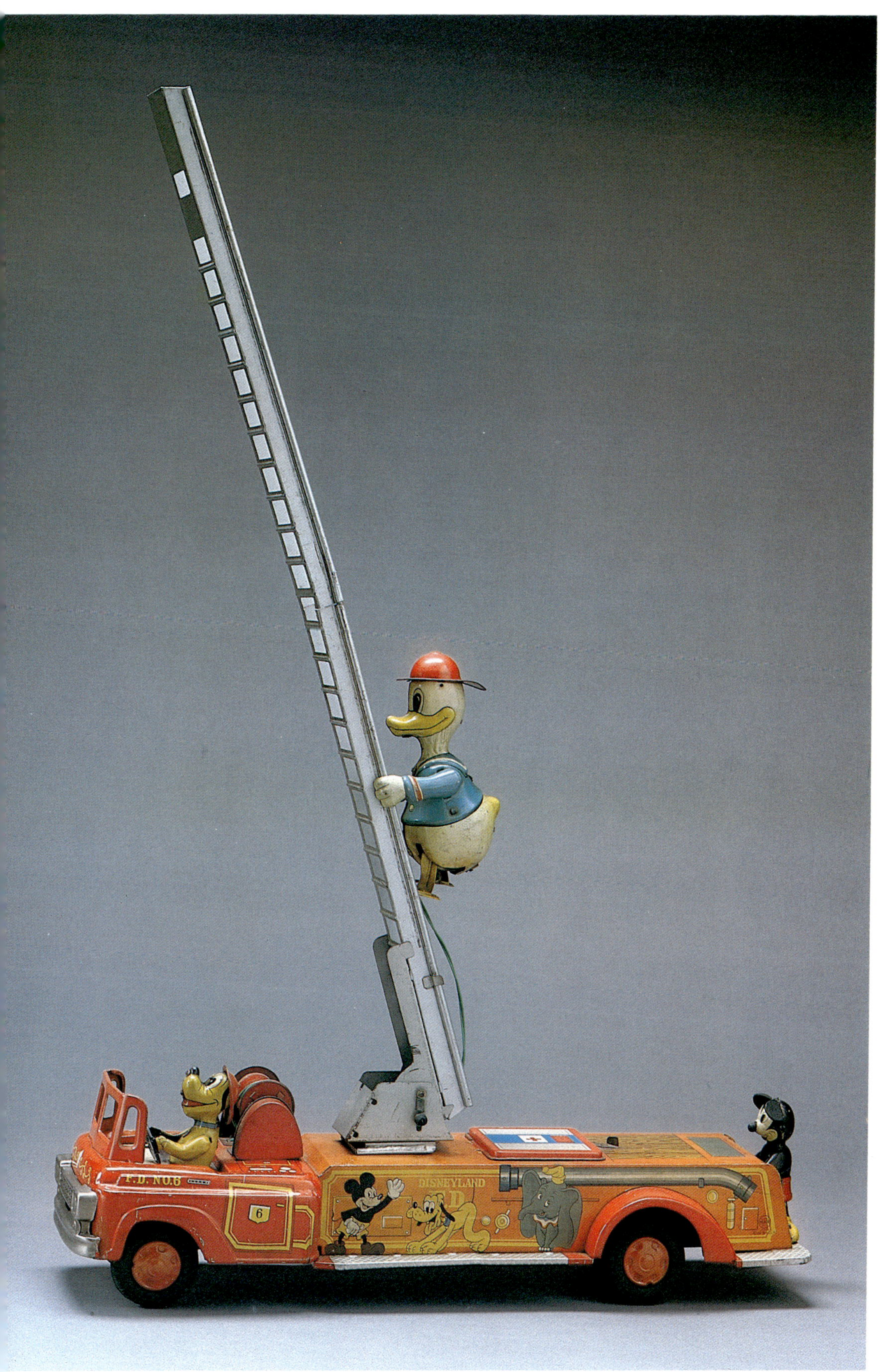

(59) 1950'S／DISNEY FIRE ENGINE／LINE MAR／460×133×705

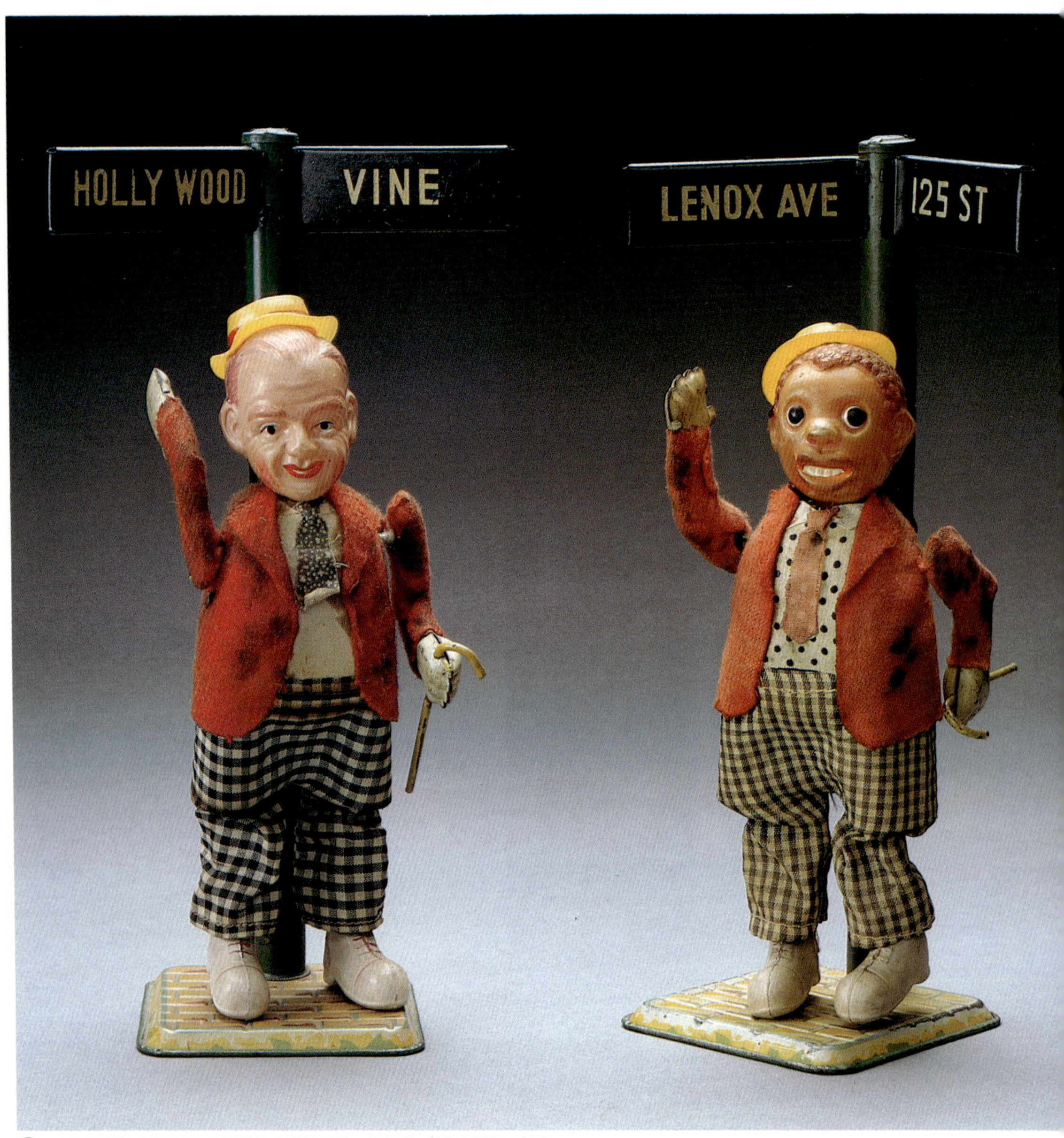

⑥⓪ OCCUPIED JAPAN／FRED ASTAIRE／ALPS／75×110×210
⑥① OCCUPIED JAPAN／TAP DANCER／ALPS／75×110×210

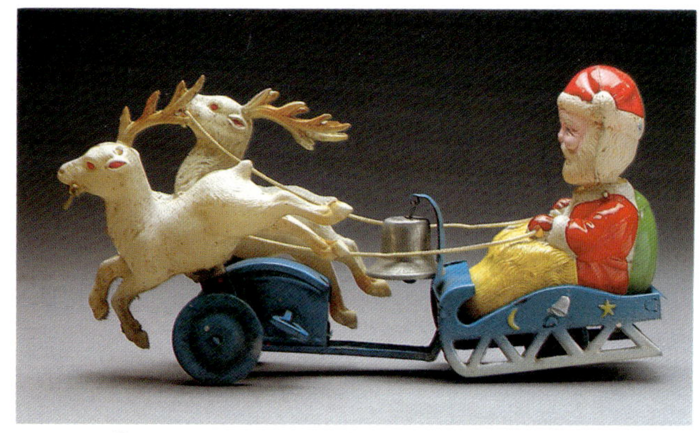

⑥② OCCUPIED JAPAN／SANTA CLAUS IN HIS SLEIGH／UNKNOWN／190×60×90

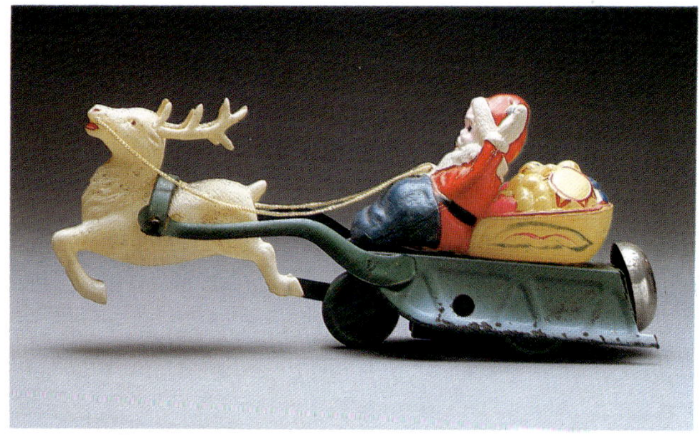

⑥③ OCCUPIED JAPAN／SANTA CLAUS IN HIS SLEIGH／UNKNOWN／205×45×85

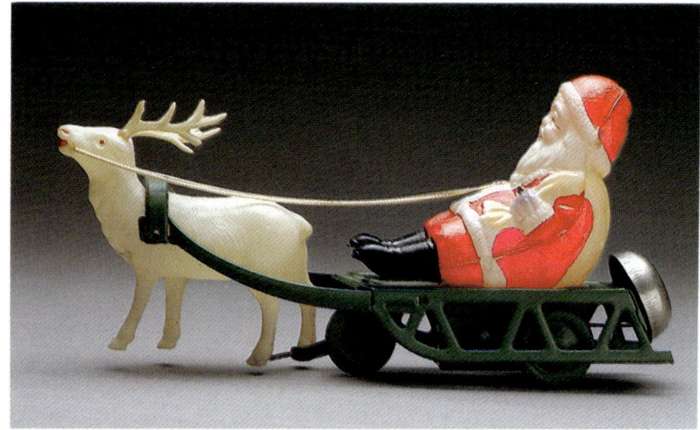

⑥④ OCCUPIED JAPAN／SANTA CLAUS IN HIS SLEIGH／UNKNOWN／205×45×100

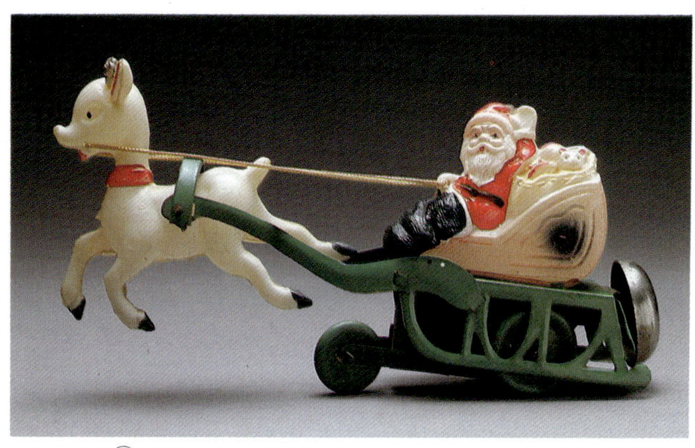

⑥⑤ OCCUPIED JAPAN／SANTA CLAUS IN HIS SLEIGH／UNKNOWN／170×45×95

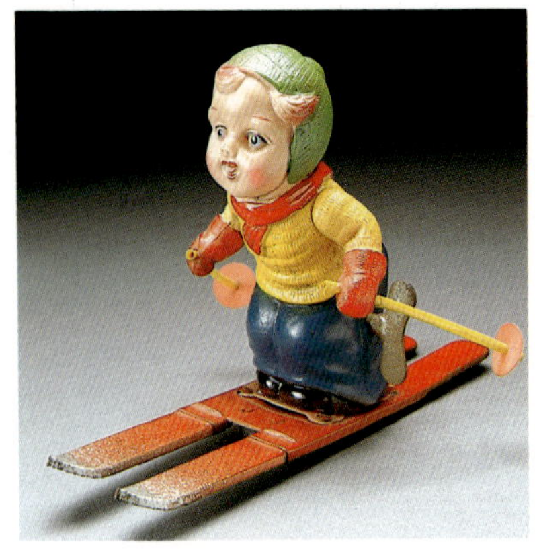

66 OCCUPIED JAPAN / SKIER / UNKNOWN / 160×120×115

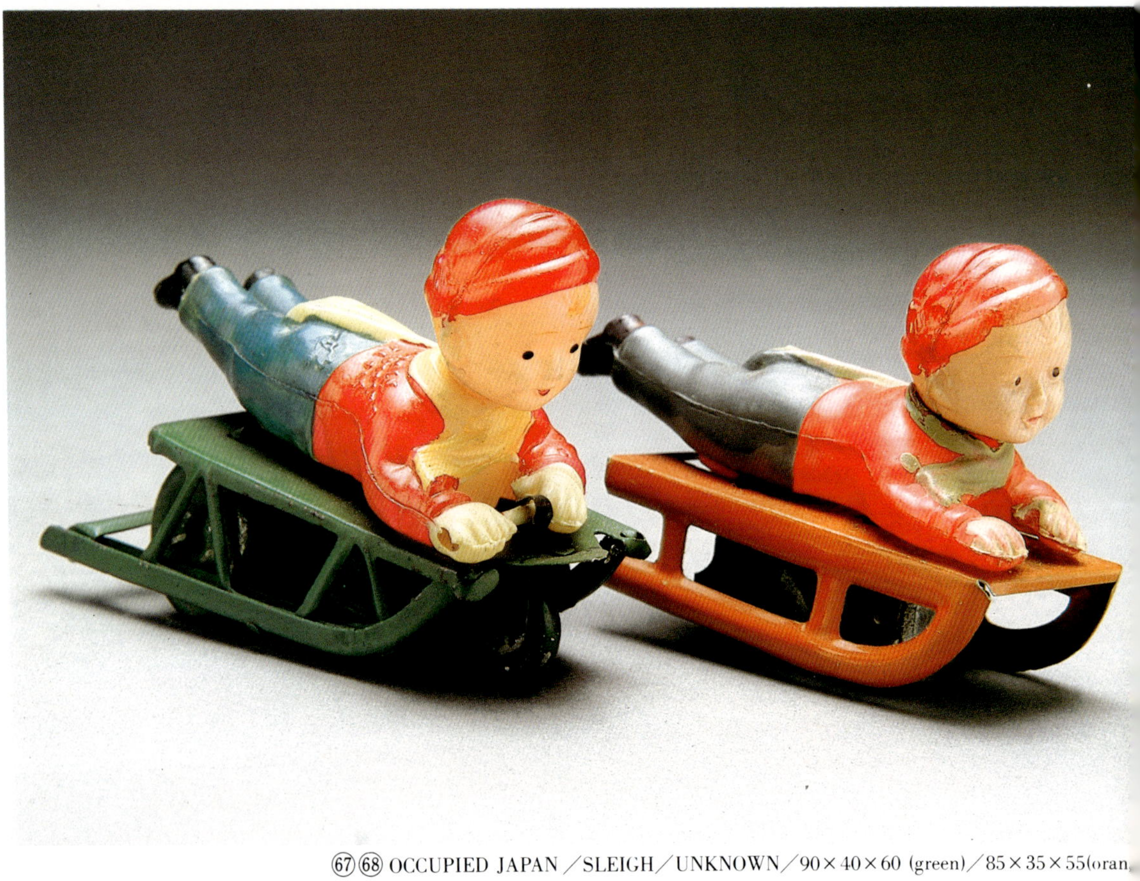

67 68 OCCUPIED JAPAN / SLEIGH / UNKNOWN / 90×40×60 (green) / 85×35×55(oran

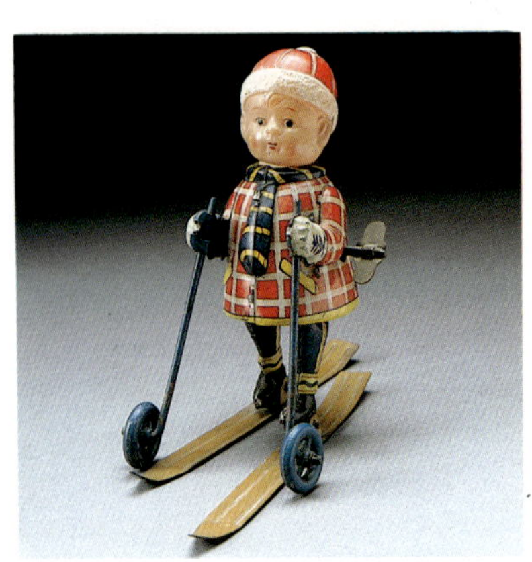

69 OCCUPIED JAPAN / SKIER / NIKKO KOGYO / 140×50×125

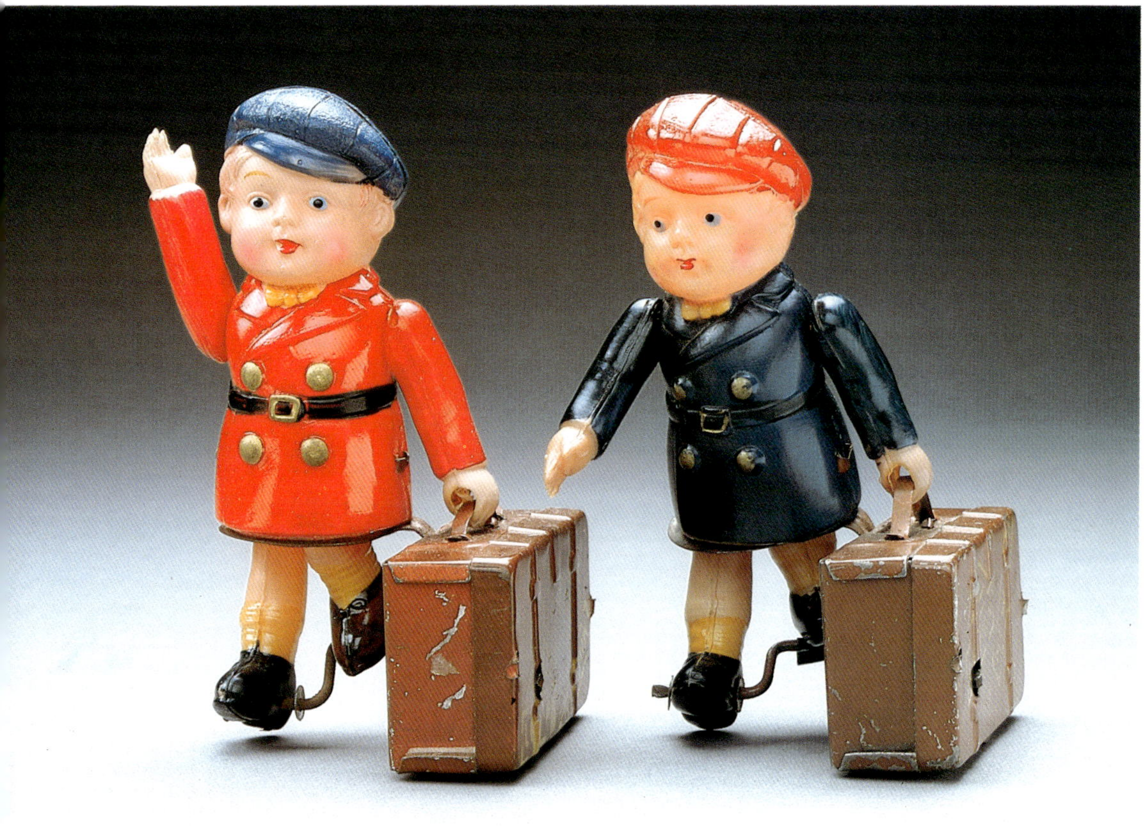

⑦⓪⑦① OCCUPIED JAPAN／BOYS CARRYING SUITCASE／ALPS／70×55×110

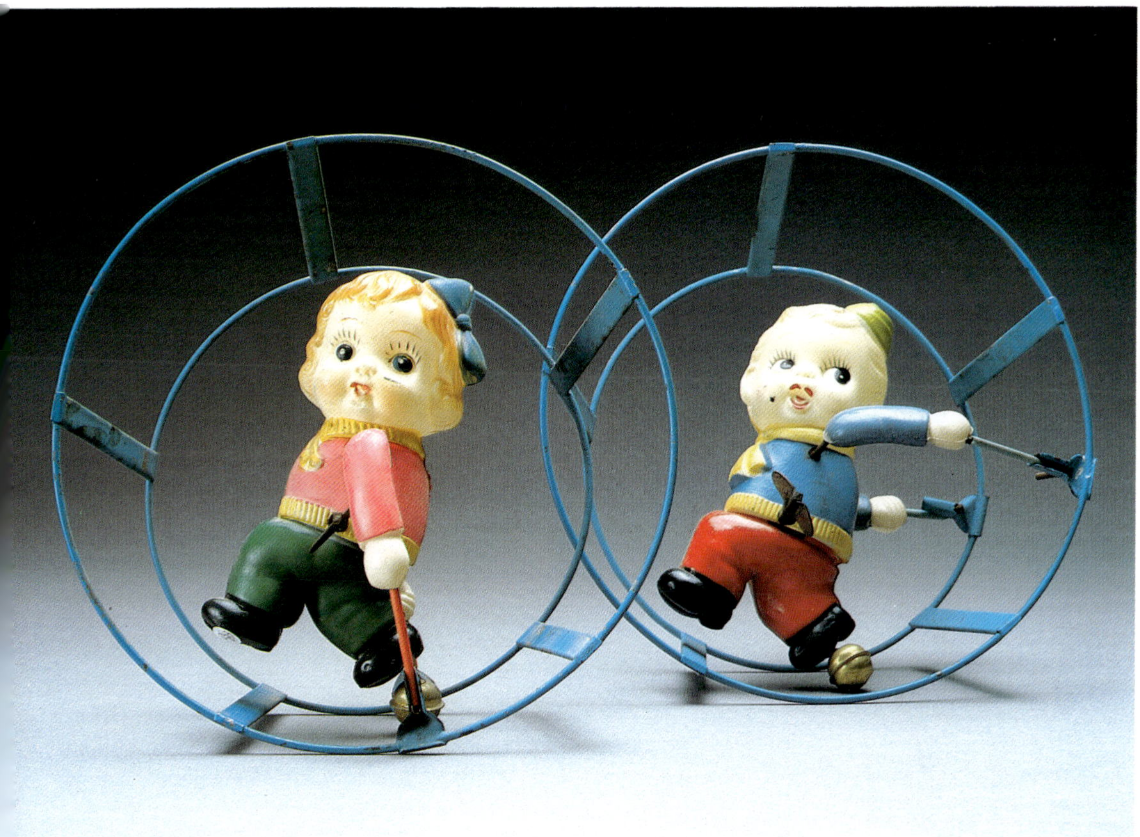

⑦②⑦③ OCCUPIED JAPAN／CHILDREN PLAYING WITH CYCLE／MASUDAYA／65×160×160

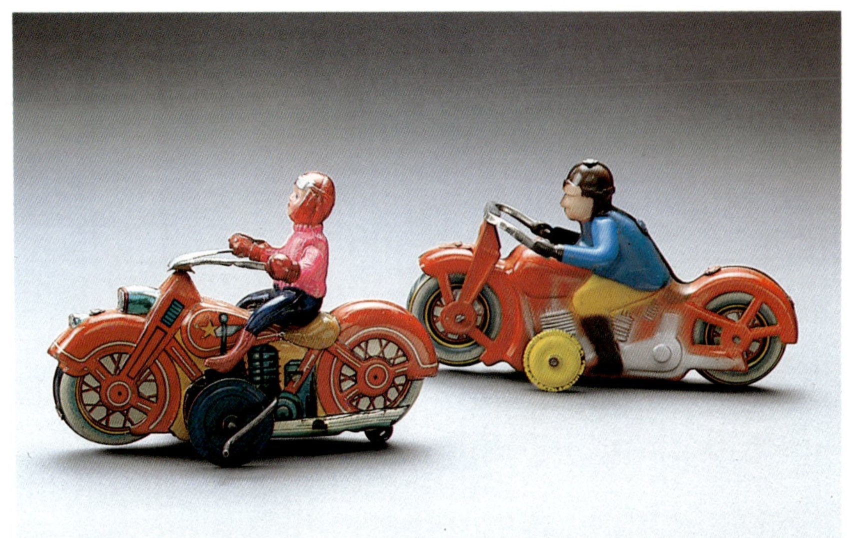

⑭⑮ OCCUPIED JAPAN／CIRCUS MOTORBIKE／YOSHIYA, UNKNOWN／
115×50×75, 130×35×75

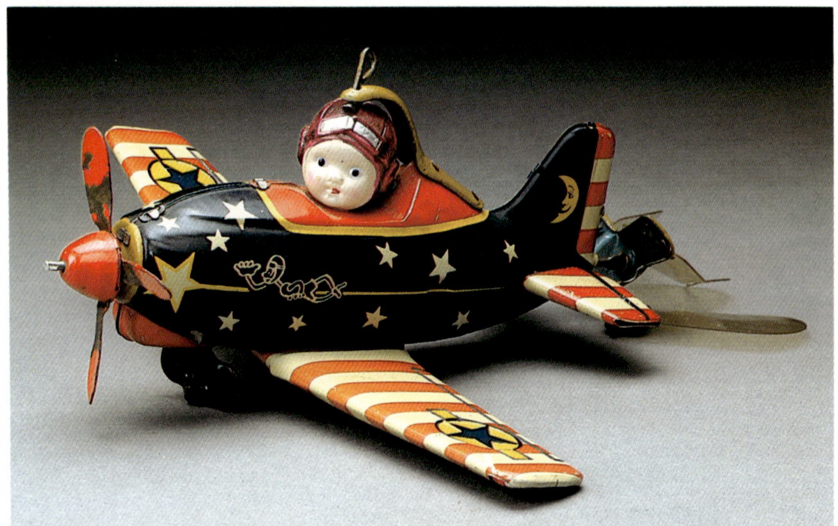

⑯ OCCUPIED JAPAN／AIRPLANE／NIKKO GANGUKOGYO／165×180×80

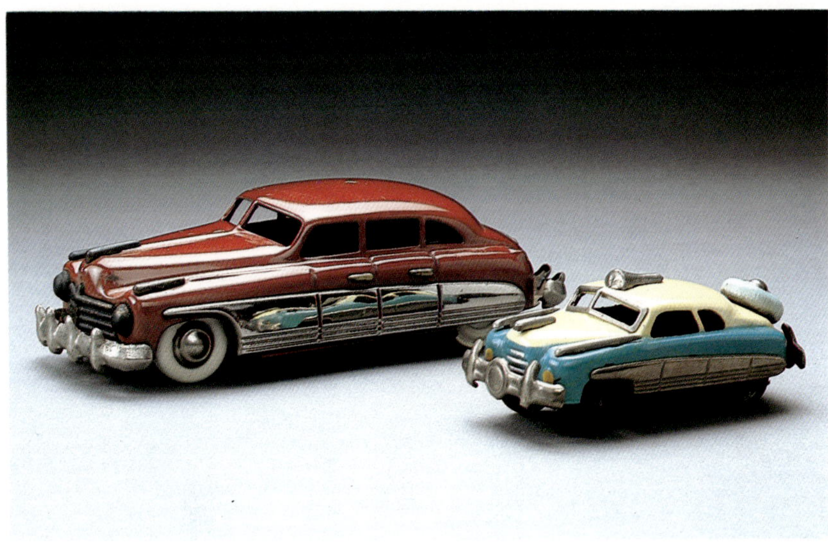

⑰ OCCUPIED JAPAN／AUTOMOBILE／UNKNOWN／170×70×55
⑱ OCCUPIED JAPAN／AUTOMOBILE／UNKNOWN／100×50×40

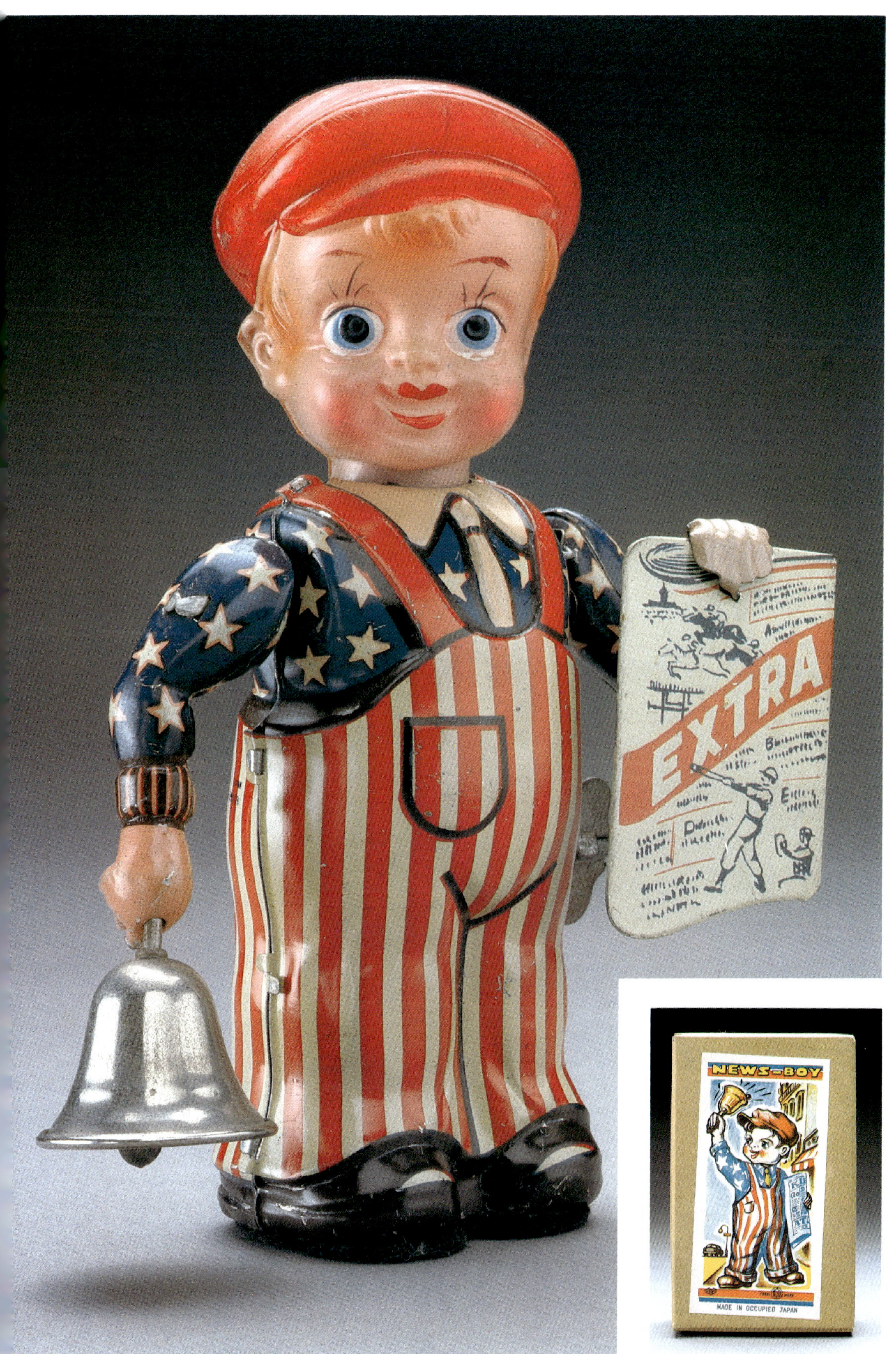

OCCUPIED JAPAN／NEWS BOY／NIKKO KOGYO／55×100×150

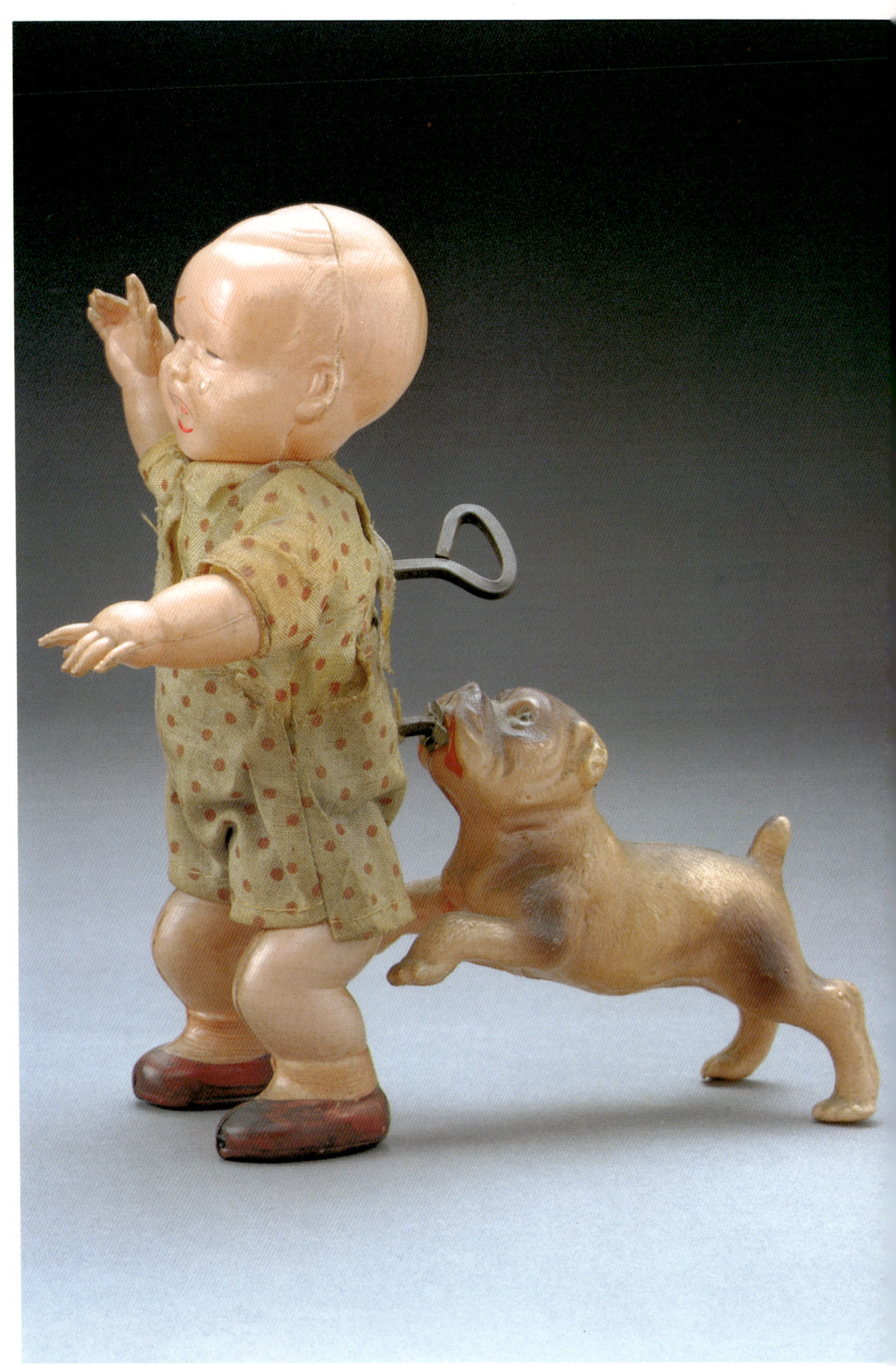

⑧⓪ OCCUPIED JAPAN／BOY WITH DOG／ALPS／115×75×145

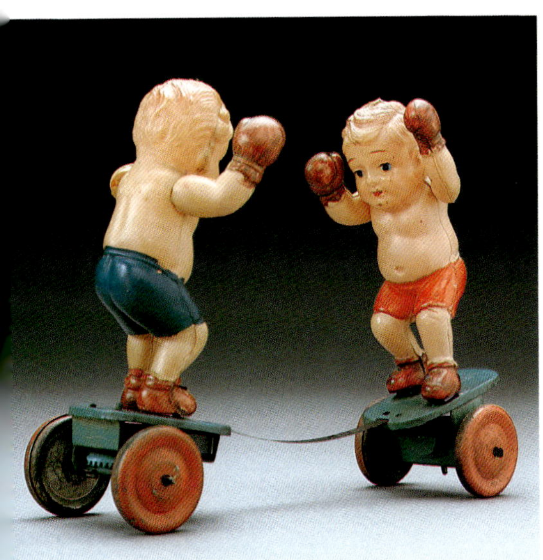

OCCUPIED JAPAN／BOXER／UNKNOWN／160×50×120

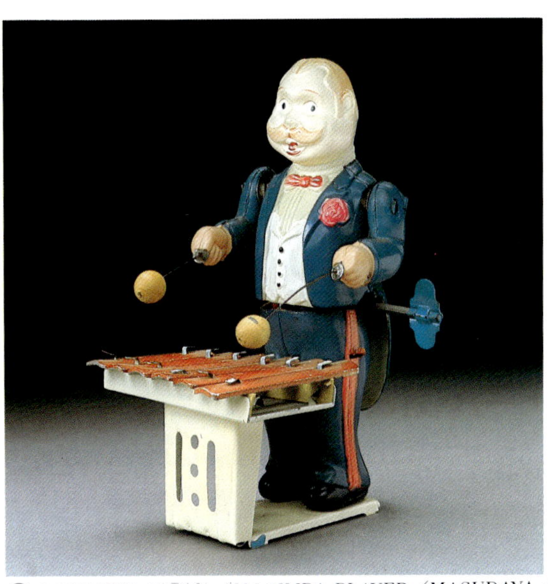

82 OCCUPIED JAPAN／MARIMBA PLAYER／MASUDAYA／90×85×145

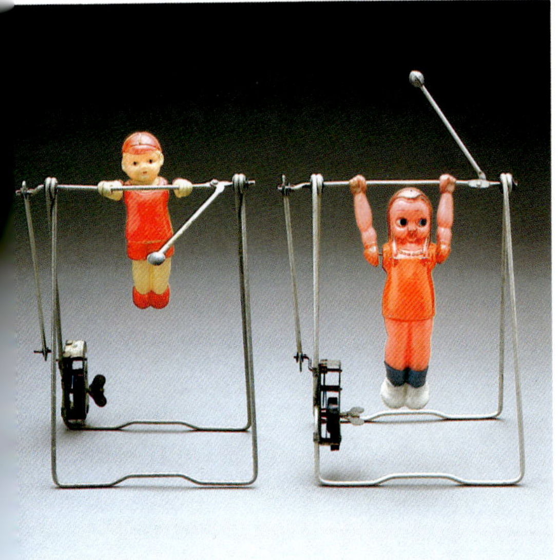

84 OCCUPIED JAPAN／CHILDREN ON HORIZONTAL BAR／FUJII／60×140×200

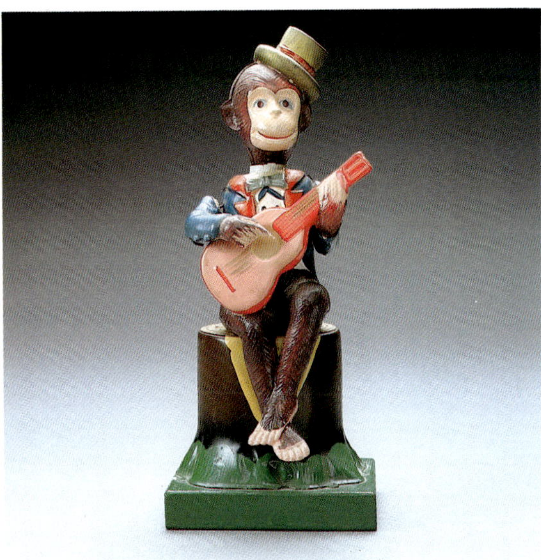

85 OCCUPIED JAPAN／MONKEY GUITARIST／ALPS／75×85×190

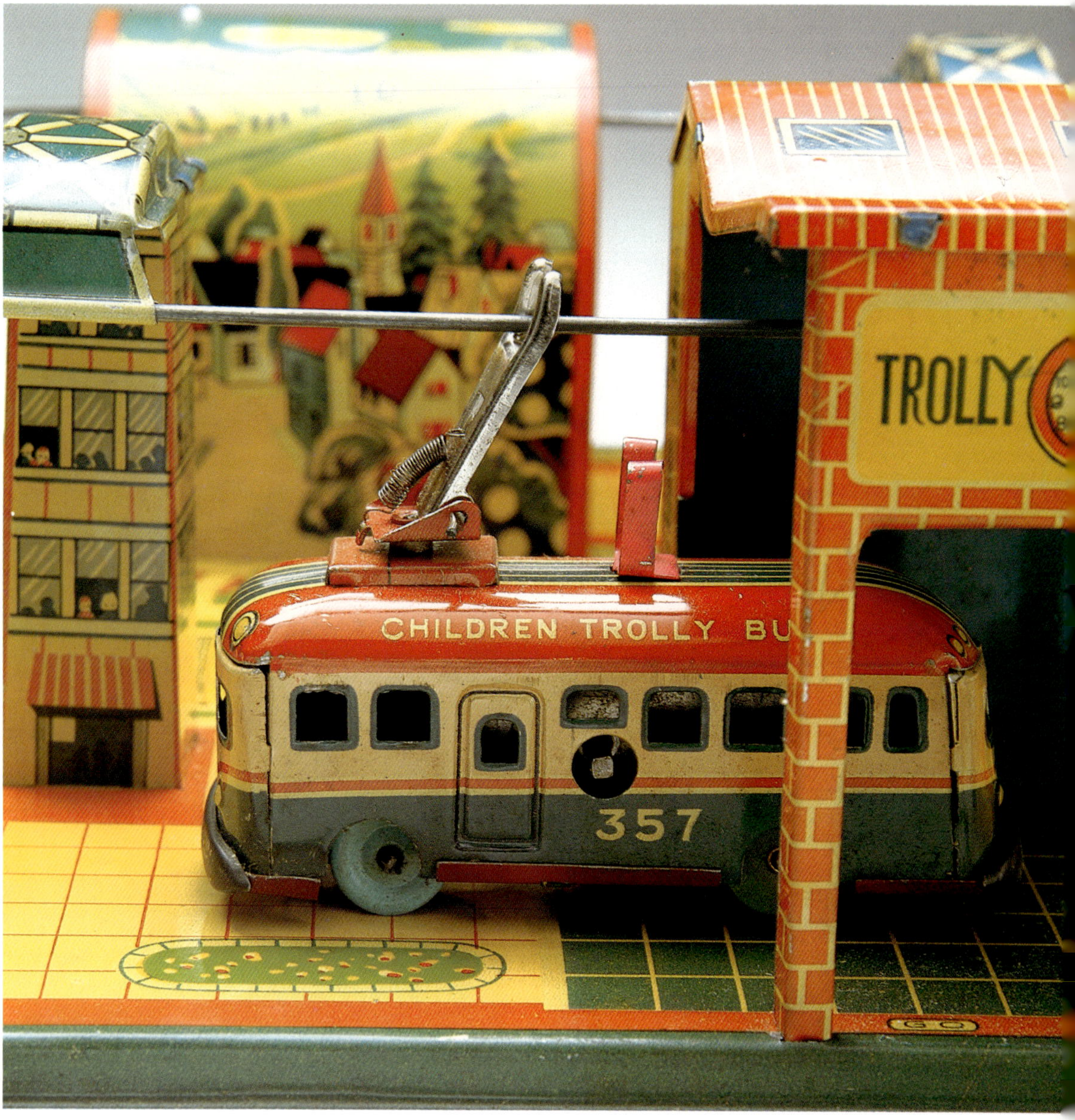

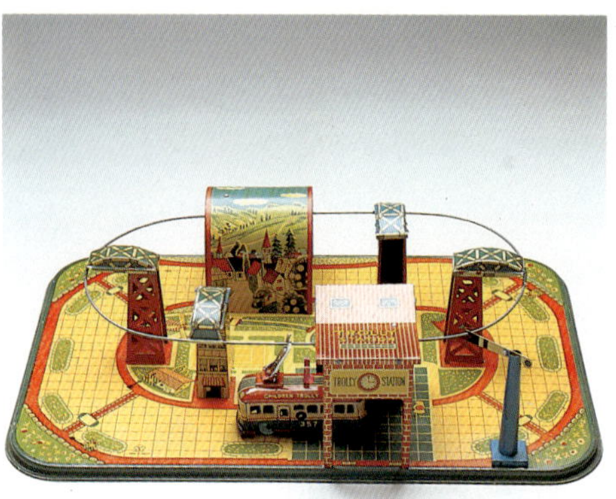

⑧⑥1950'S／TROLLEY BUS／YONEZAWA／430×280×100

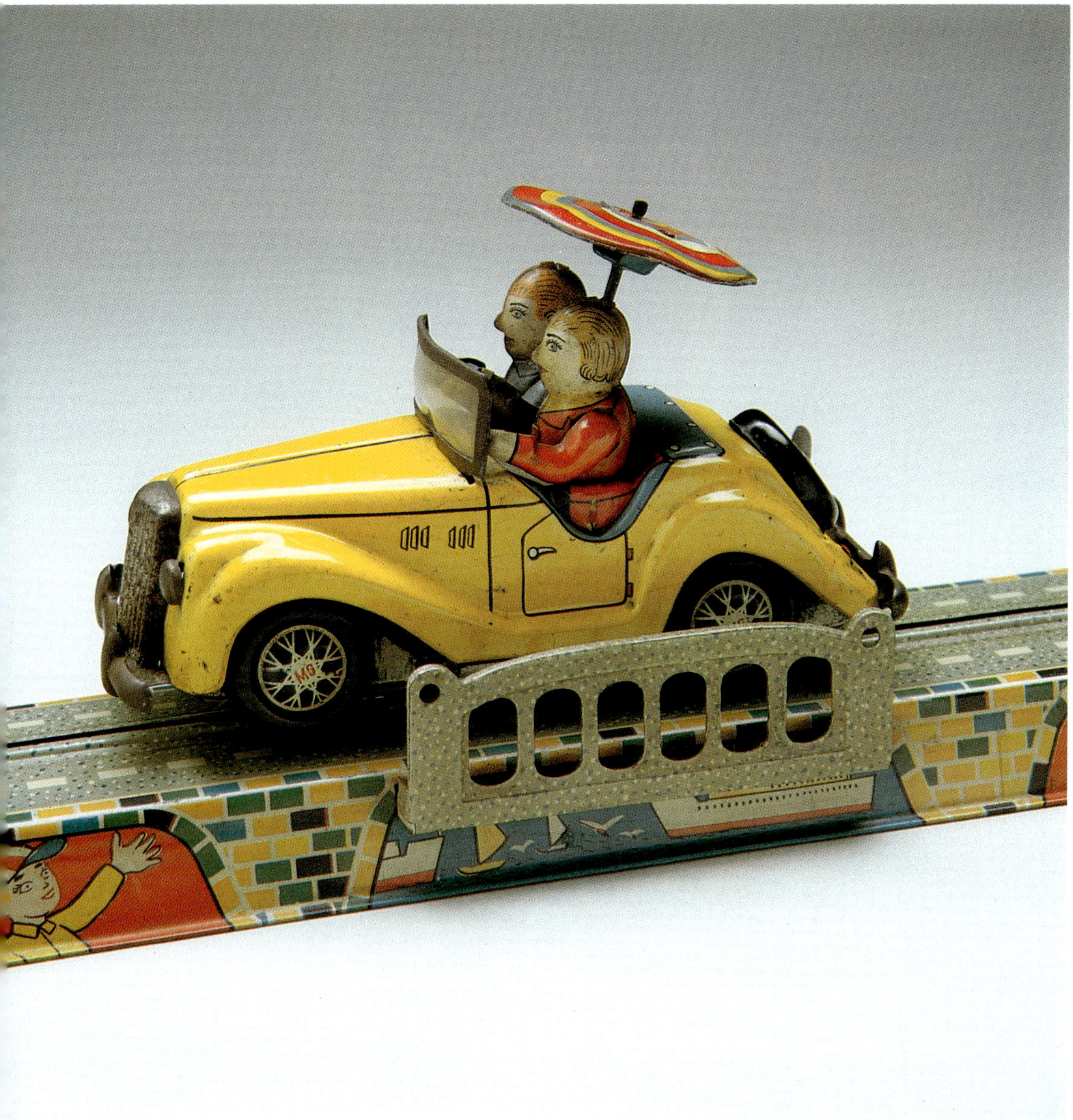

(87) 1950'S／M. G.／MARUSAN／315×65×100

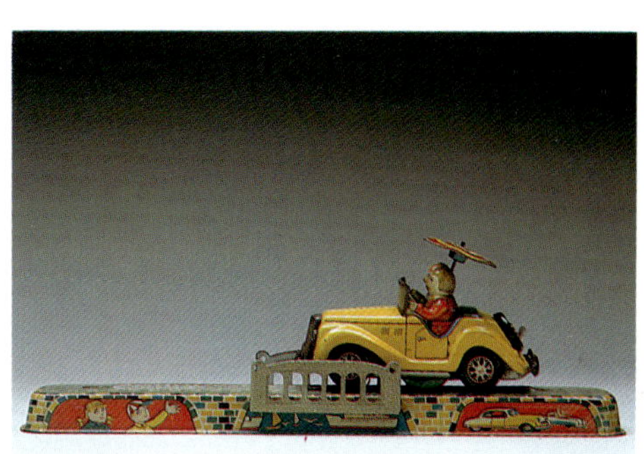

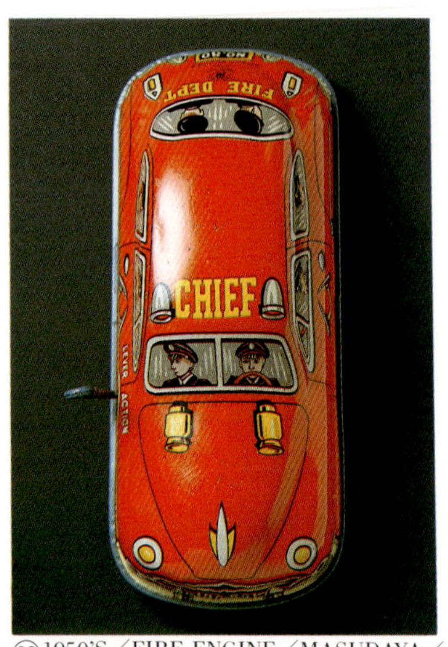

⑧⑧ 1950'S／FIRE ENGINE／MASUDAYA／
163×78×53

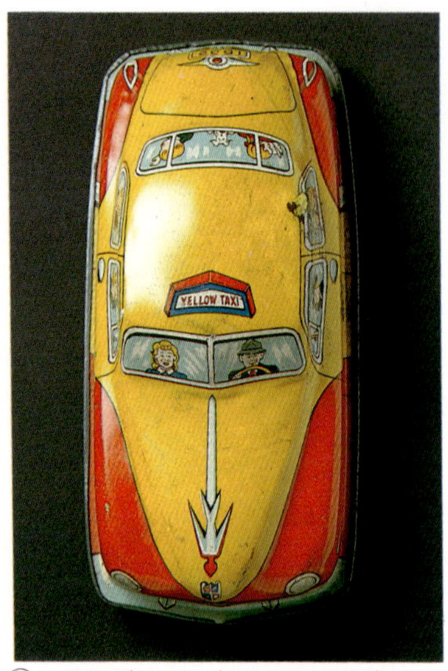

⑧⑨ 1950'S／TAXI ／MASUDAYA／
163×78×53

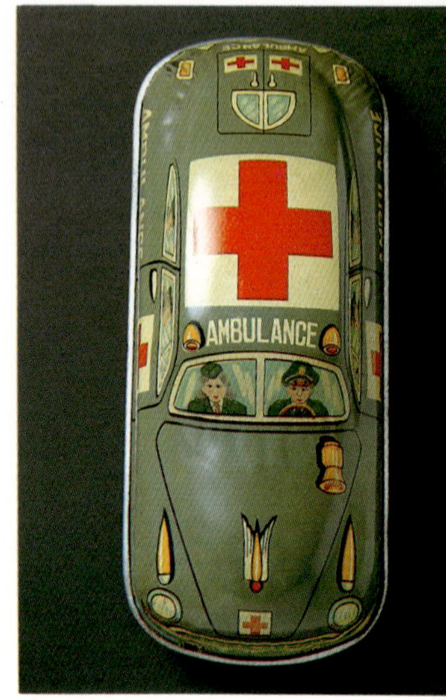

⑨⓪ 1950'S／AMBULANCE／MASUDAY
190×80×58

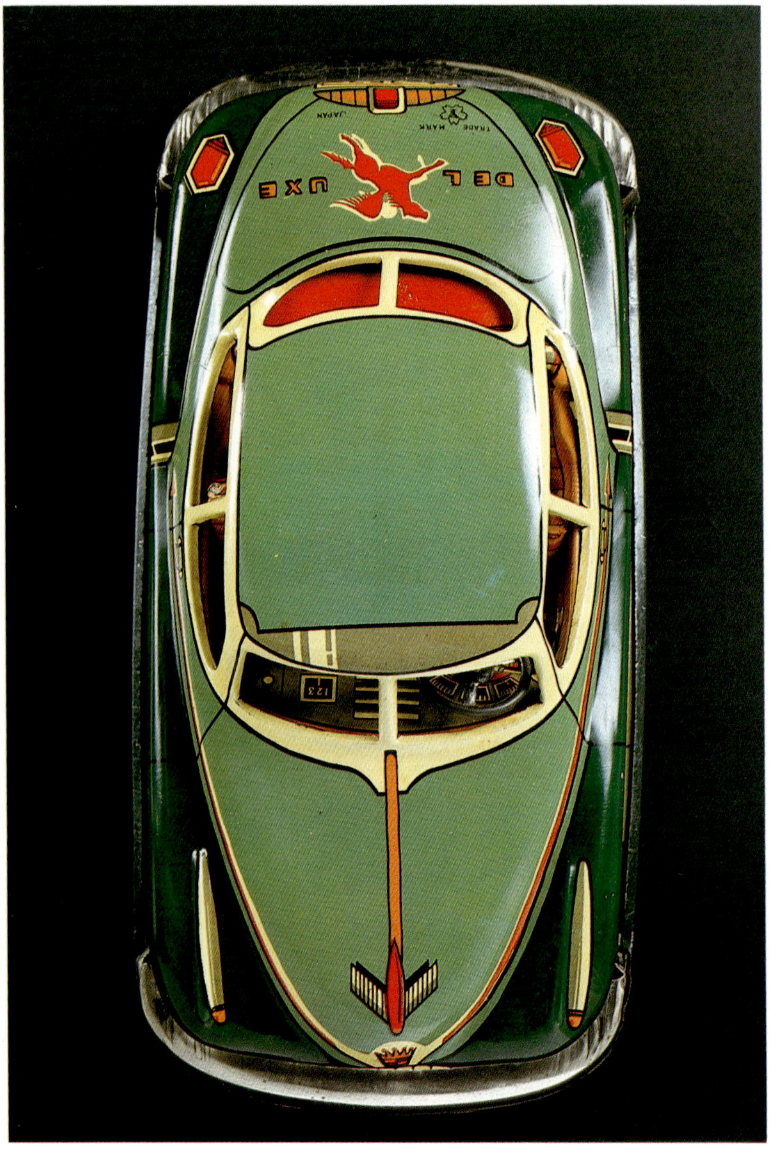

⑨① 1950'S／PEGASUS／YONEZAWA／
220×100×70

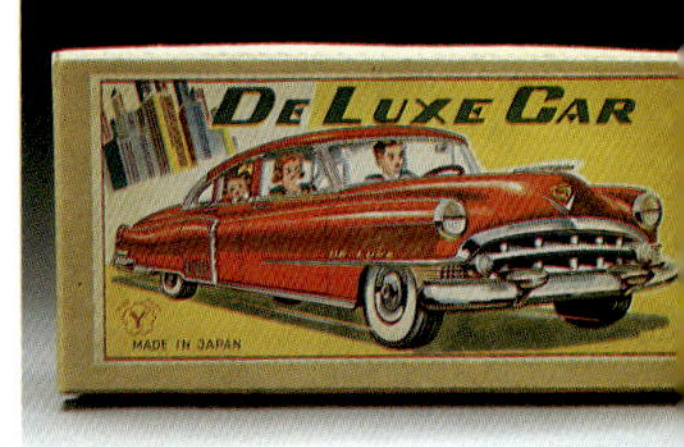

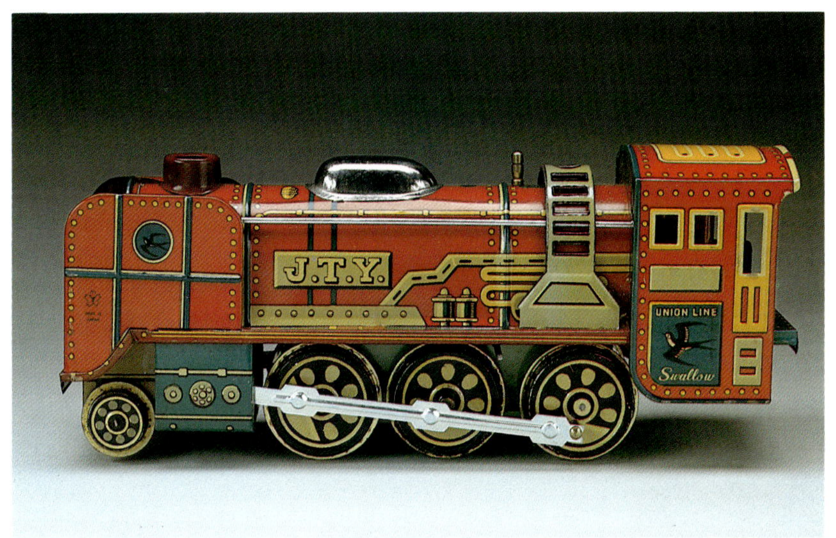

(92) 1950'S / LOCOMOTIVE / YONEZAWA / 290 × 75 × 120

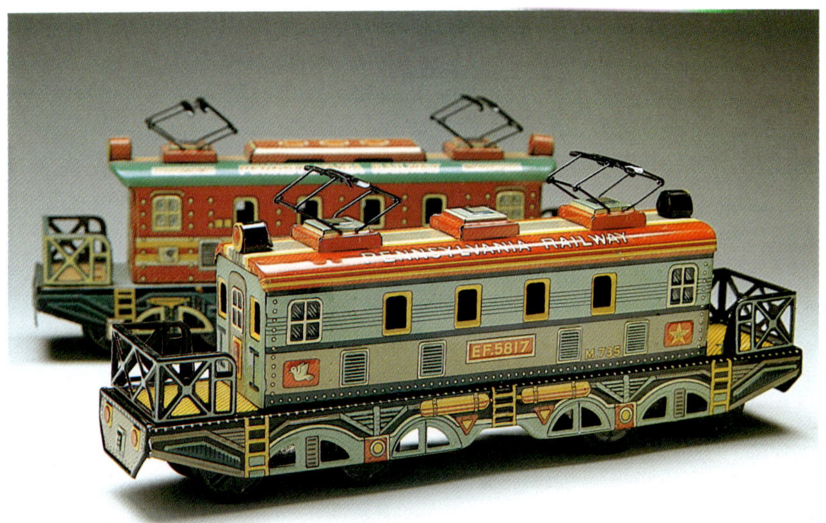

(93)(94) 1950'S / STREET CAR / ASAKUSA GANGU NINGYO, YONEZAWA / 335 × 65 × 125

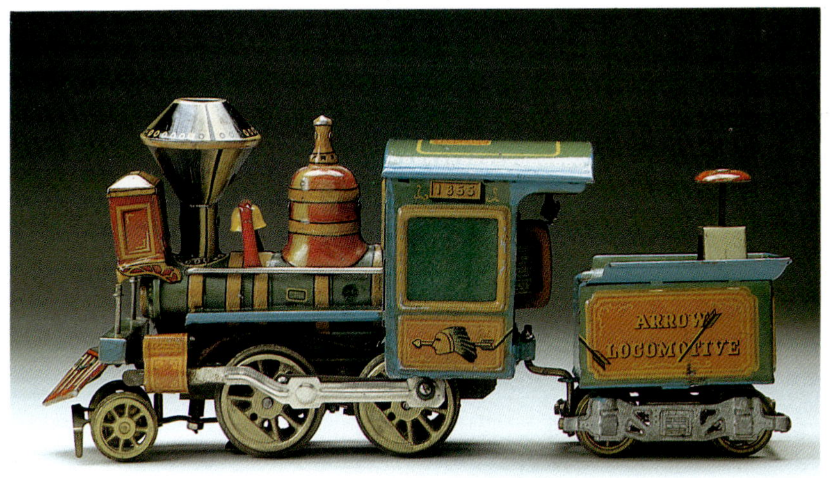

(95) 1950'S / LOCOMOTIVE / TOMIYAMA / 230 × 60 × 110

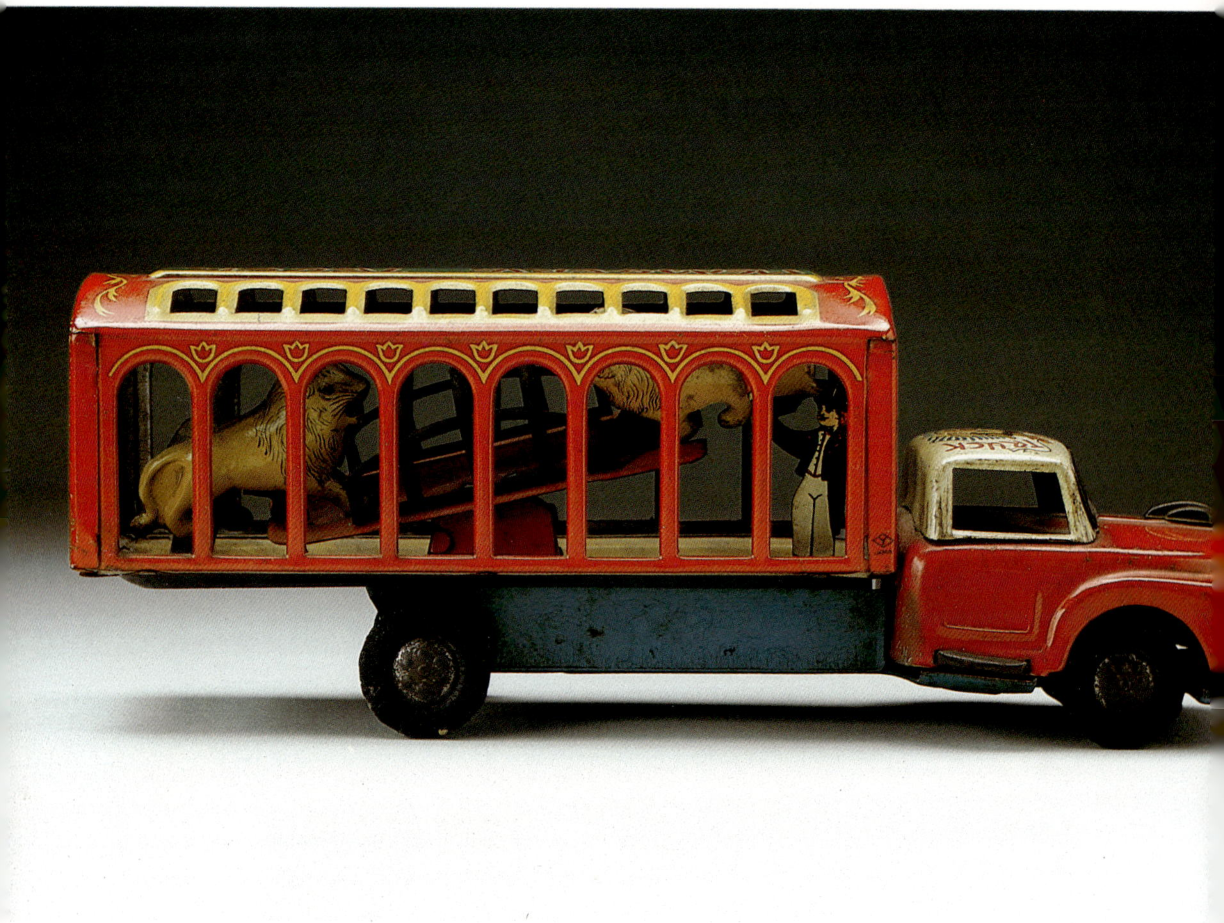

(96) 1950'S／CIRCUS TRUCK／YOSHI1／250×60×95

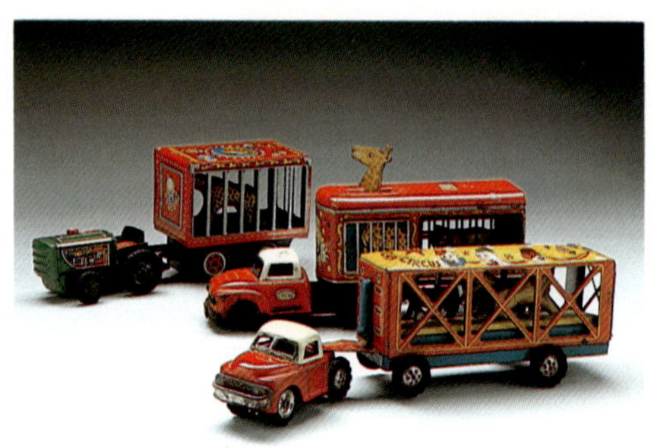

(97) 1950'S／CIRCUS TRUCK／SANKEI／225×70×95
(98) 1950'S／CIRCUS TRUCK／MITSUHASHI／230×60×125
(99) 1950'S／CIRCUS TRUCK／UNKNOWN／280×65×85

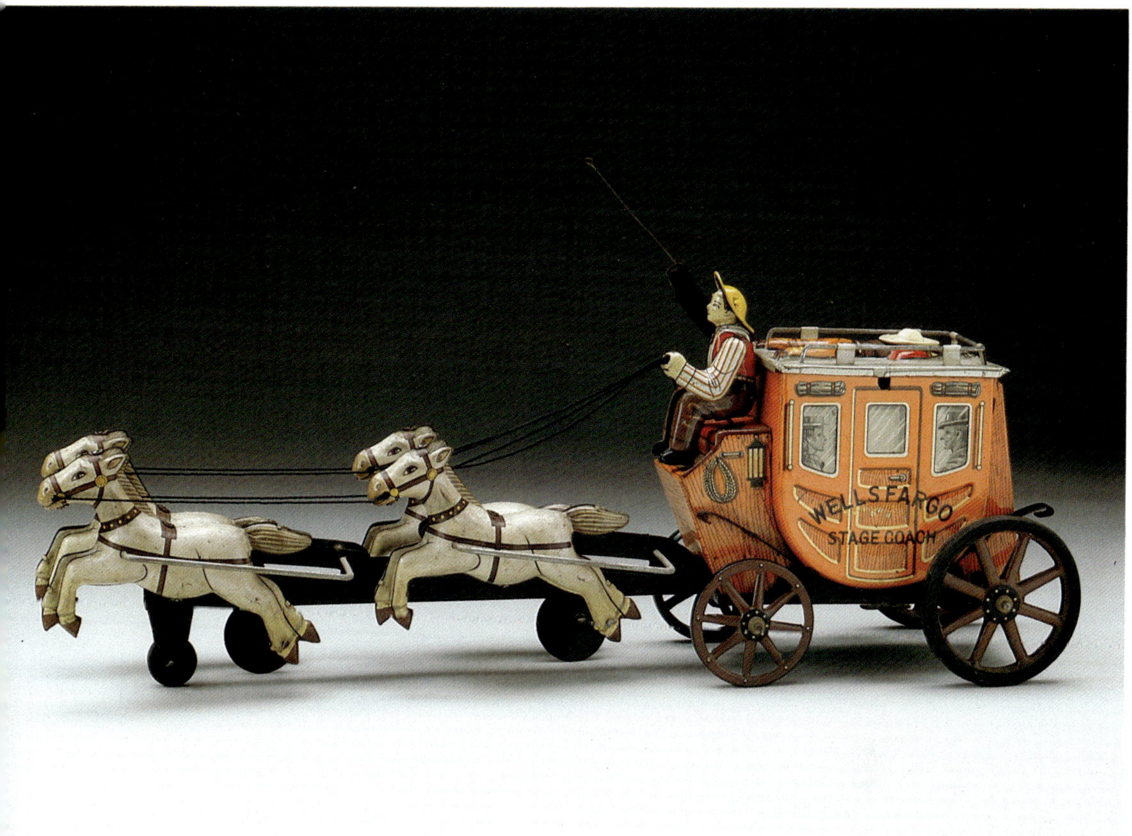

(100) 1950'S／STAGECOACH／NOMURA／380×90×110

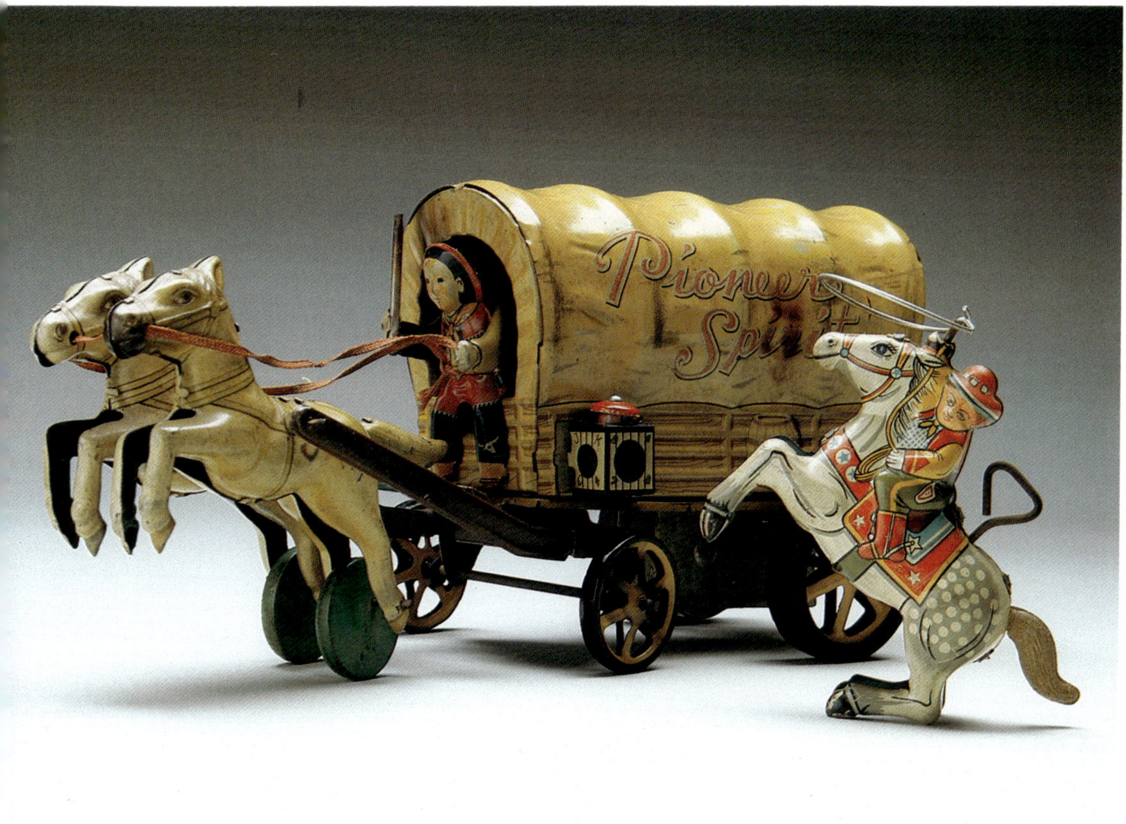

(101) (102) 1950'S／COVERED WAGON AND COWBOY／ALPS, UNKNOWN／270×80×113, 105×25×80

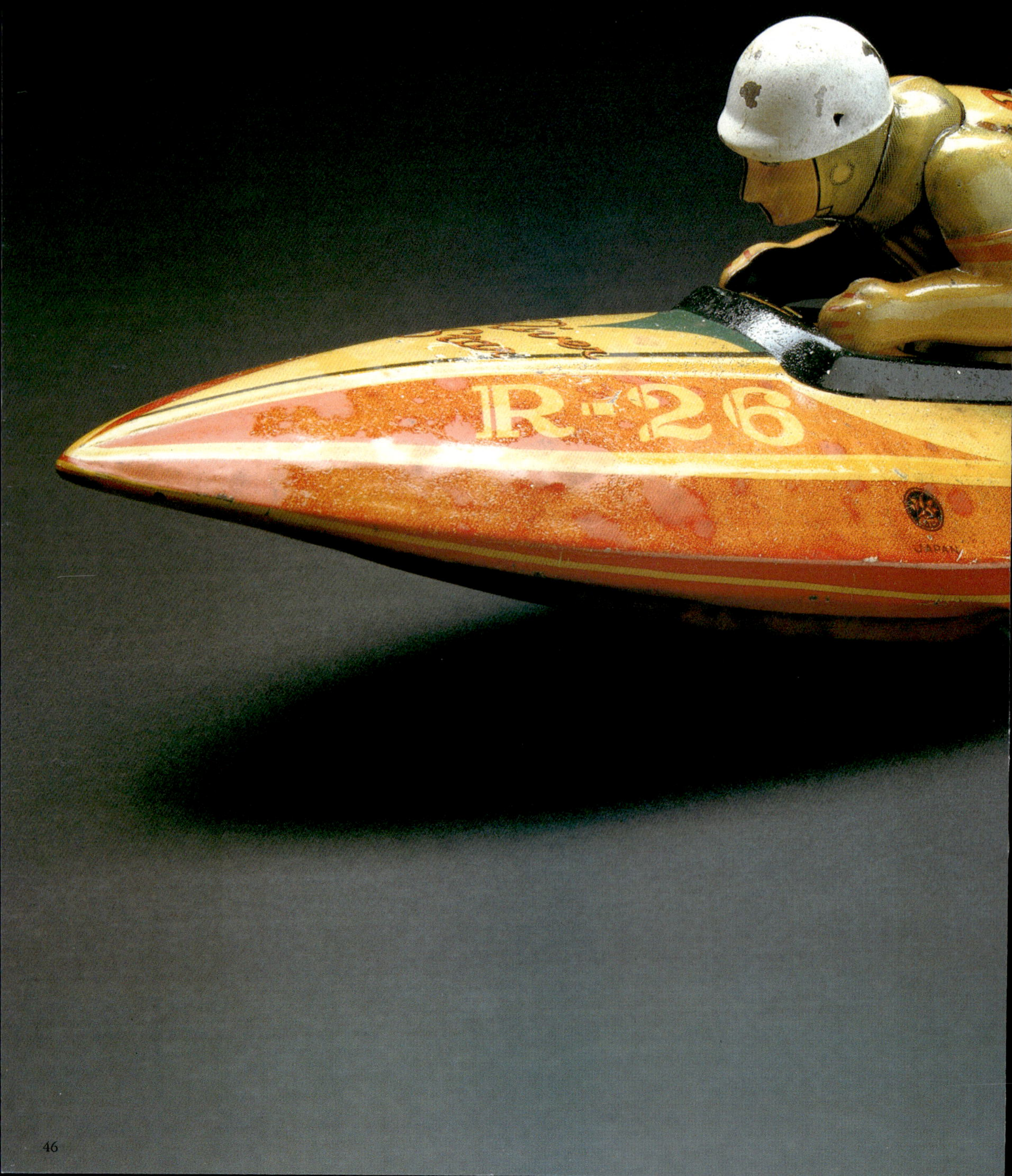
R-26

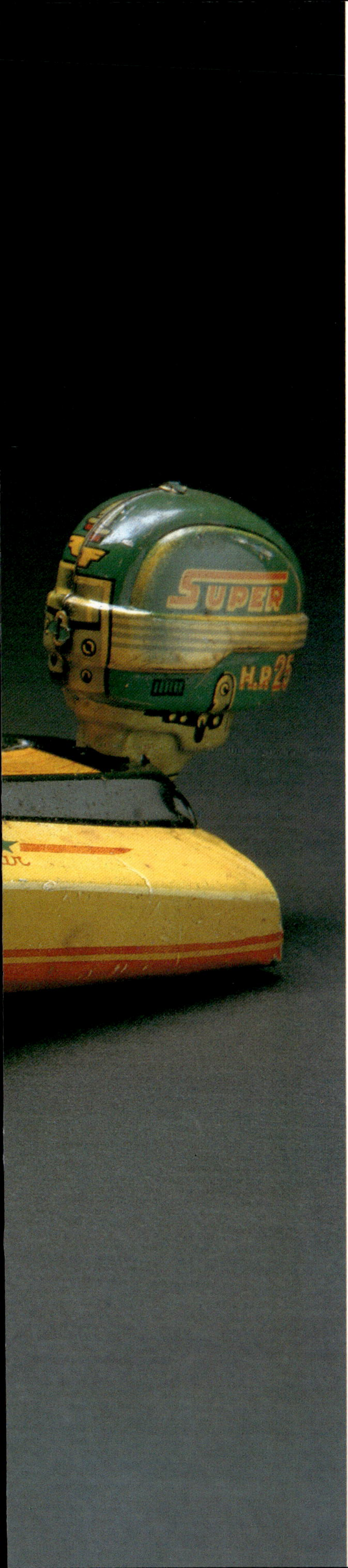

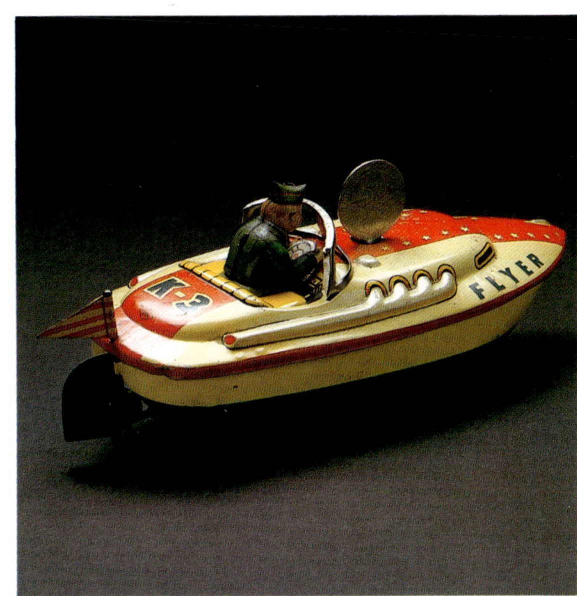

(104) 1950'S／MOTOR BOAT／NIHON BOEKI／205×75×70

(105) 1950'S／ROW BOAT／**MOMOYA**／200×95×105

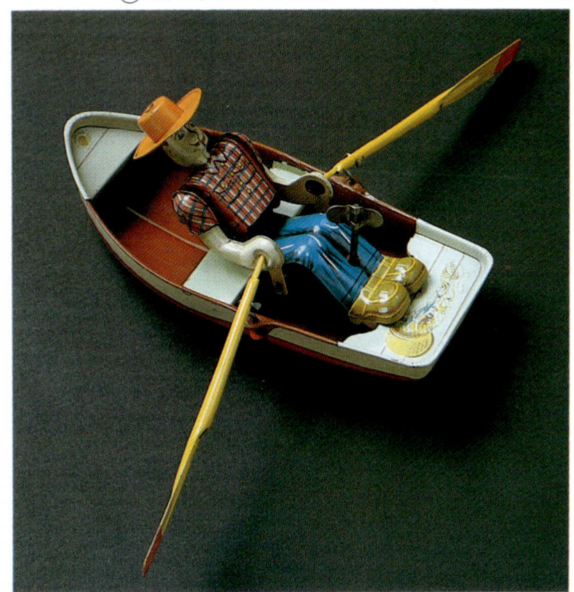

(103) 1950'S／RACING BOAT／TOMIYAMA／238×90×82

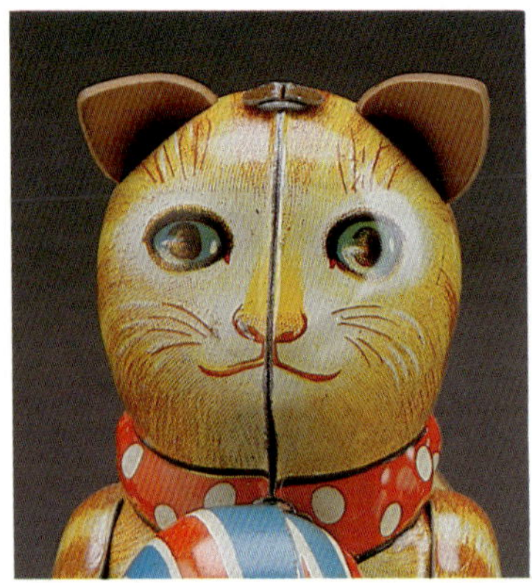

⑩⑥ 1950'S／CAT／KANTO TOY／ 115 (length)

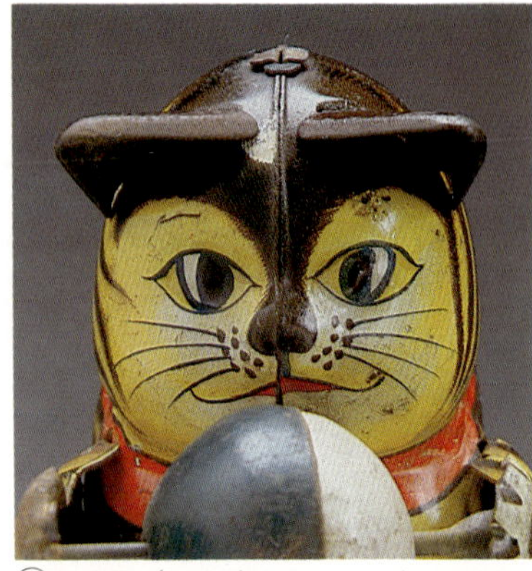

⑩⑦ 1950'S／CAT／FUKUDA ／135 (length)

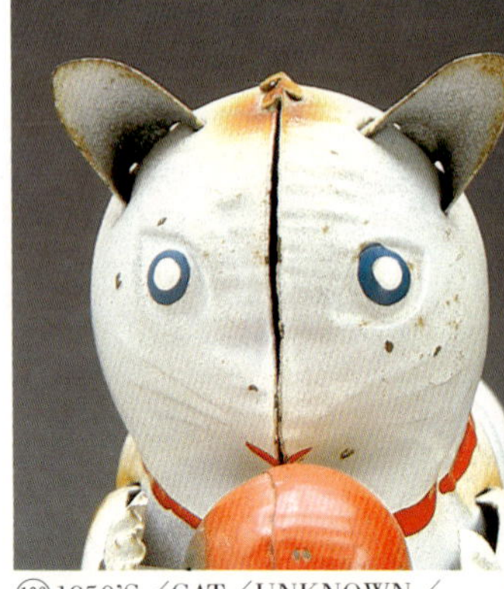

⑩⑧ 1950'S／CAT／UNKNOWN／ 140 (length)

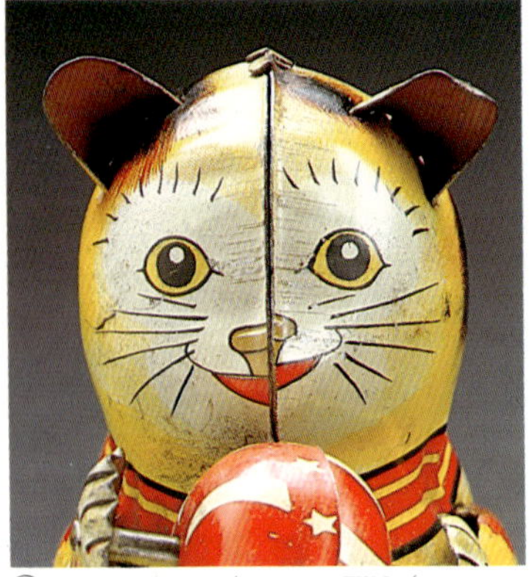

⑩⑨ 1950'S／CAT／UNKNOWN／ 135 (length)

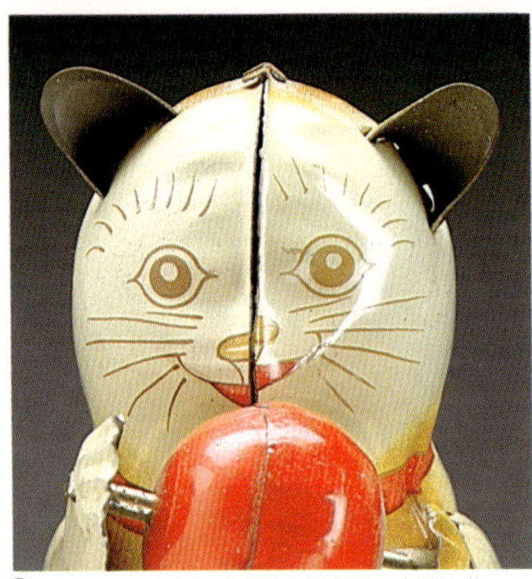

⑪⓪ 1950'S／CAT／UNKNOWN／135 (length)

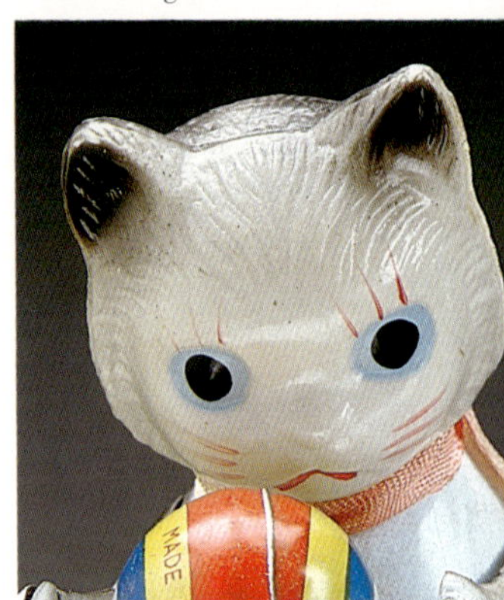

⑪⑪ 1950'S／CAT／UNKNOWN／130 (l

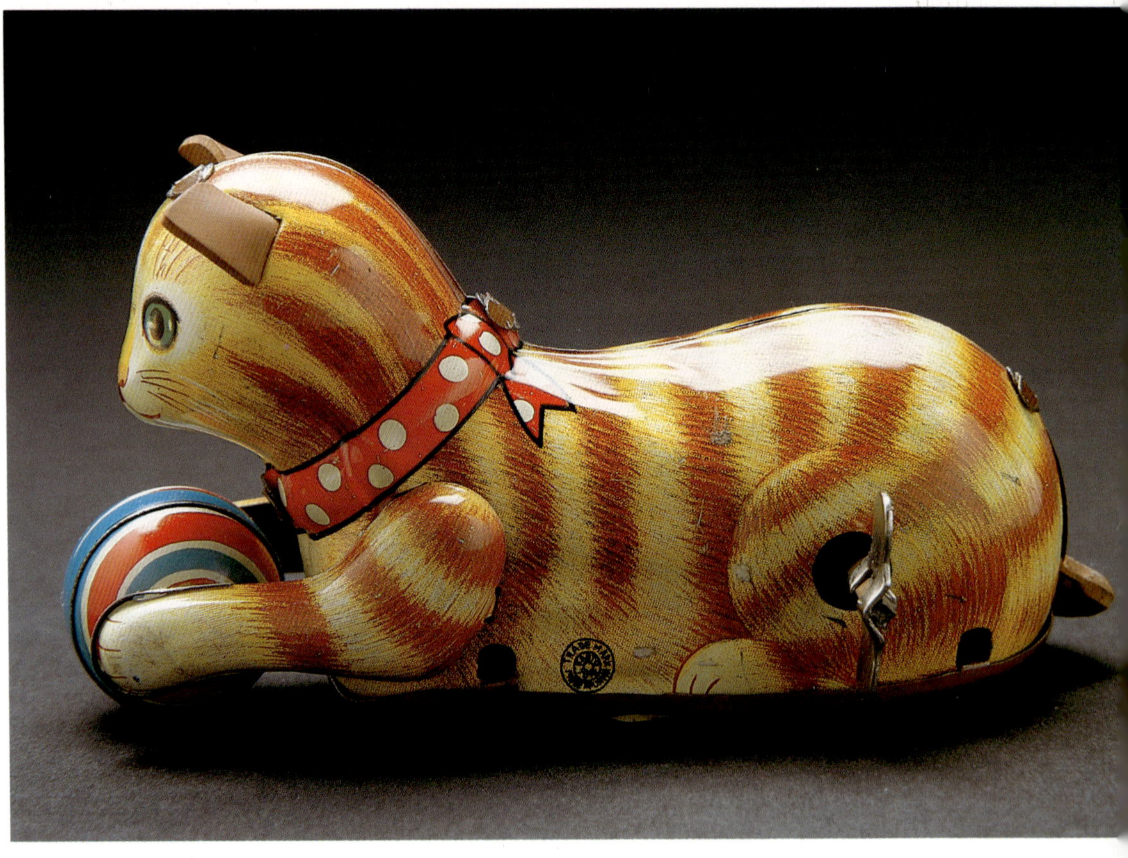

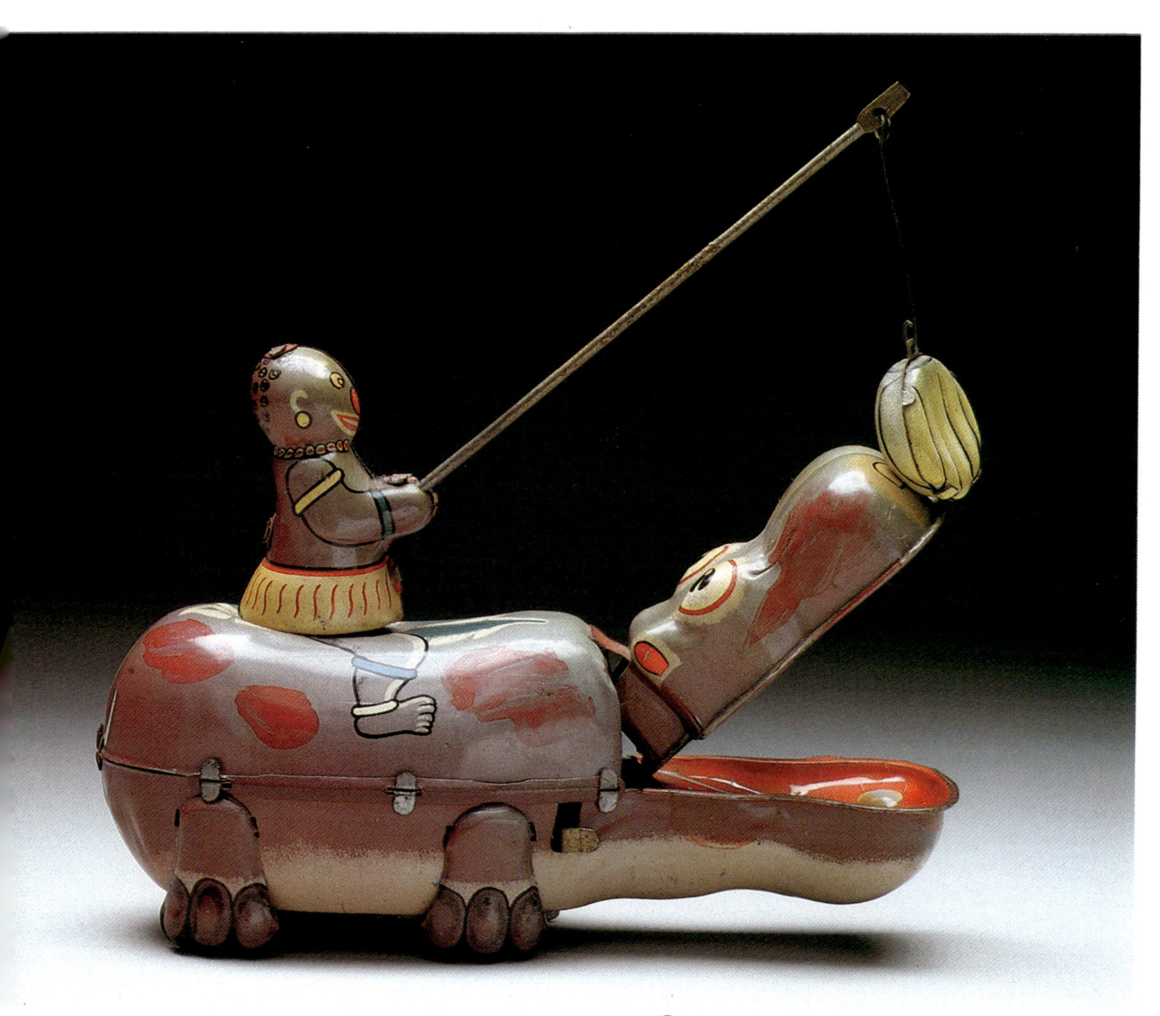

⑪② 1950'S／HIPPOPOTAMUS／TOPLY／142×50×140

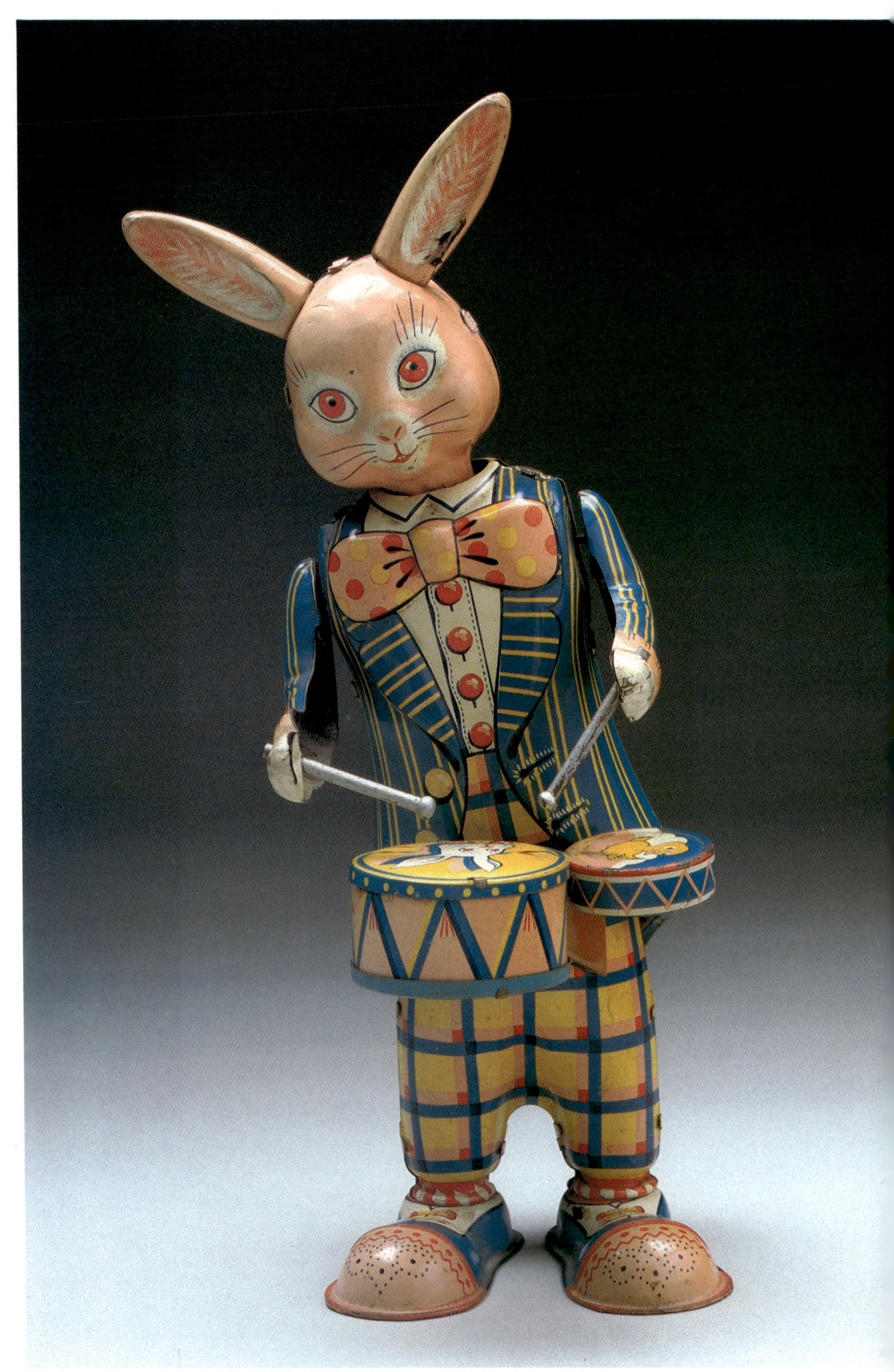

⑪③ 1950'S／RABBIT DRUMMER／ALPS／85×75×210

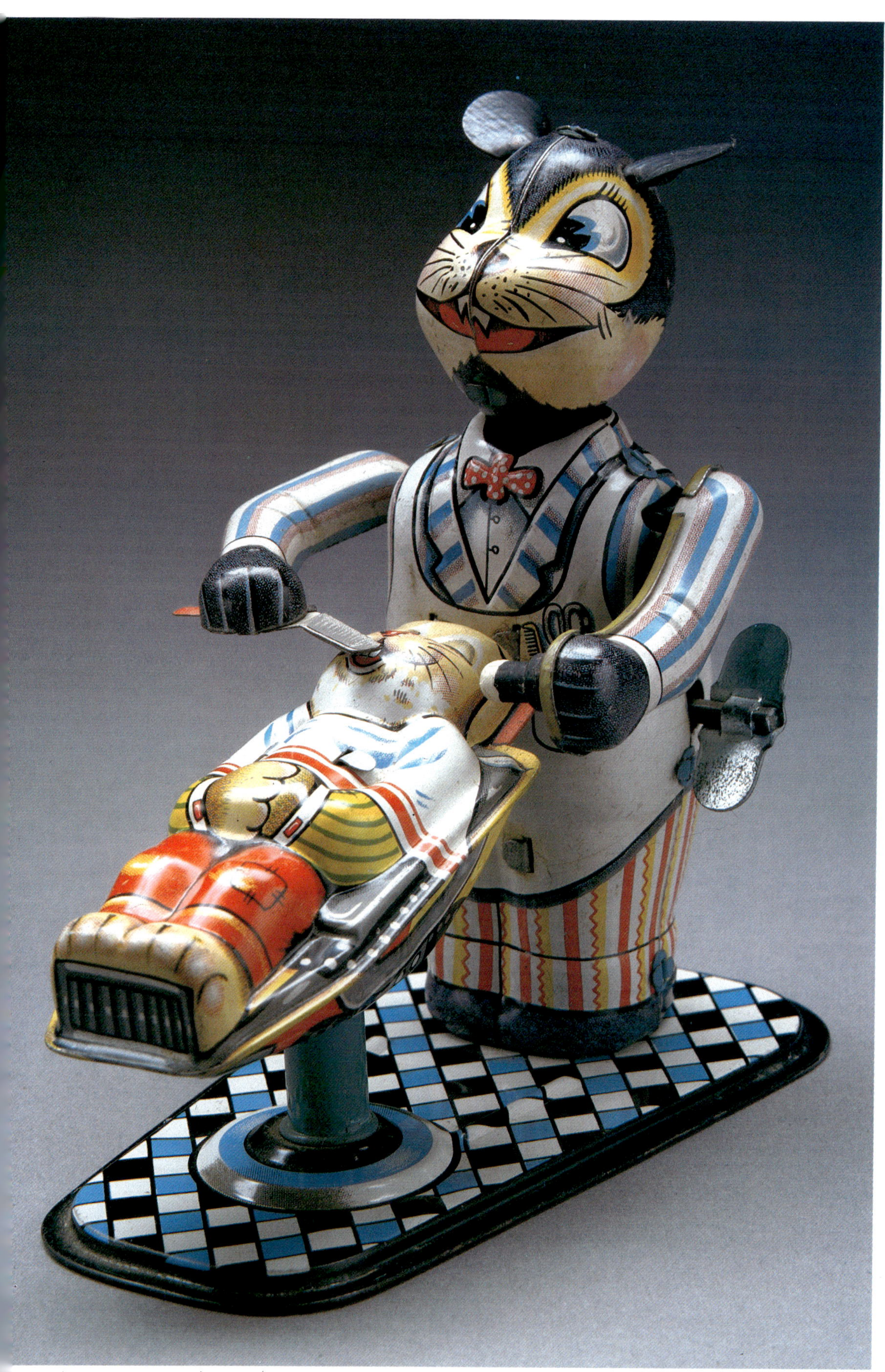

950'S/ANIMAL BARBER/TOPLY/120×70×120

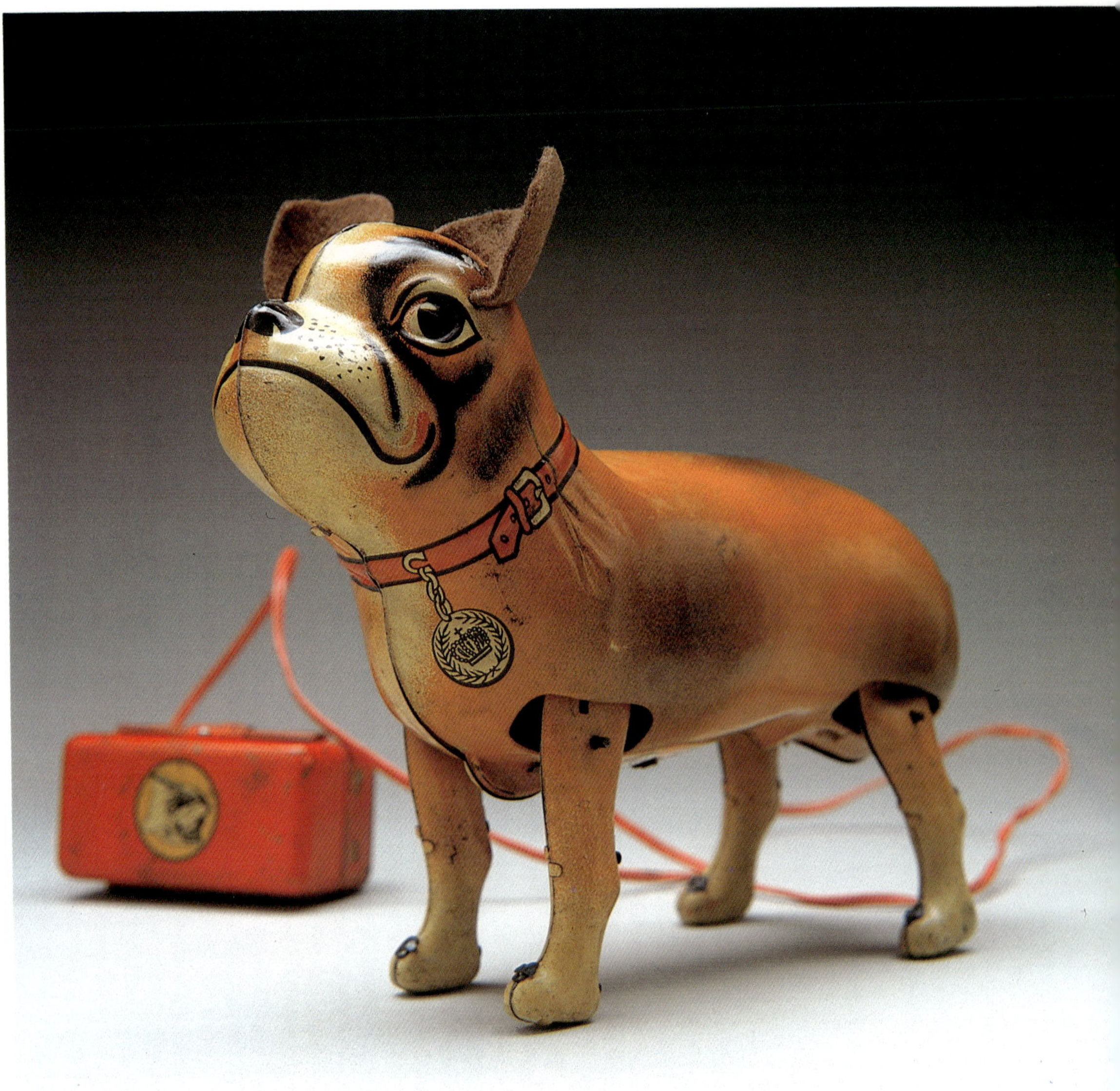

(115) 1950'S／BULLDOG／MARUSAN／190×65×155

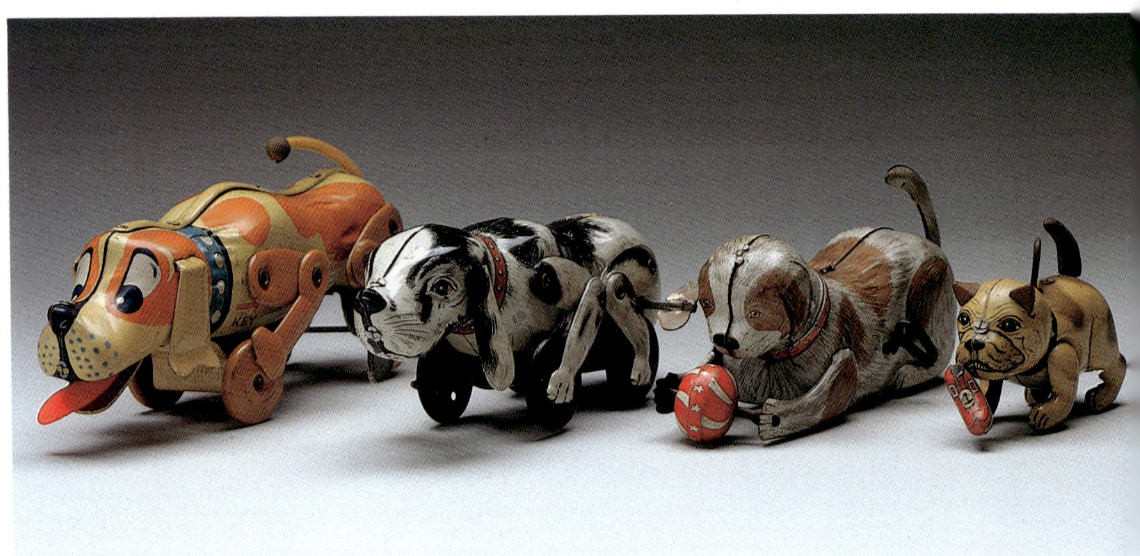

(116)(117)(118)(119) 1950'S／DOGS／KANTO TOY, NOMURA, KANTO TOY, UNKNOWN

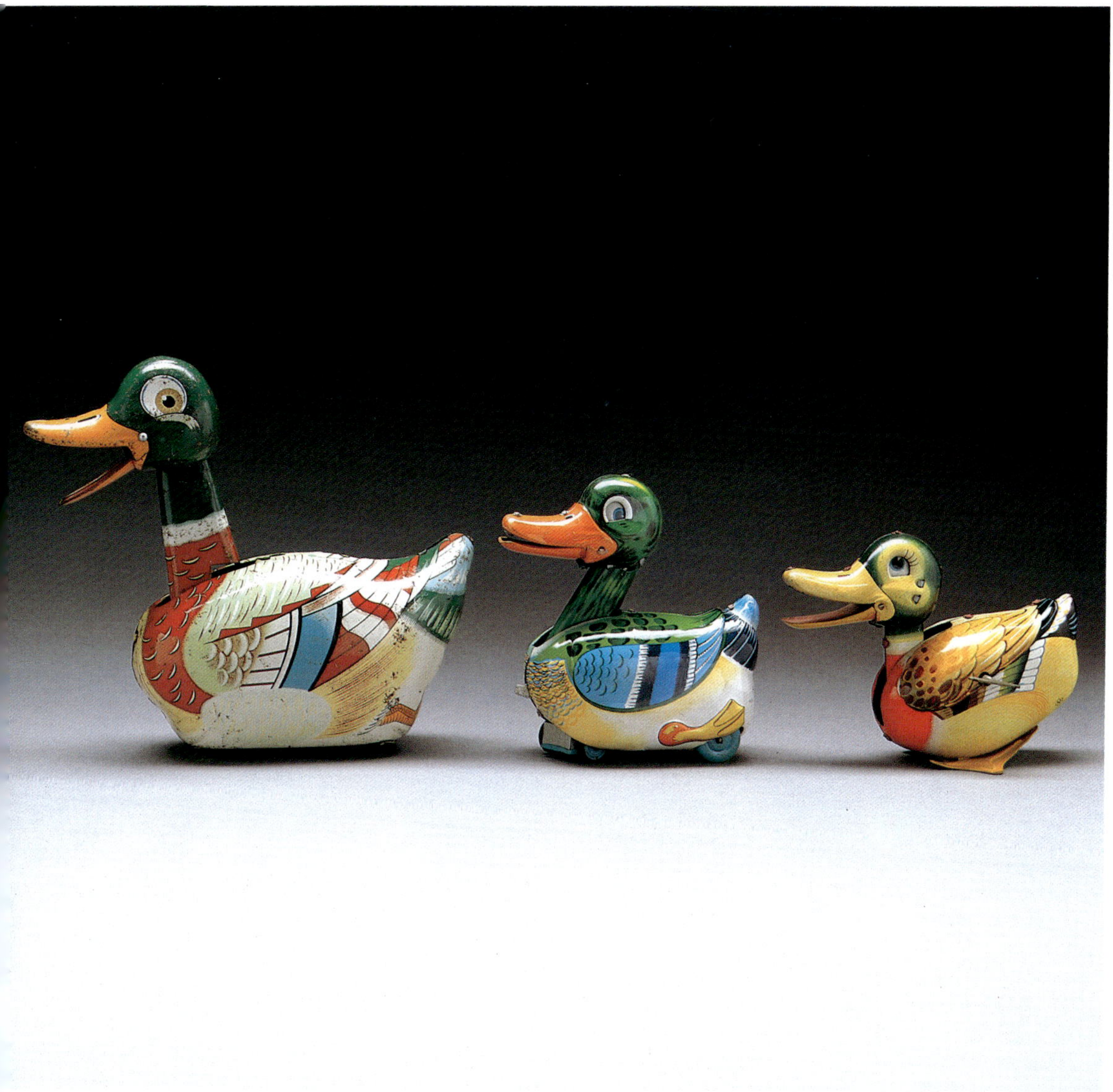

(120)(121)(122) 1950'S／DUCK／TERAI, TOMIYAMA, NOMURA／200×70×180, 150×75×110, 130×60×130

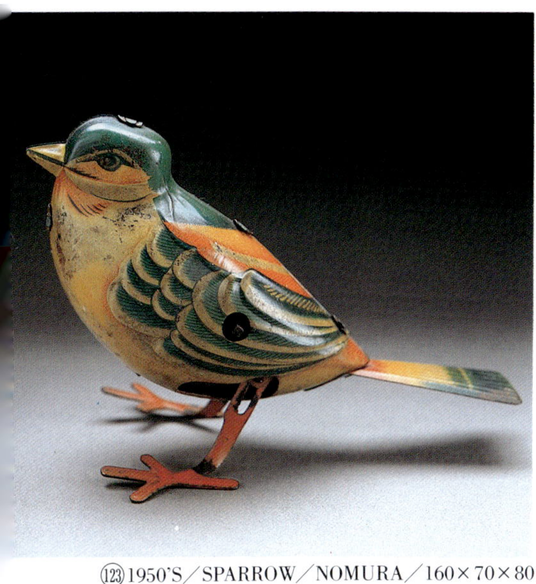

(123) 1950'S／SPARROW／NOMURA／160×70×80

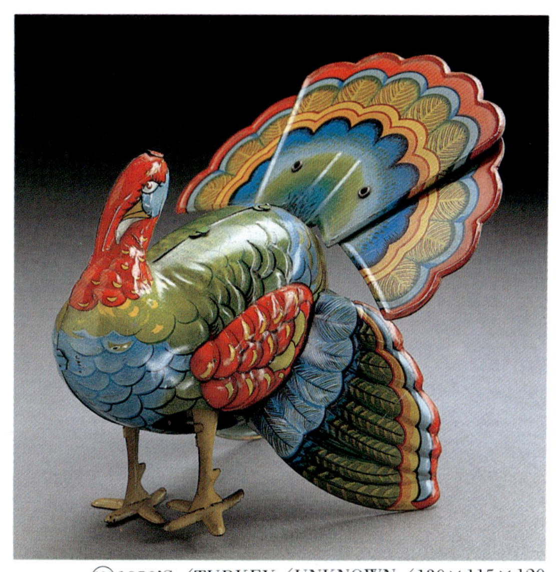

(124) 1950'S／TURKEY／UNKNOWN／130×115×120

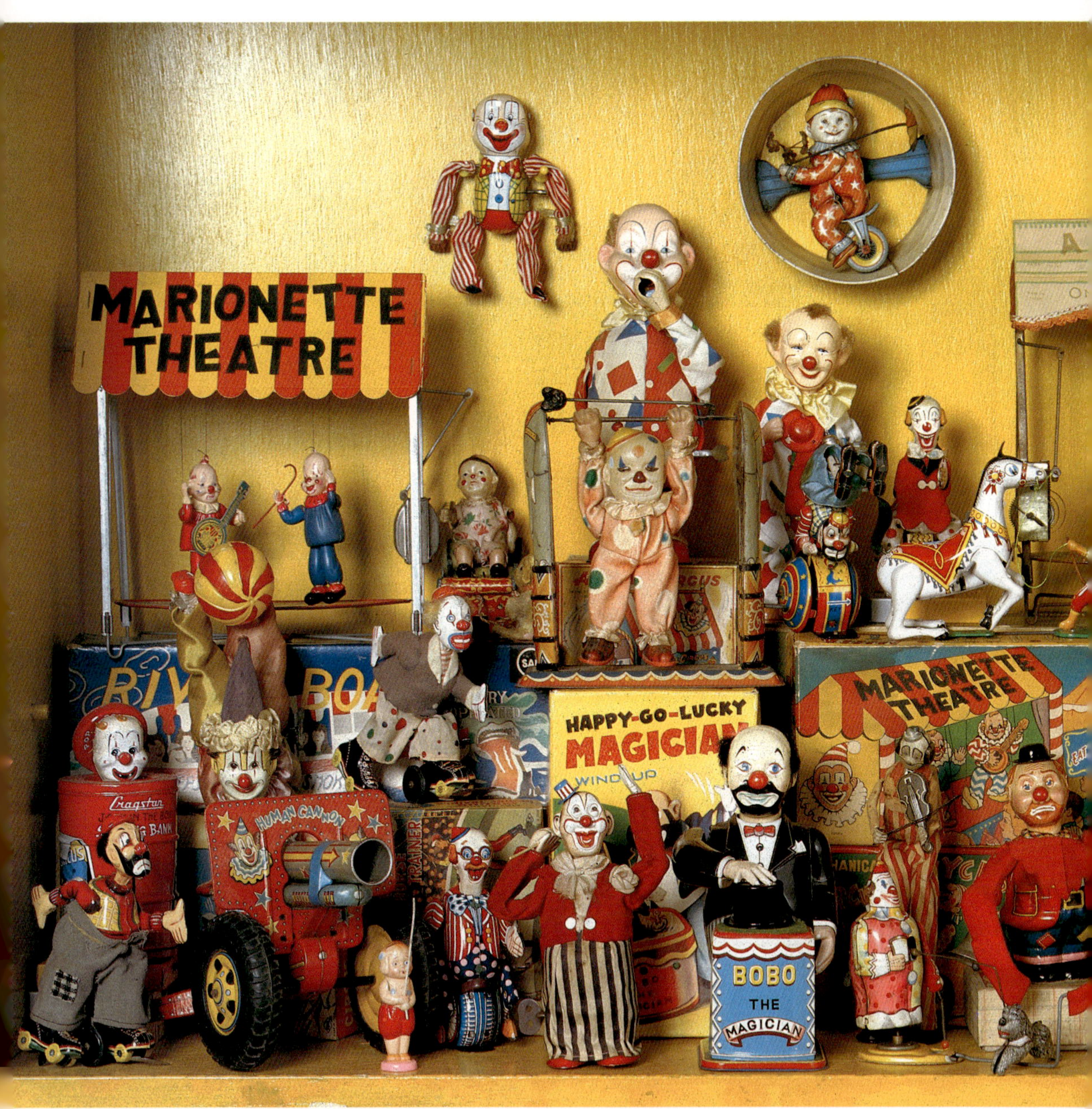
MARIONETTE THEATRE
HAPPY-GO-LUCKY MAGICIAN
WIND UP
BOBO THE MAGICIAN
HUMAN CANNON
Cragstan
MARIONETTE THEATRE

125 CLOWNS

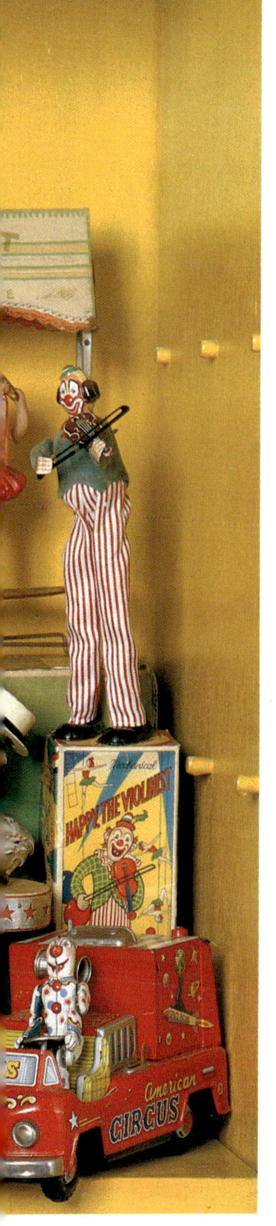

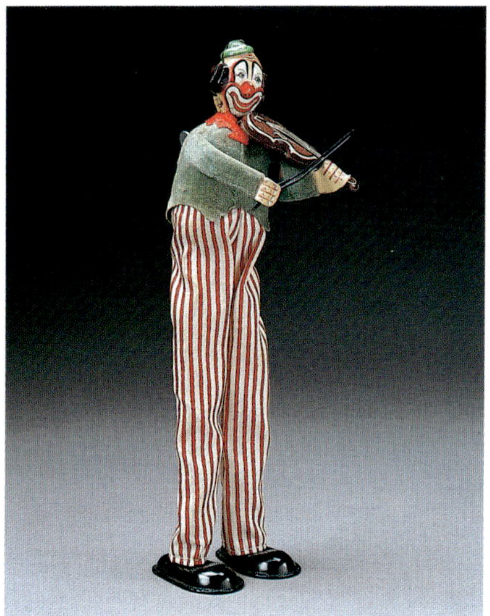

⑫⑥ 1950'S／CLOWN VIOLINIST／TOPLY／
75×75×220

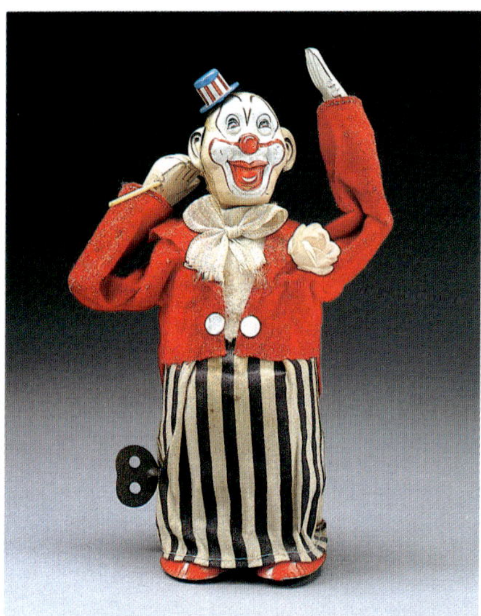

⑫⑦ 1950'S／JOLLY CLOWN／MASUDAYA／
70×110×183

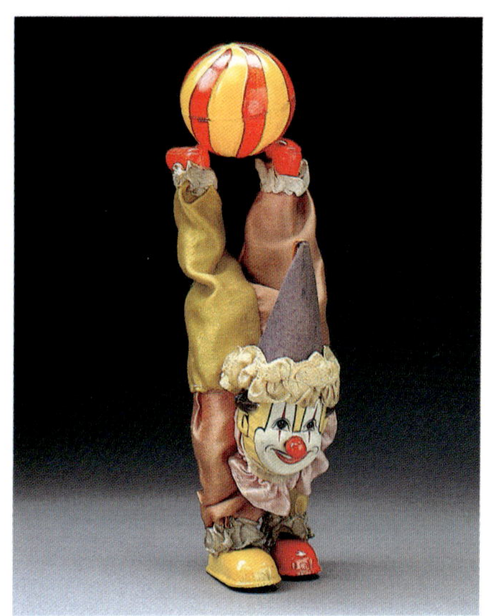

⑫⑧ 1950'S／HANDSTANDING CLOWN／
UNKNOWN／95×80×245

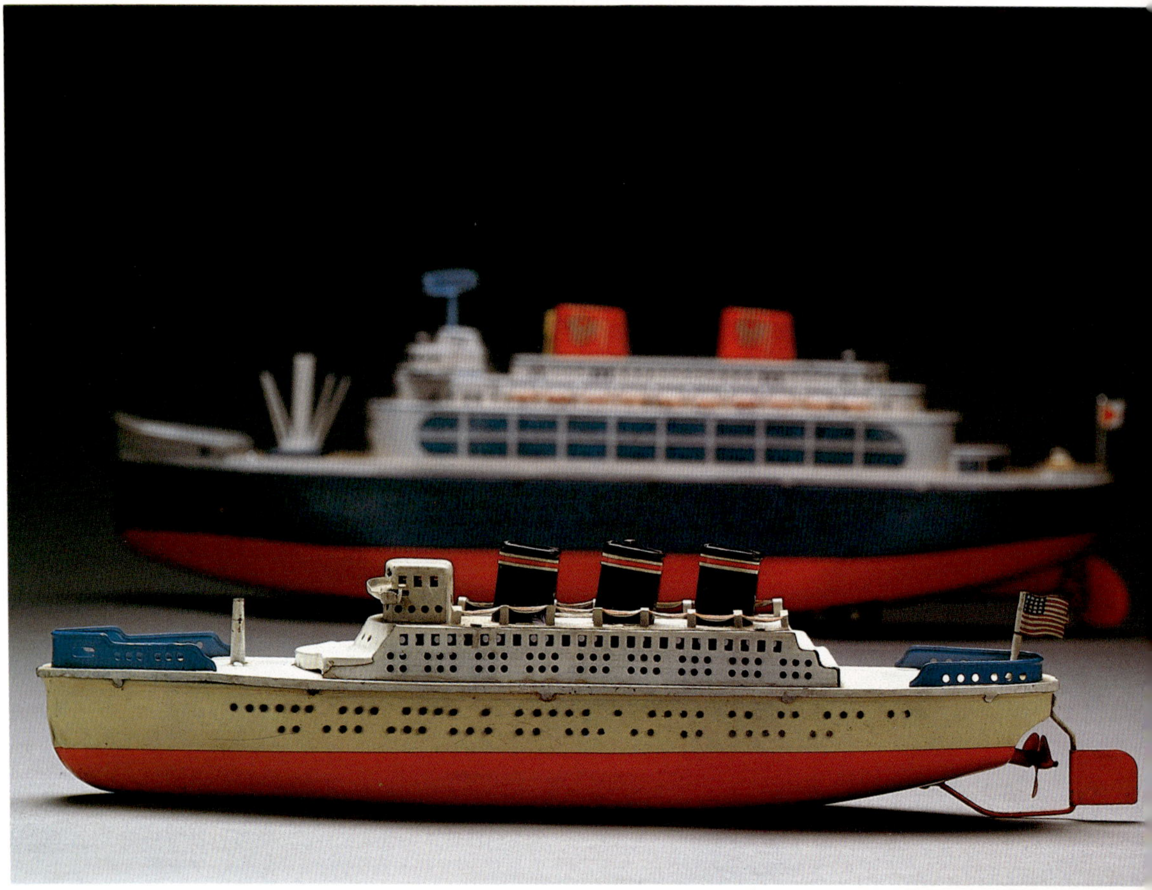

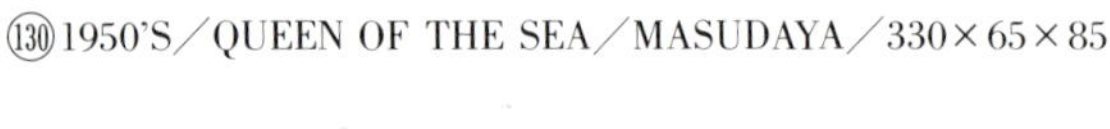

⑫⑨1950'S／QUEEN OF THE SEA／MASUDAYA／545×110×170
⑬⓪1950'S／QUEEN OF THE SEA／MASUDAYA／330×65×85

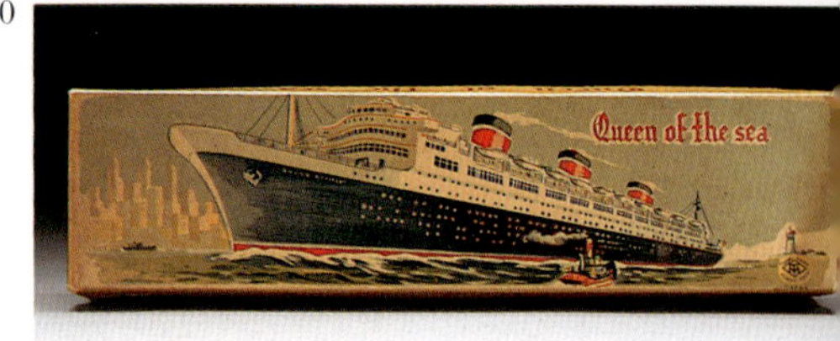

⑬⓪CASE ATTACHED

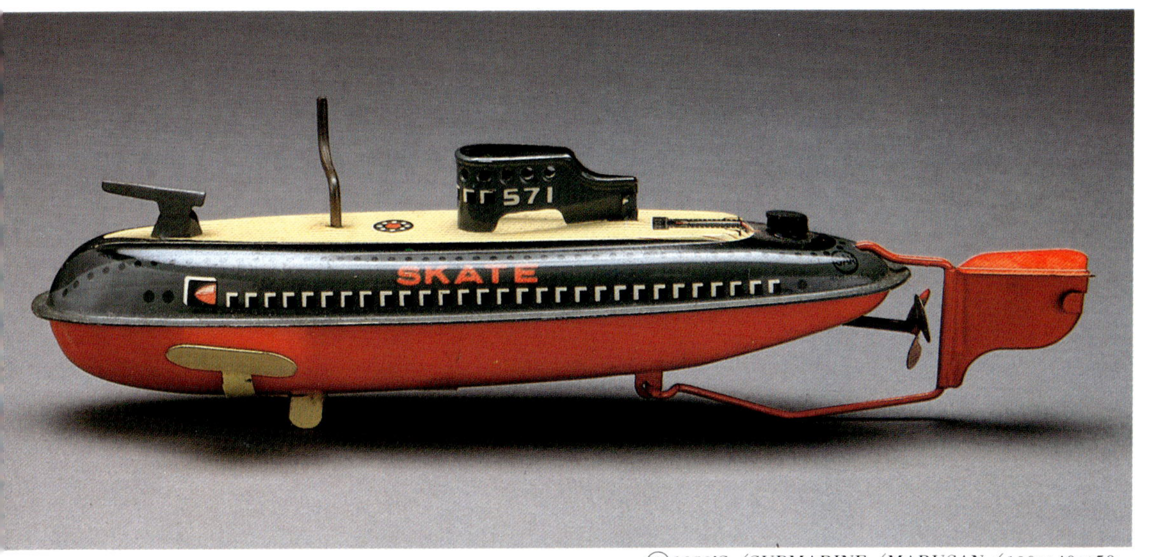

(131) 1950'S／SUBMARINE／MARUSAN／190×40×50

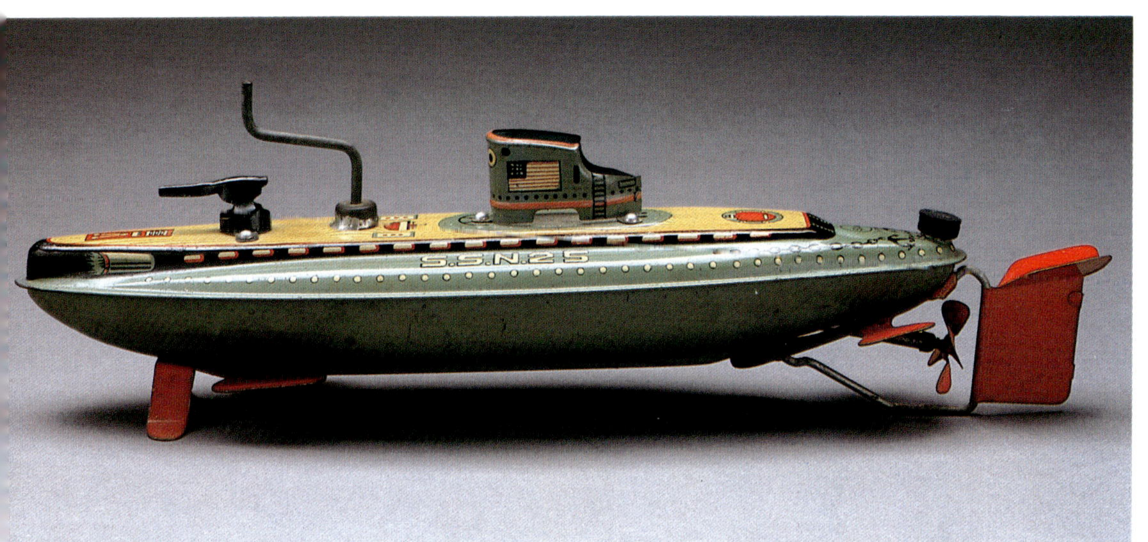

(132) 1950'S／SUBMARINE／MARUSAN／255×55×70

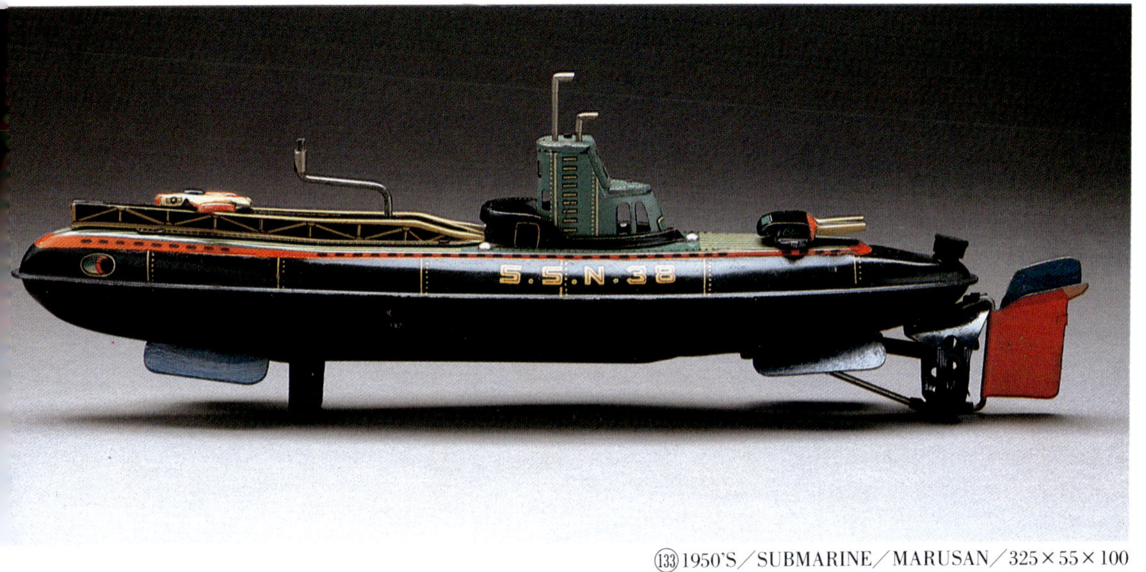

(133) 1950'S／SUBMARINE／MARUSAN／325×55×100

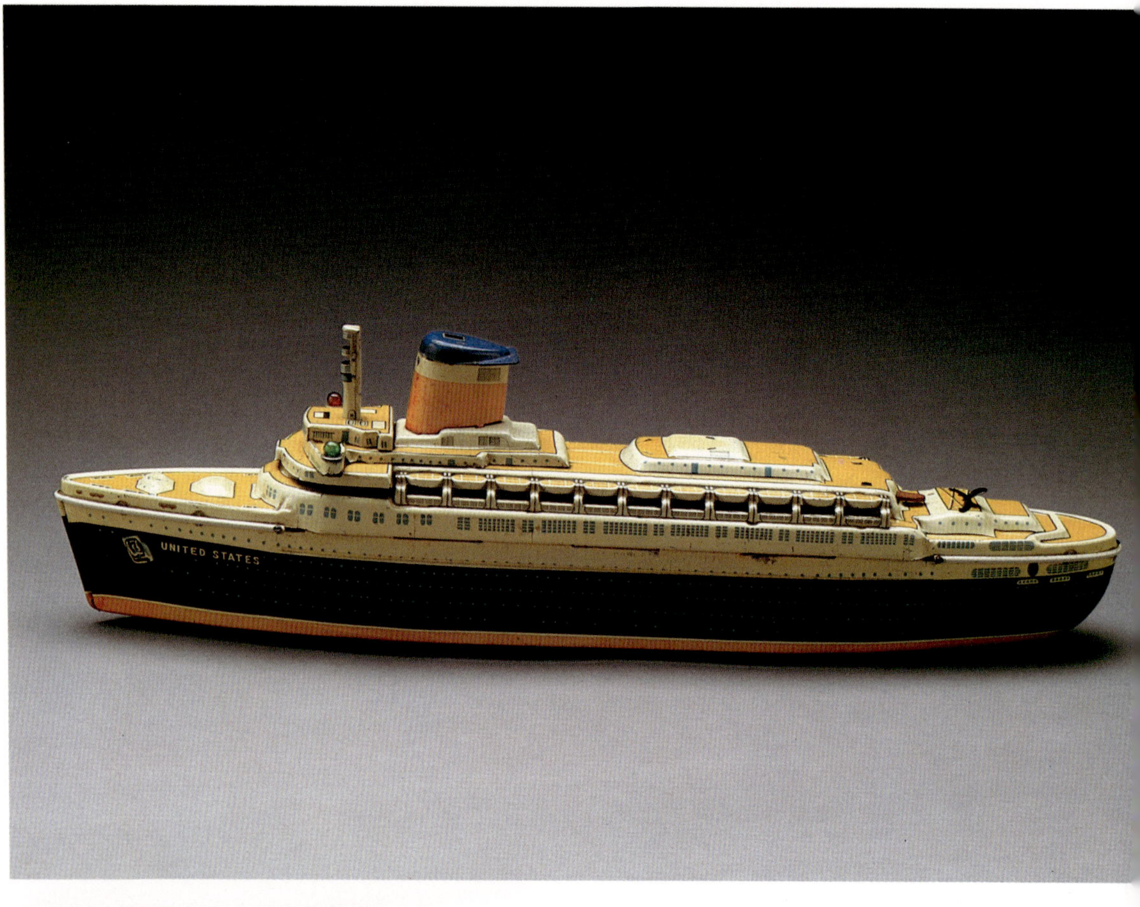

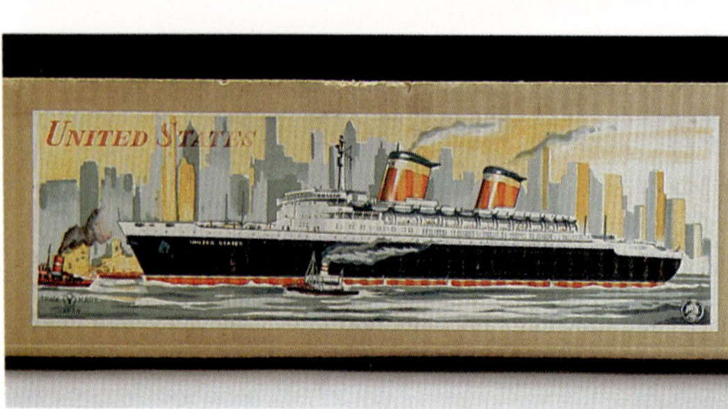

(134) 1950'S／UNITED STATES／TOMIYAMA／480×70×130

CASE ATTACHED

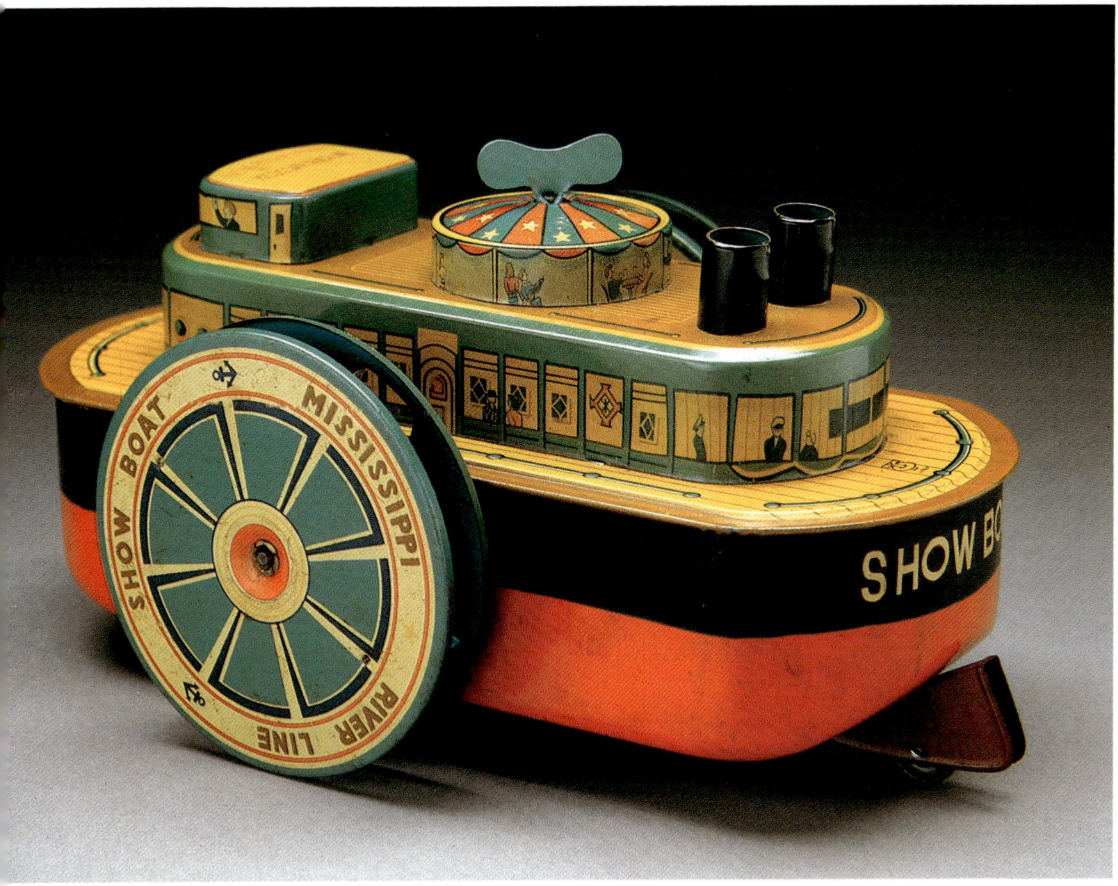

⑬⑤ OCCUPIED JAPAN／SHOWBOAT／UNKNOWN／225×140×120

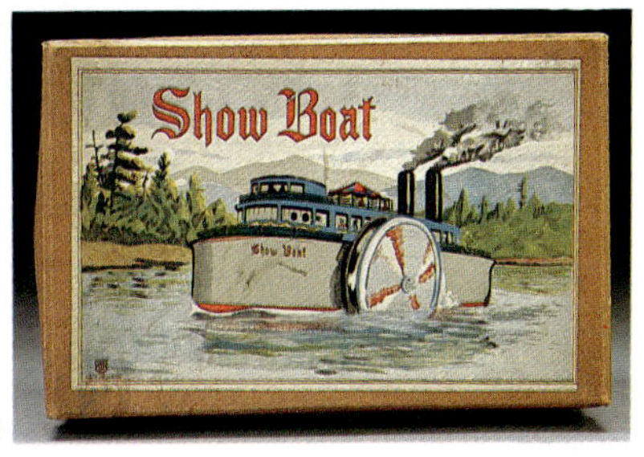

CASE ATTACHED

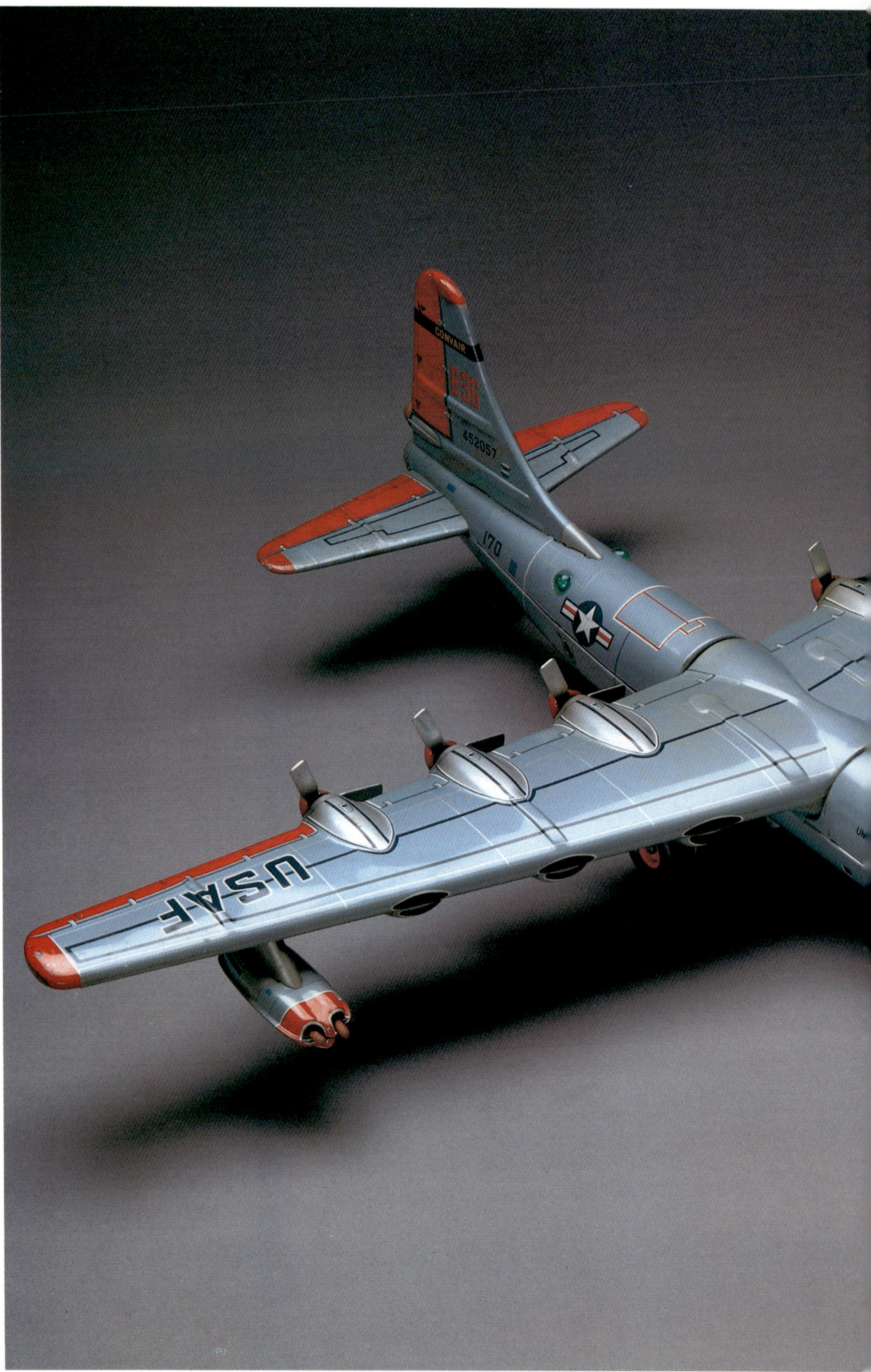
CONVAIR
B36
452057
170
USAF

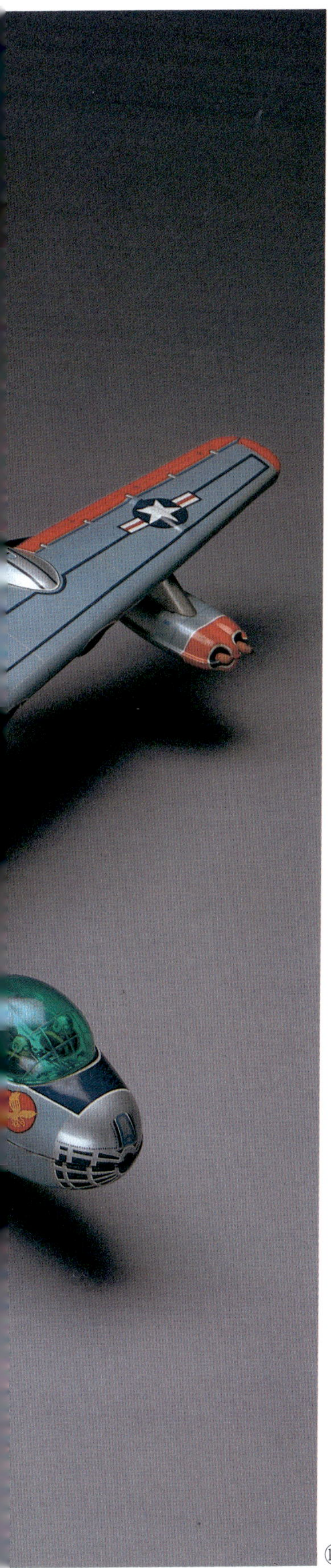

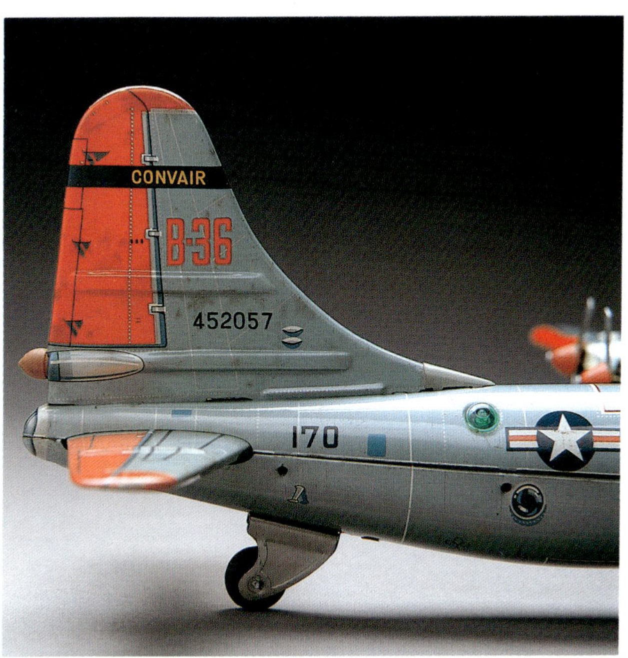

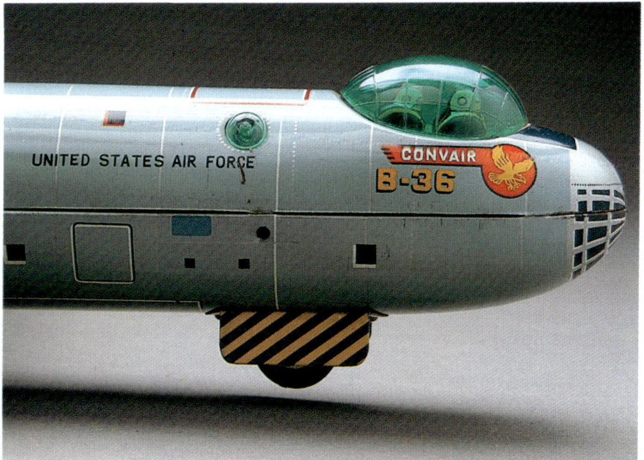

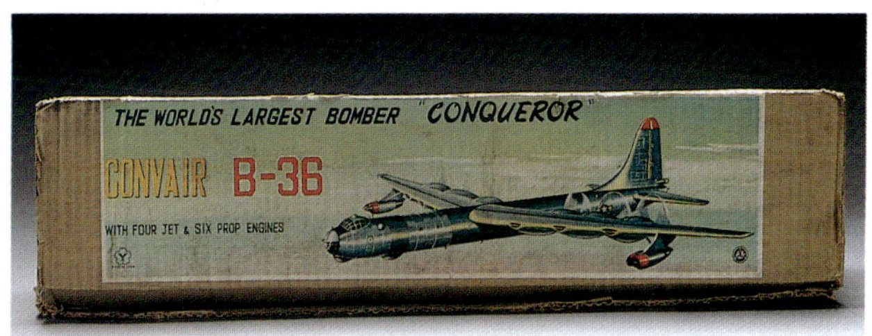

CASE ATTACHED

(136) 1950'S／B-36／TOMIYAMA／490×660×155

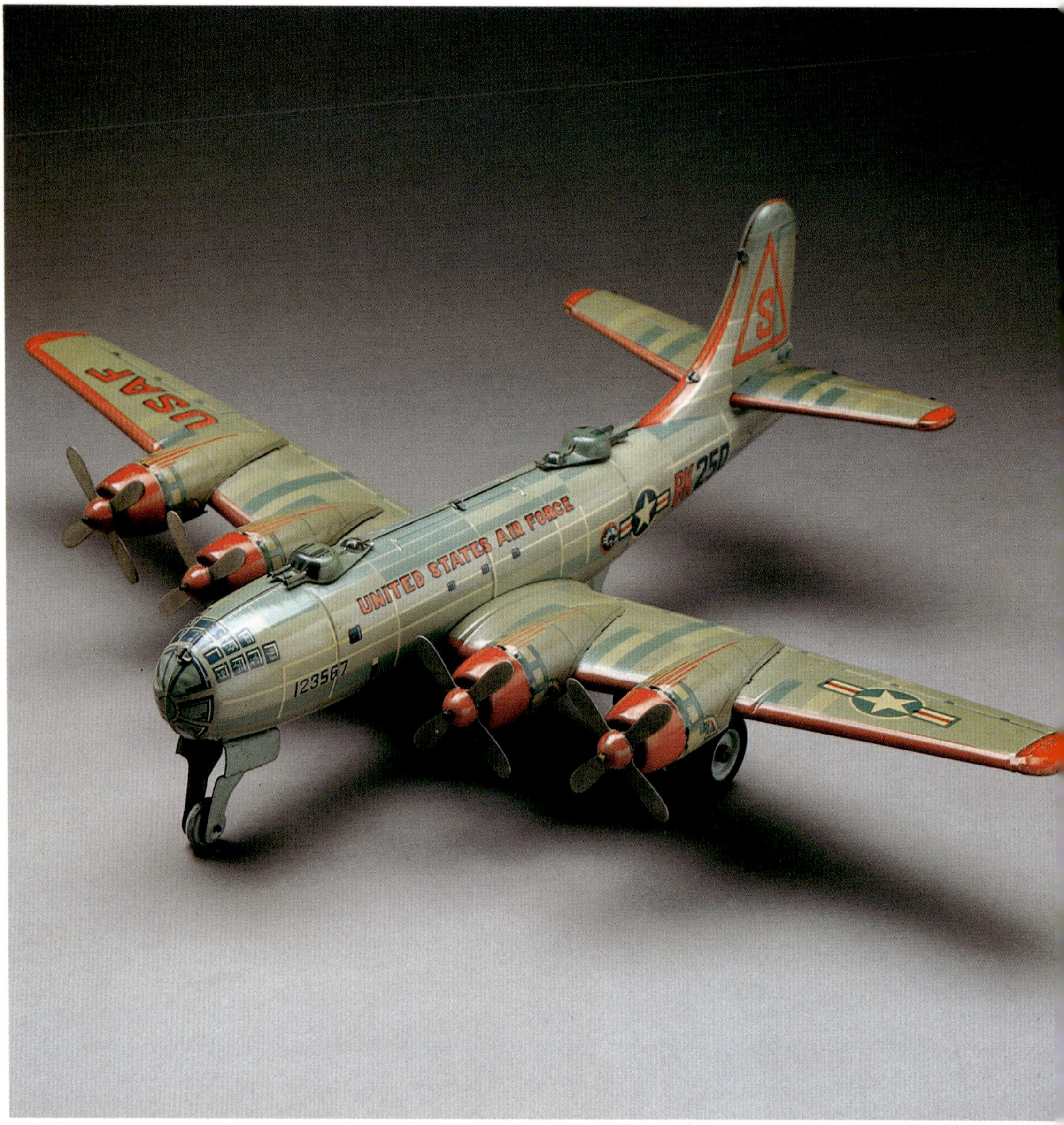

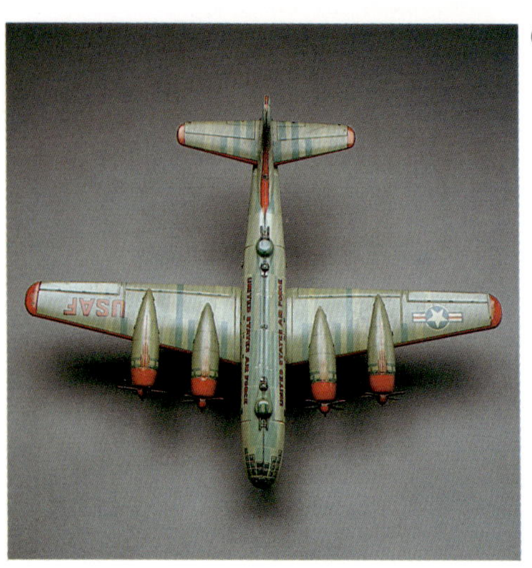

⑬⑦ 1950'S／B-29／TOMIYAMA／375×480×145

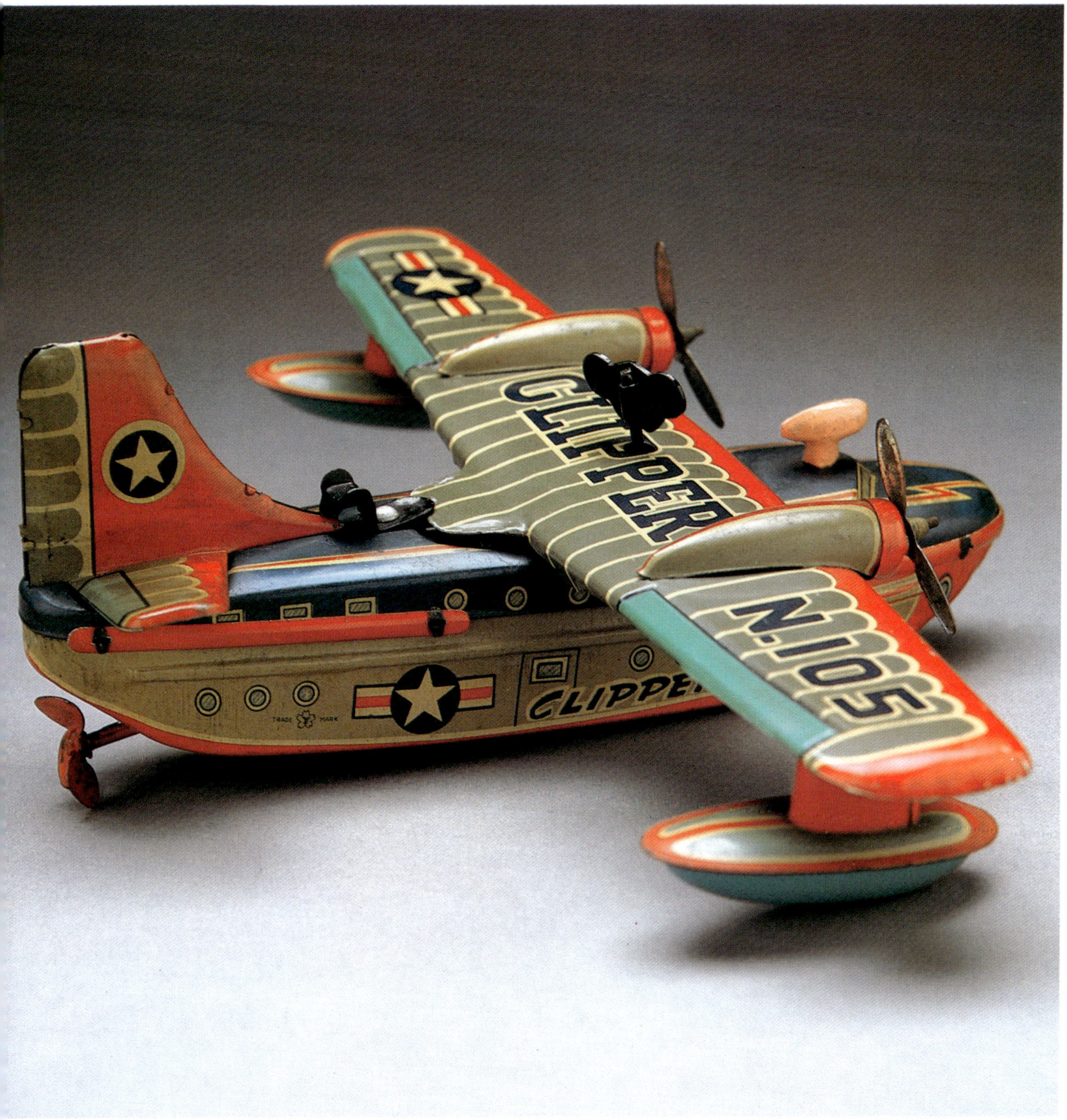

(138) 1950'S／CLIPPER／YONEZAWA／220×295×95

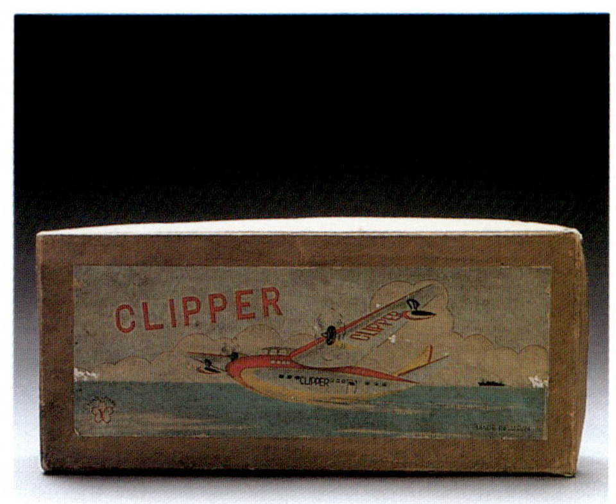

CASE ATTACHED

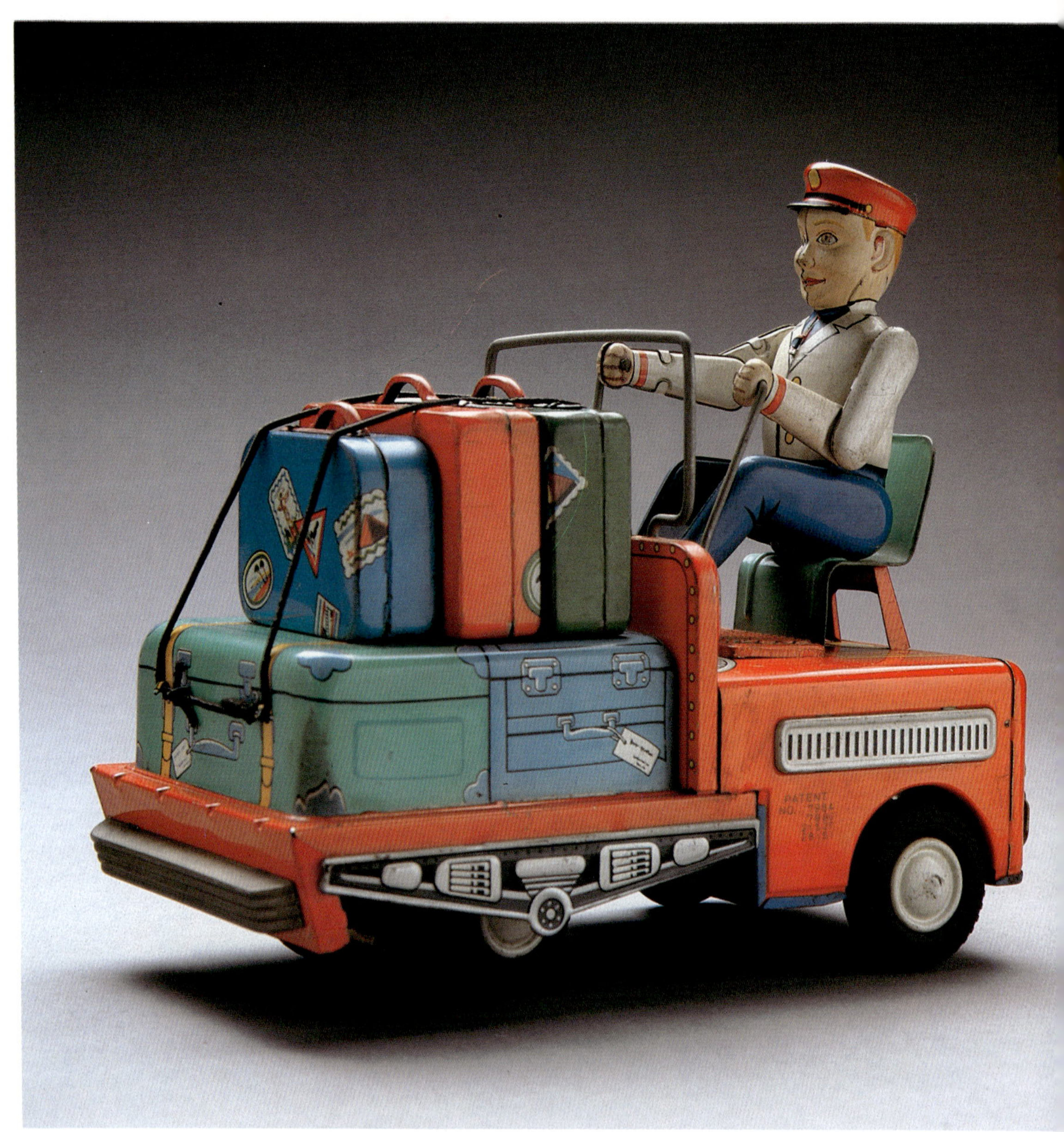

(139) 1950'S／TRANSPORTER TROLLEY／MASUDAYA／190×95×170

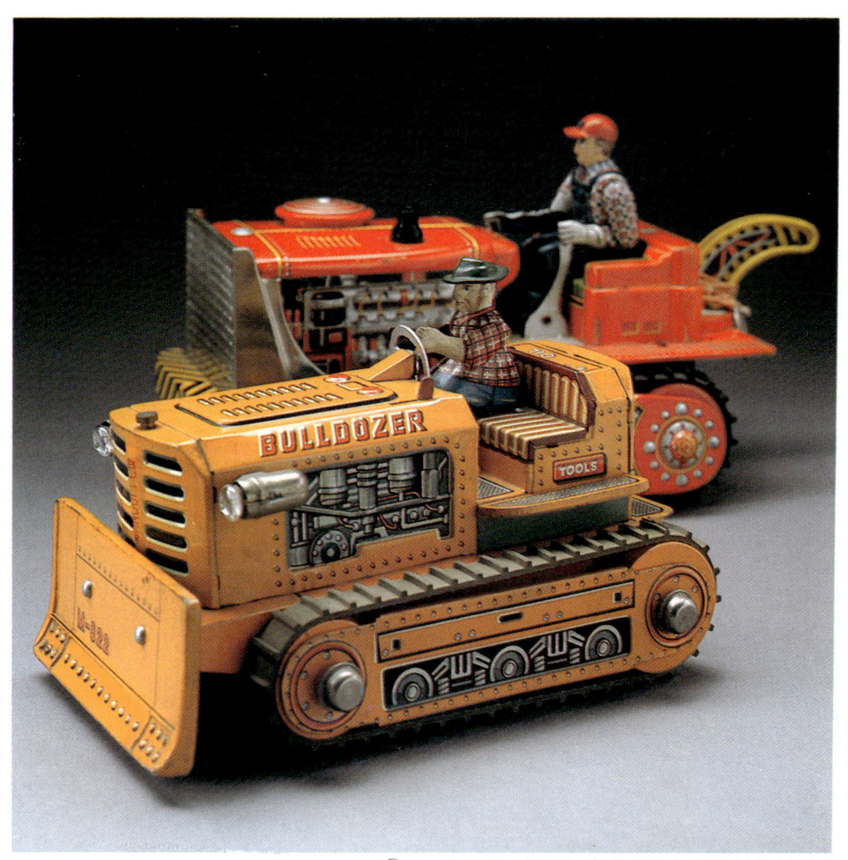

(140) 1950'S／TRACTOR／NOMURA／290×175×155

(141) 1950'S／TRACTOR／MITSUHASHI／215×140×130

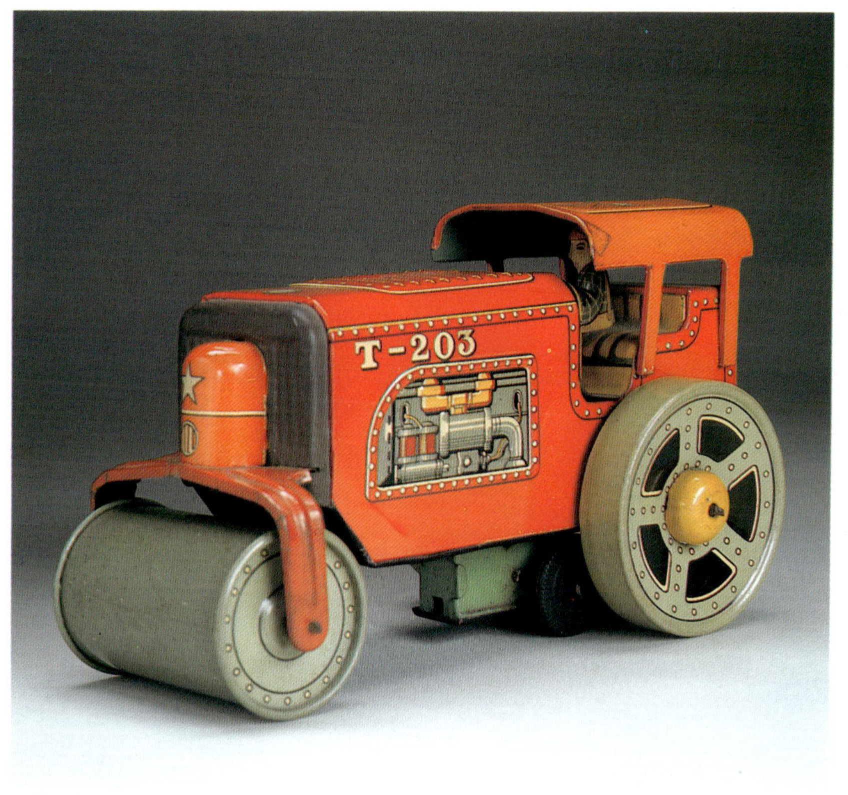

(142) 1950'S／TRACTOR／YONEZAWA／175×90×105

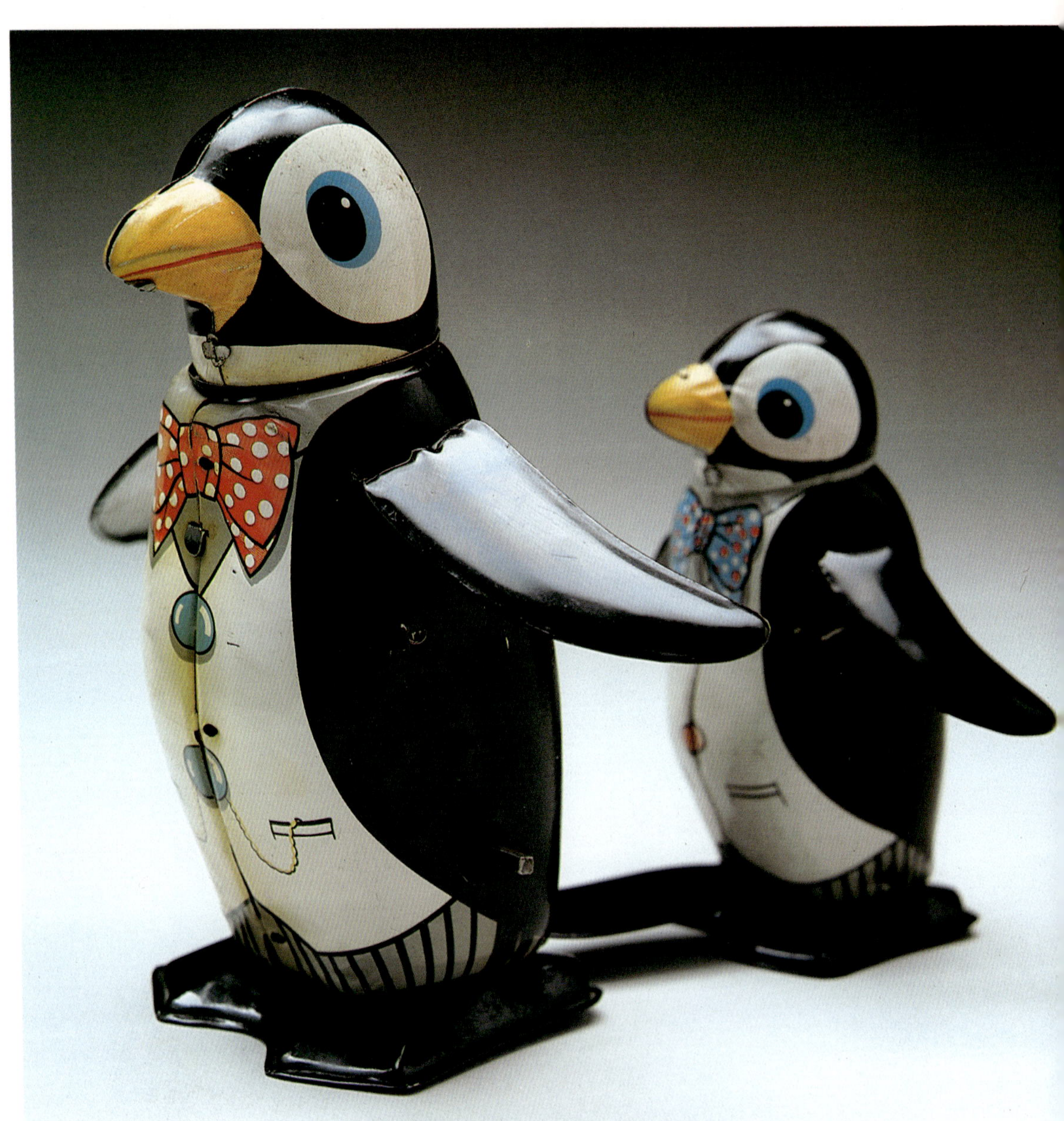

⑭③1950'S／PENGUIN FAMILY／MARUSAN／140×65×135

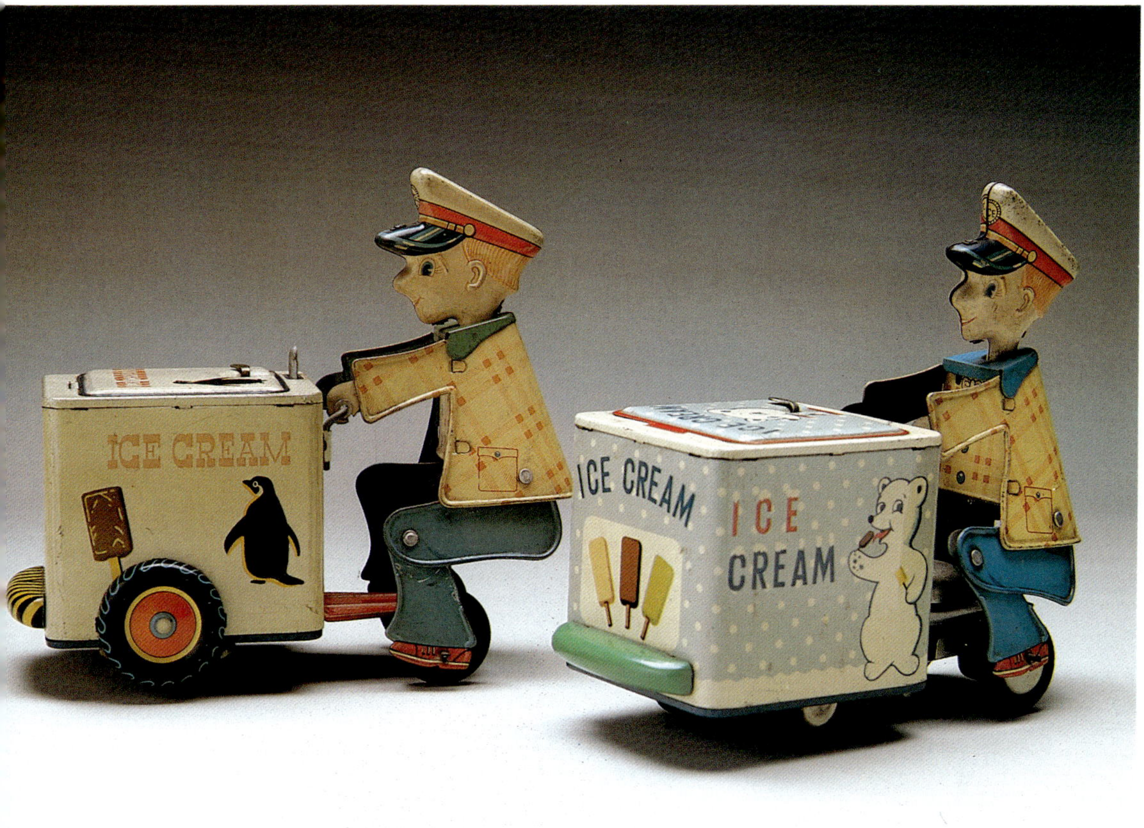

(144)(145) 1950'S／ICE CREAM VENDOR／MASUDAYA／200 × 95 × 170

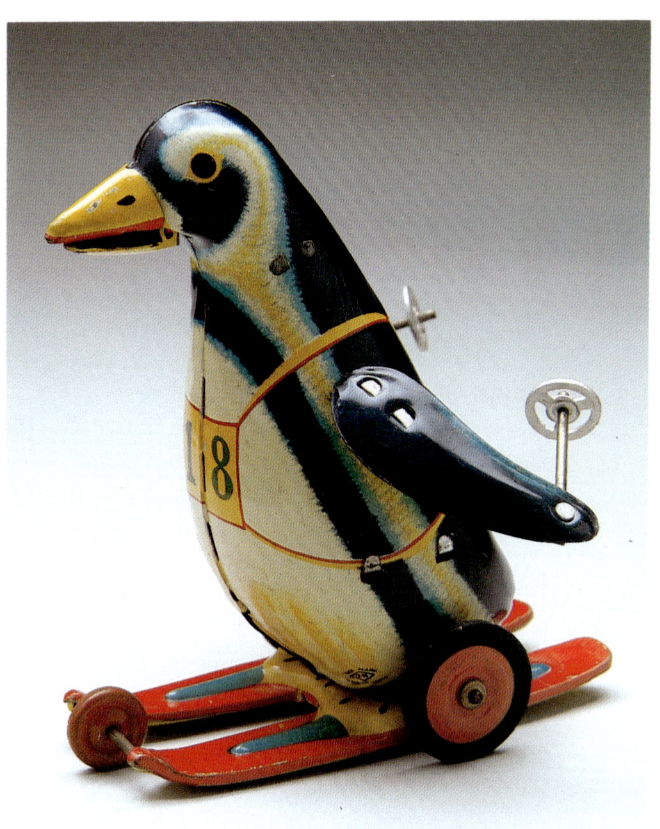

(146) 1950'S／PENGUIN SKIER／NOMURA／110 × 70 × 120

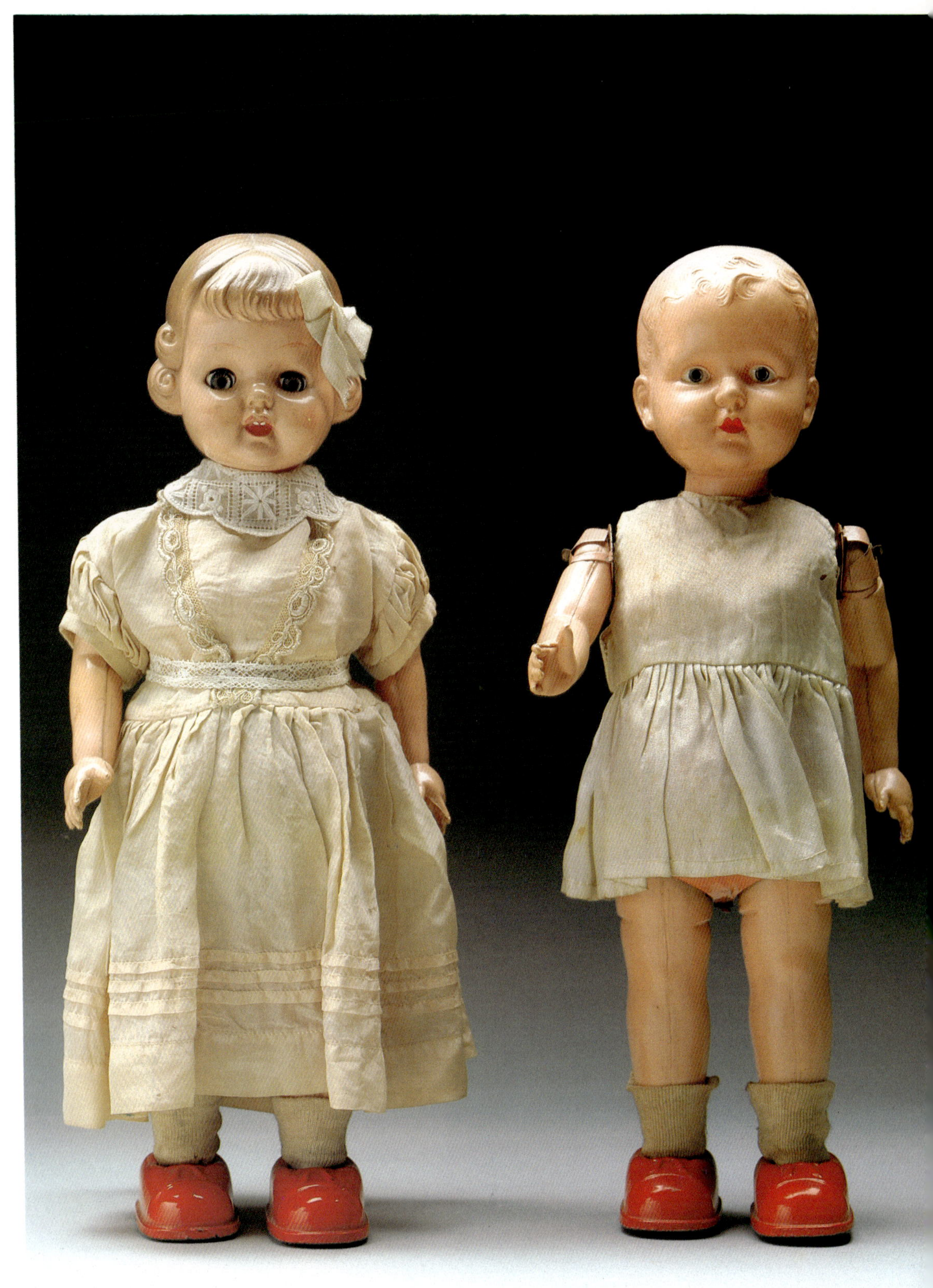

⑭⑭1950'S／WALKING DOLL／MASUDAYA／340 (height)

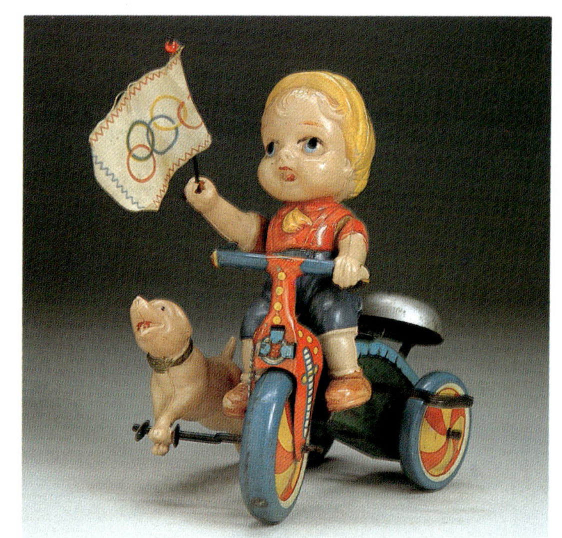

⑭⑨1950'S／BOY AND TRICYCLE／UNKNOWN／100 × 70 × 120

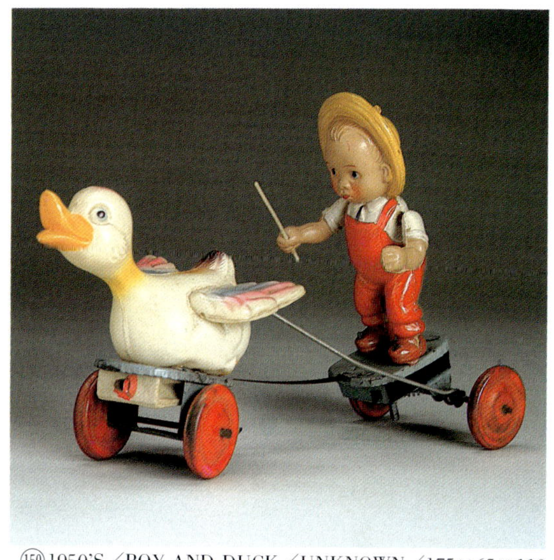

⑮⓪1950'S／BOY AND DUCK／UNKNOWN／175×65×110

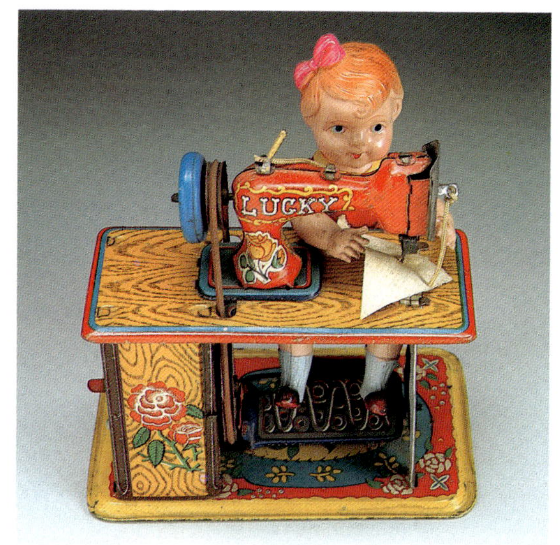

⑮①1950'S／GIRL AND SEWING MACHINE／MARUSAN／125×75×135

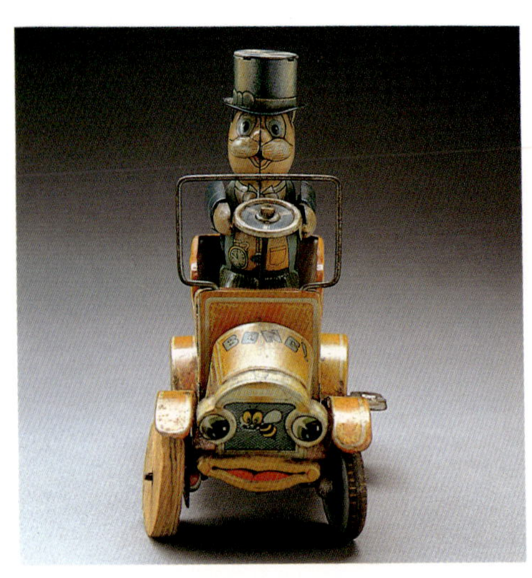

(152) 1950'S／OLD MAN IN CLASSIC AUTO ／TOMIYAMA／135×70×138

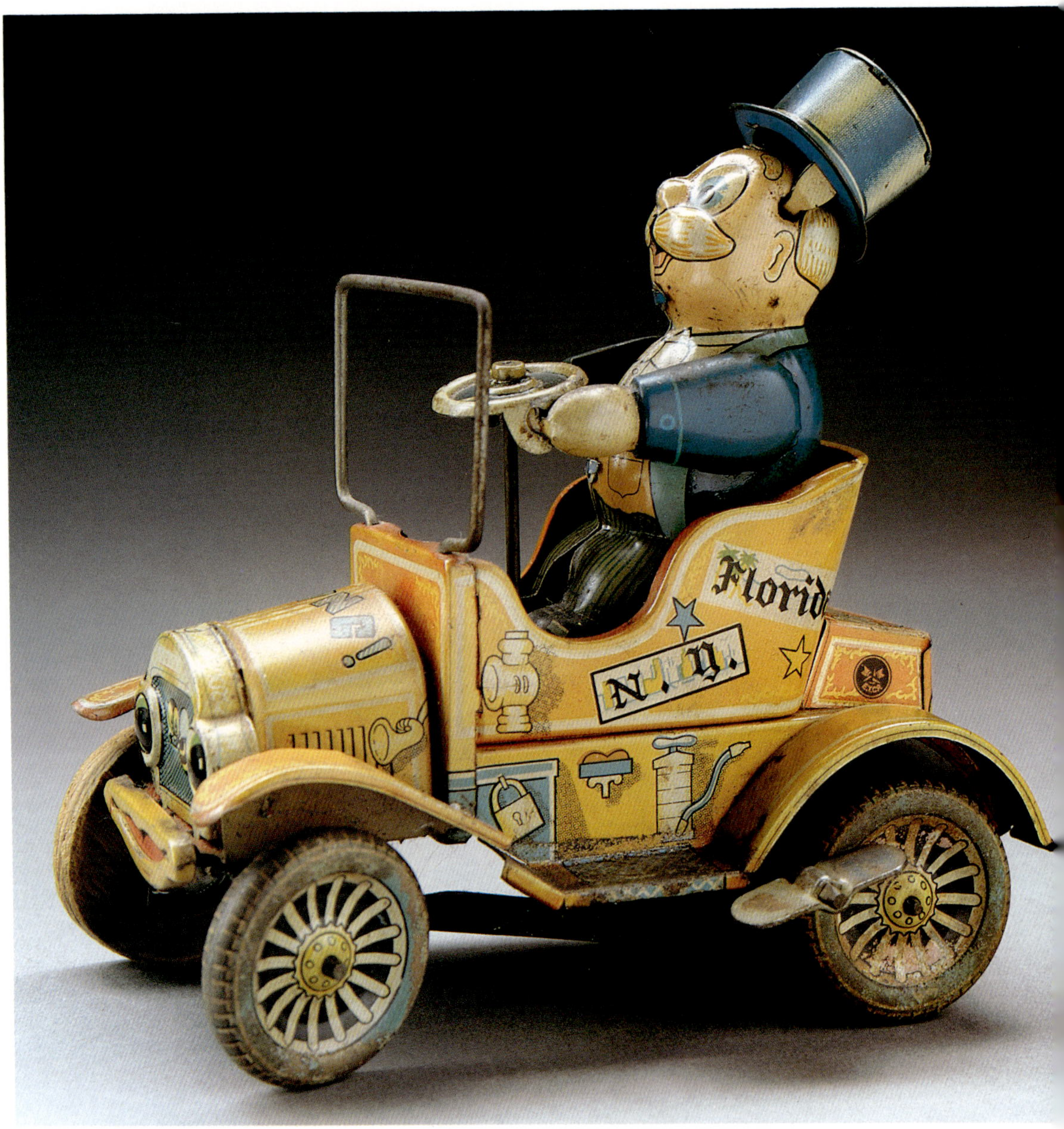

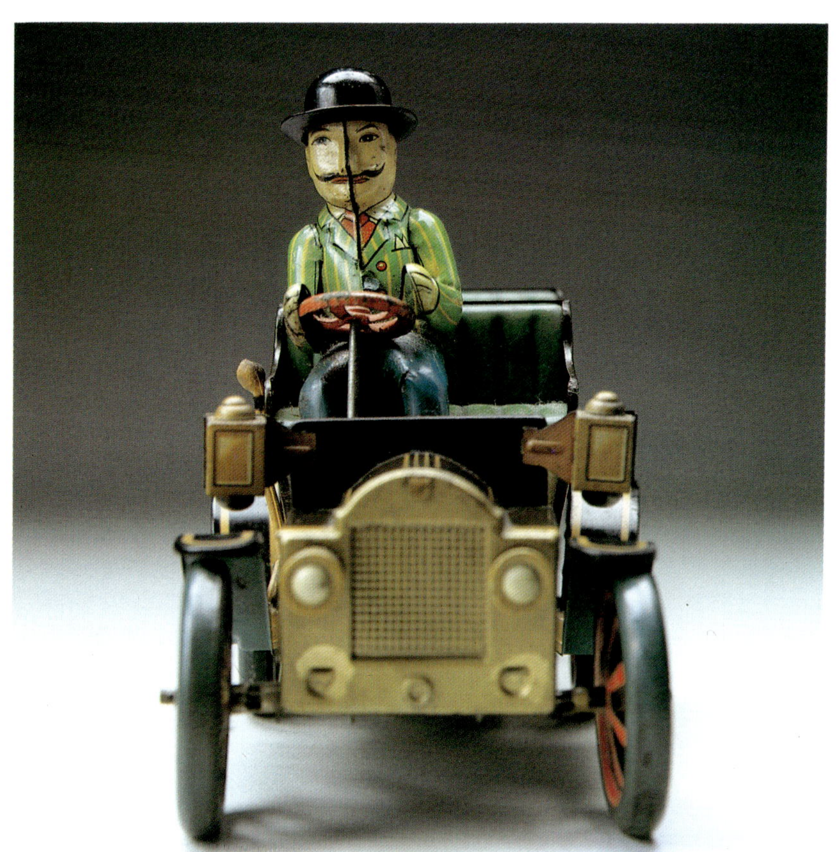

⑬1950'S／OLD MAN IN CLASSIC AUTO／MASUDAYA／180×100×150

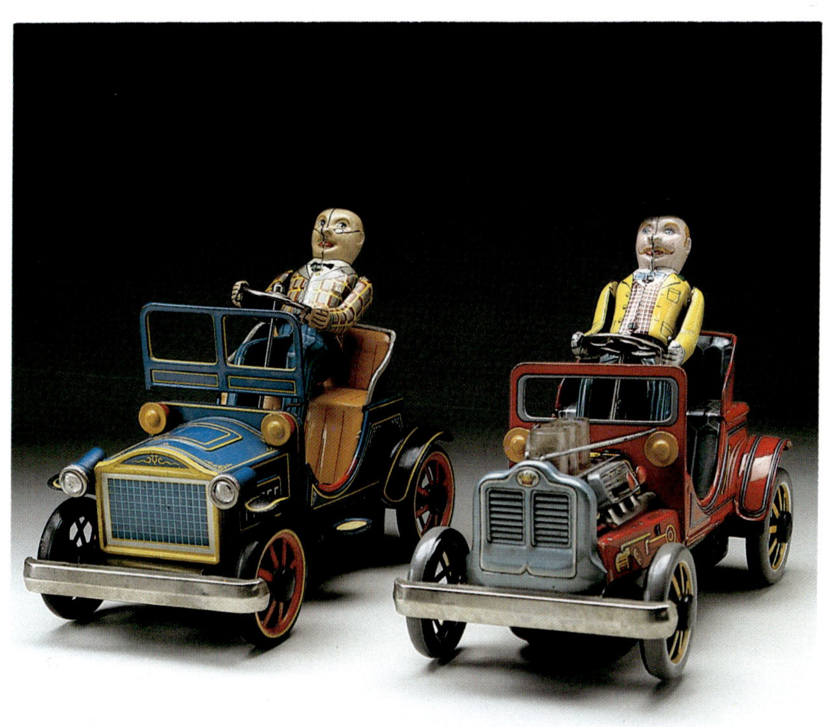

⑭⑮1950'S／OLD MAN IN CLASSIC AUTO／YONEZAWA／
230×120×180, 180×100×150

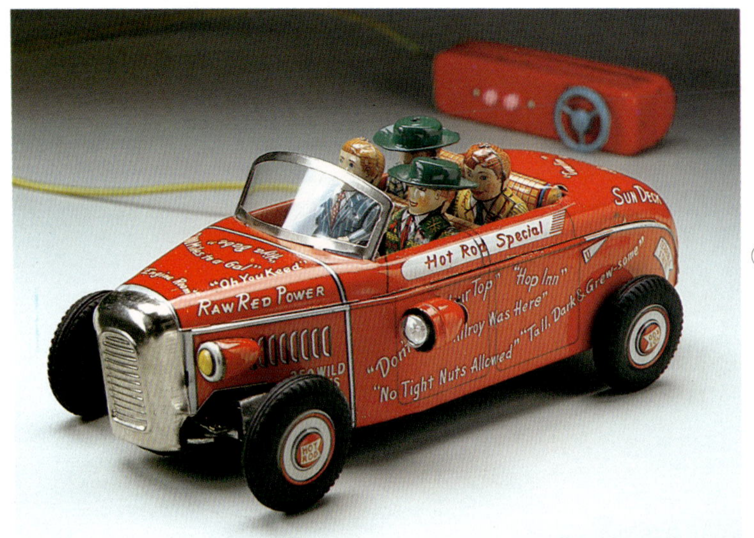

⑯1950'S／ CAR／LINE MAR／245×110×1

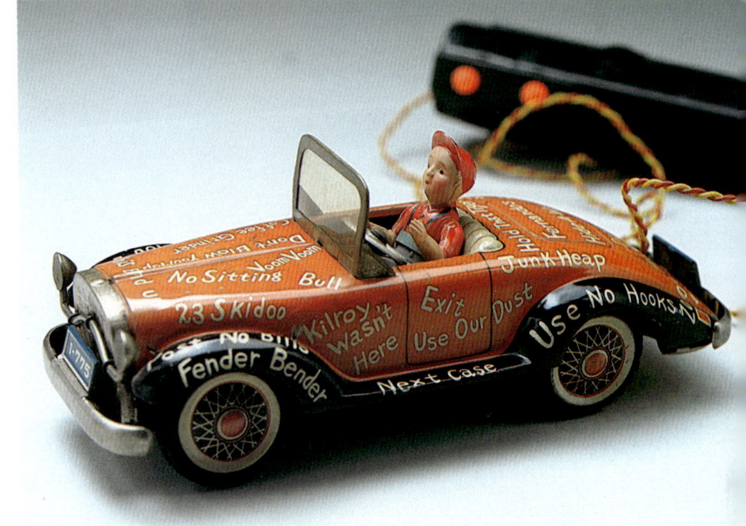

⑰1950'S／ CAR／LINE MAR／
185×75×75

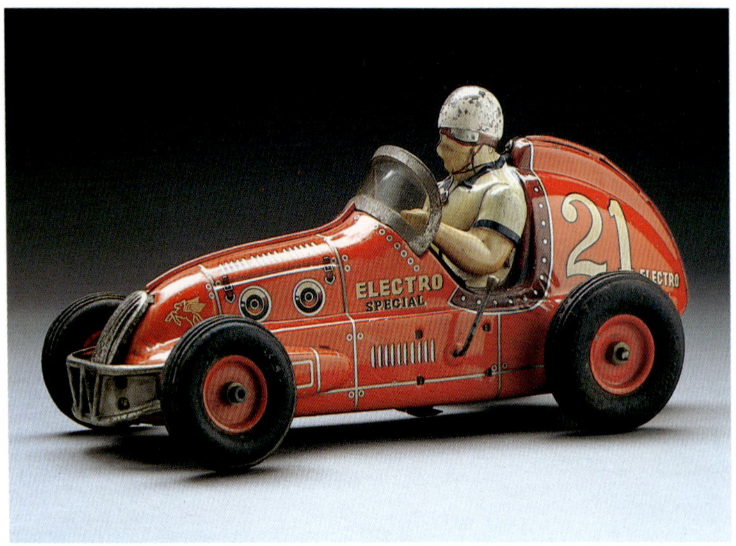

⑱1950'S／RACING CAR／TOMIYAMA／
250×120×115

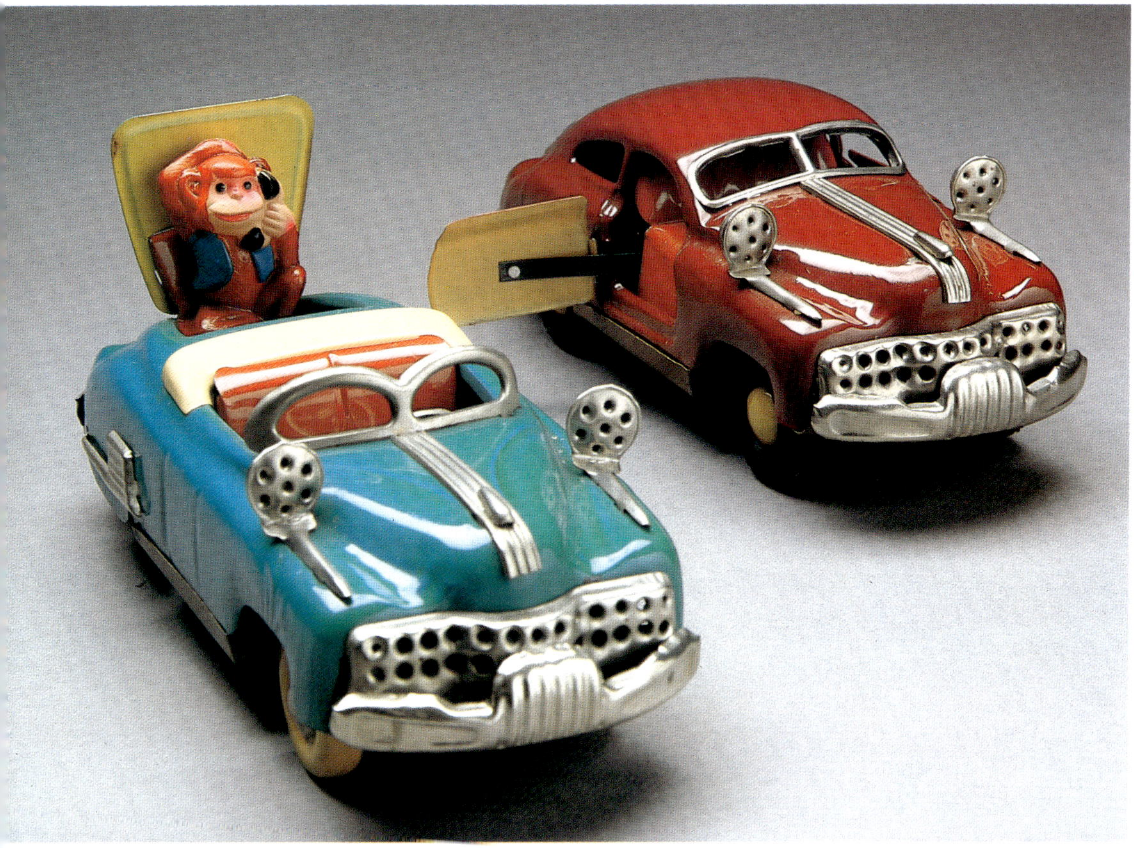

)160 1950'S／POP UP CAR／NIHON BOEKI／200×85×70

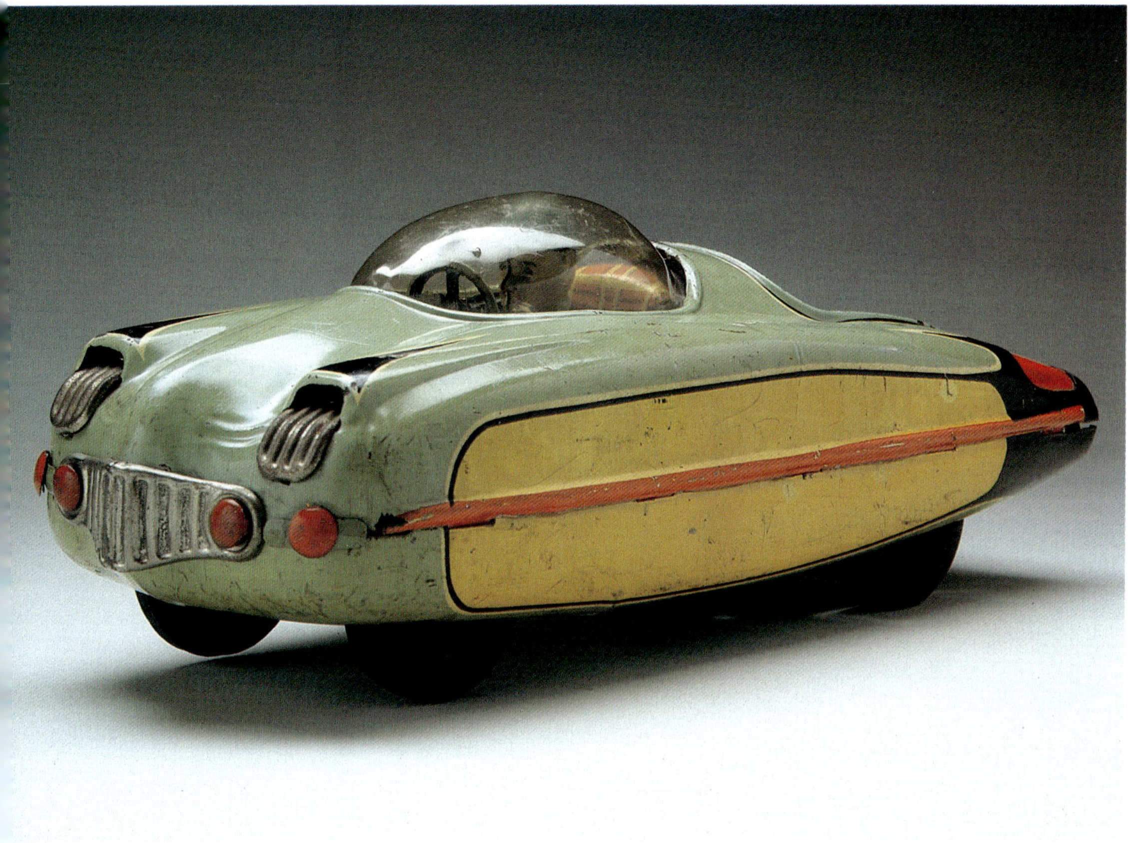

1950'S／FUTURE AUTOMOBILE／YONEZAWA／270×100×70

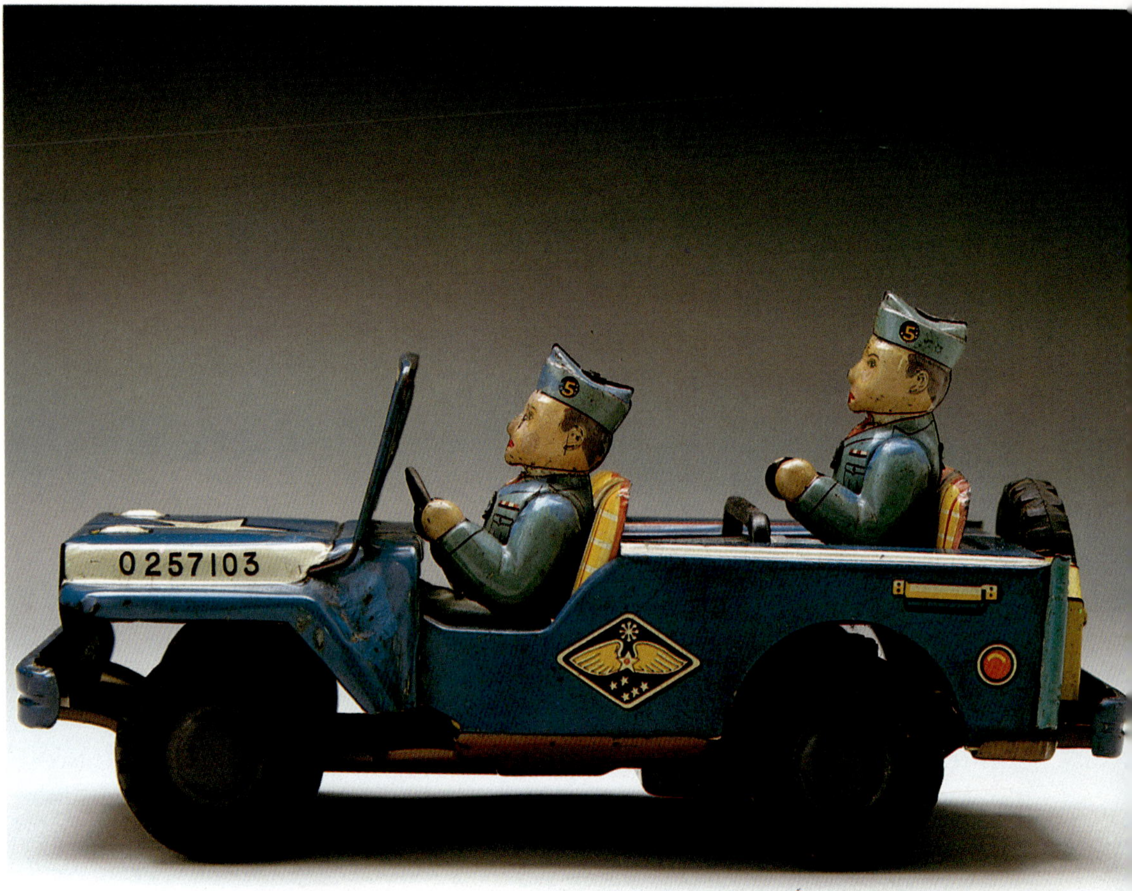

(162) 1950'S／JEEP／UNKNOWN／210×95×110

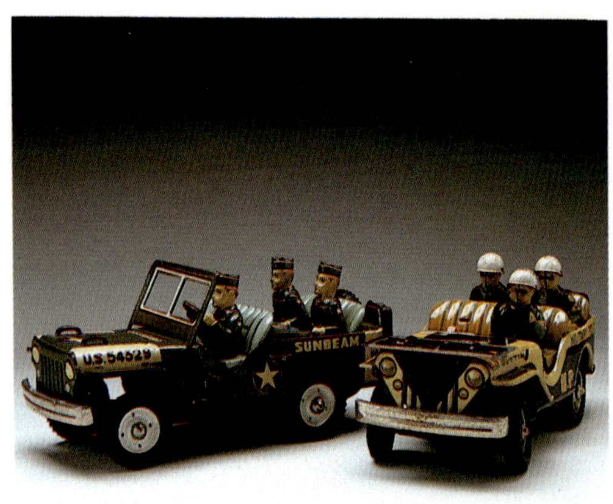

(163)(164) 1950'S／JEEP／NIHON BOEKI／260×115×115、
260×110×115

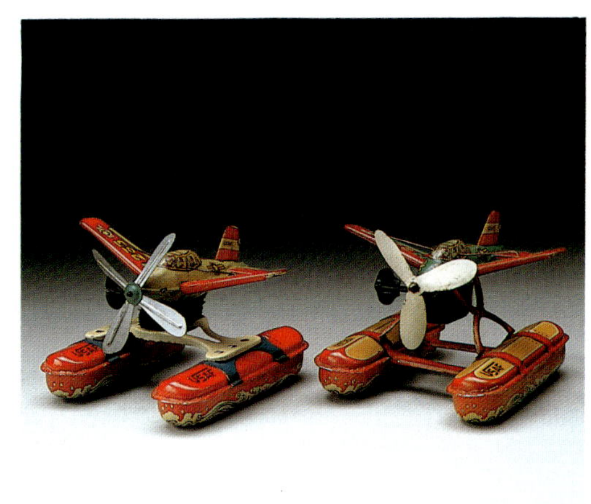

(165)(166) 1950'S／SEAPLANE／YONEZAWA／125×135×85

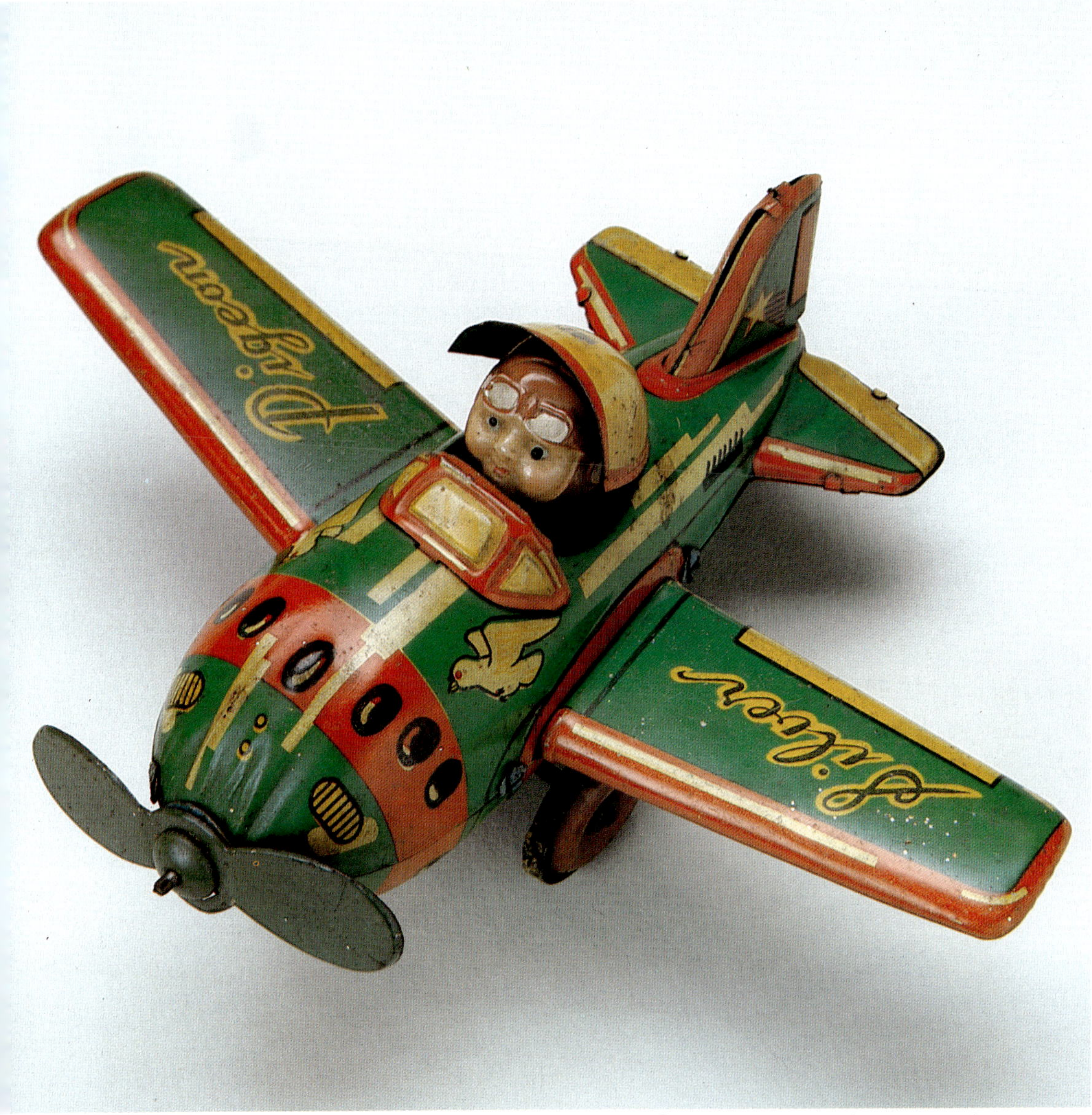

(167) 1950'S／FIGHTER ／YONEZAWA／150×185×80

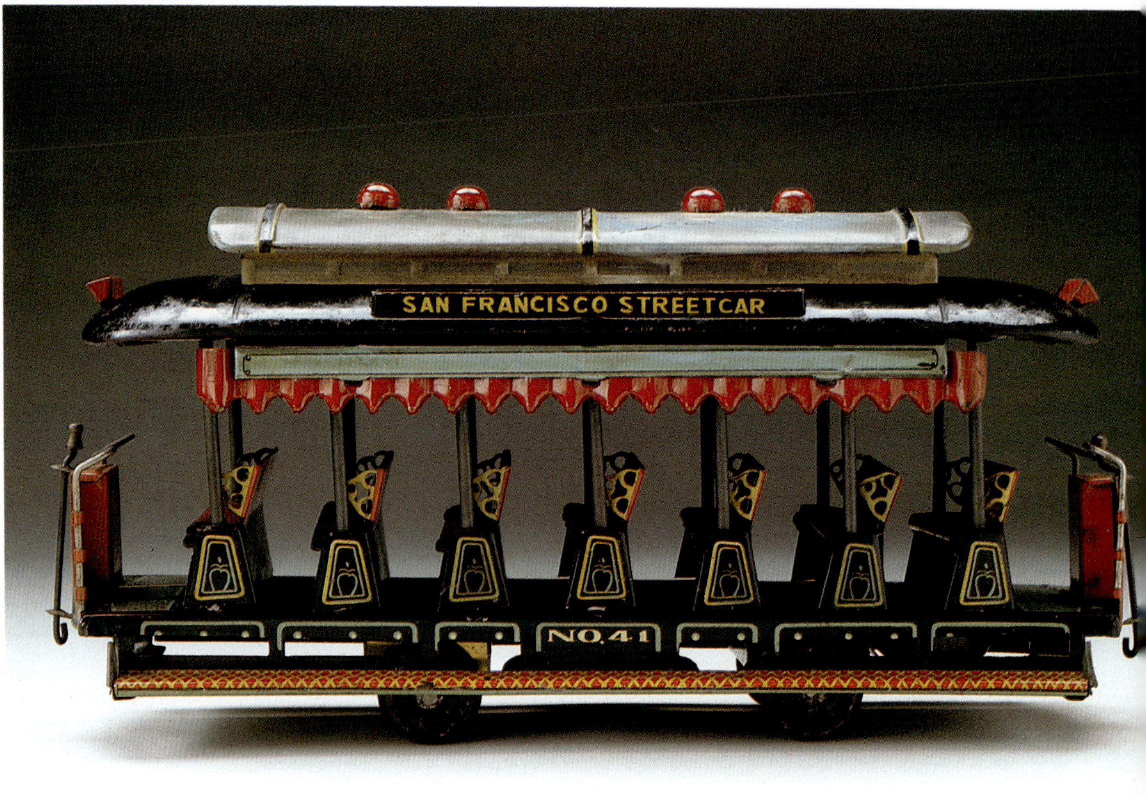

⑯1950'S／SAN FRANCISCO STREET CAR／ALPS／245×78×115

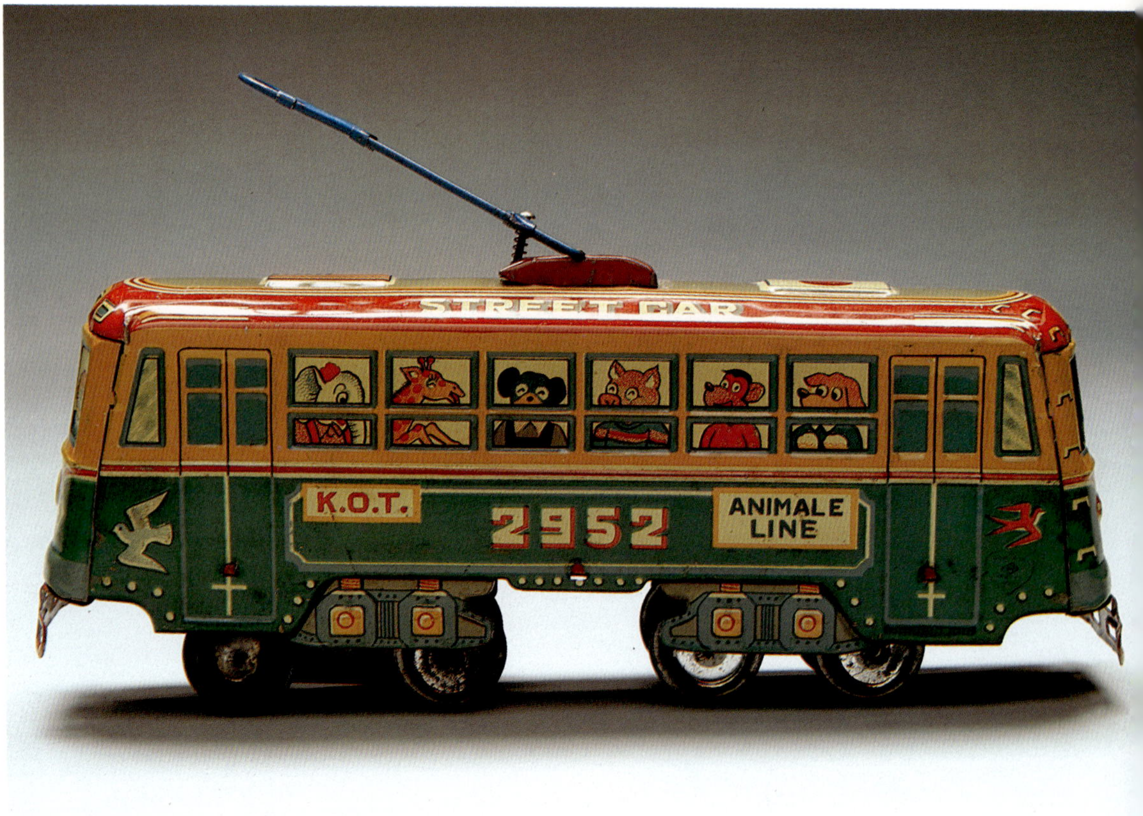

⑯1950'S／STREET CAR／YOSHIYA／250×60×145

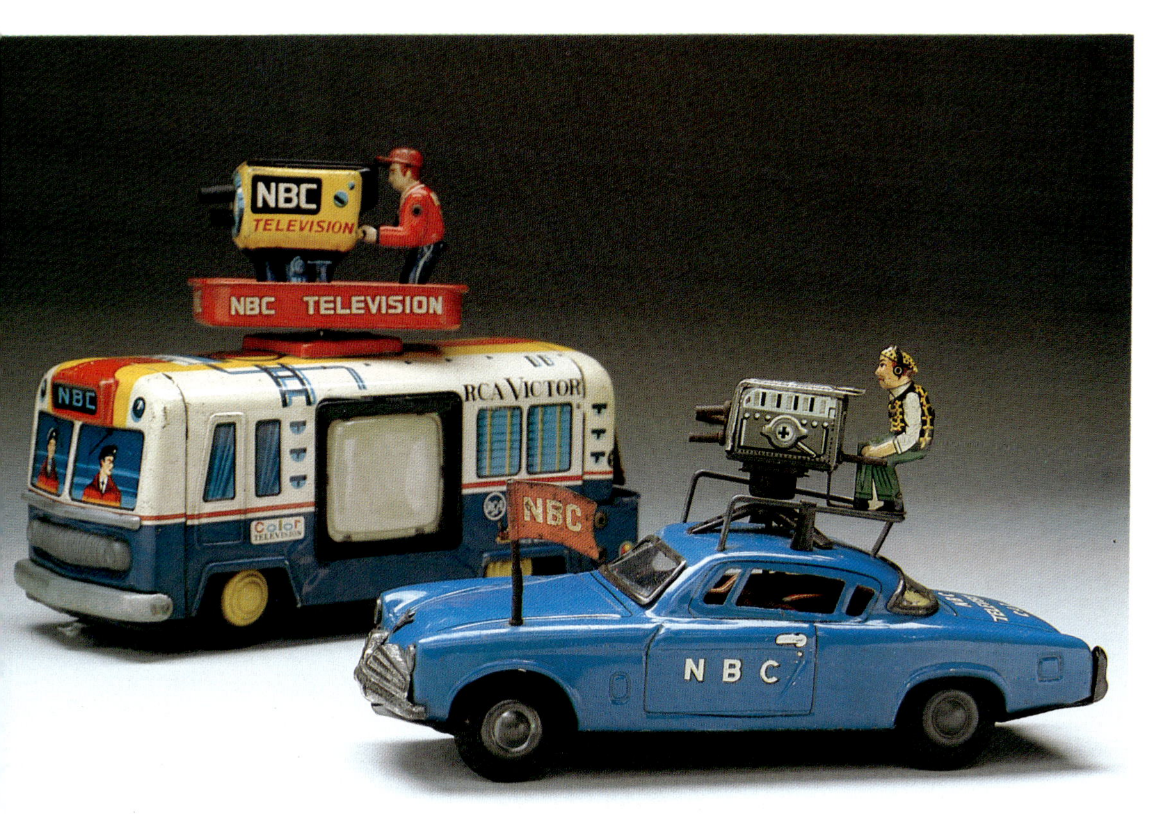

(170)(171) 1950'S／TV CREW BUS AND CAR／TOMIYAMA, UNKNOWN／215×90×155, 190×75×115

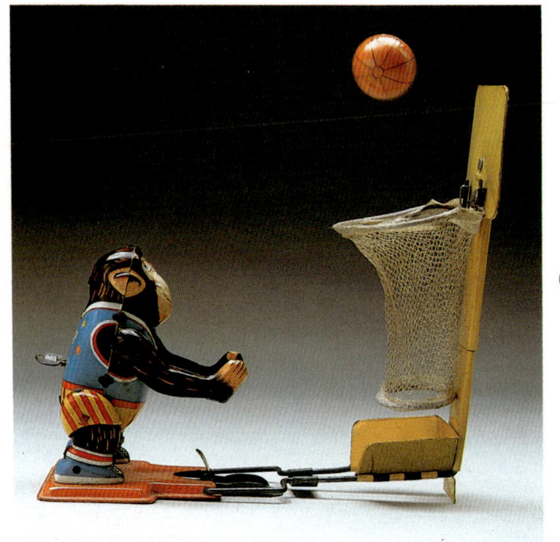

(172) 1950'S／MONKEY BASKETBALL PLAYER／TOPLY／185 × 8

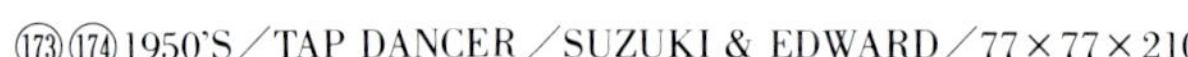

(173)(174) 1950'S／TAP DANCER／SUZUKI & EDWARD／77 × 77 × 210

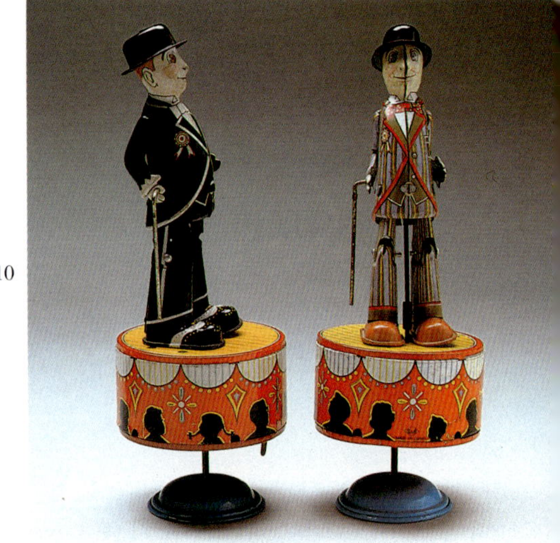

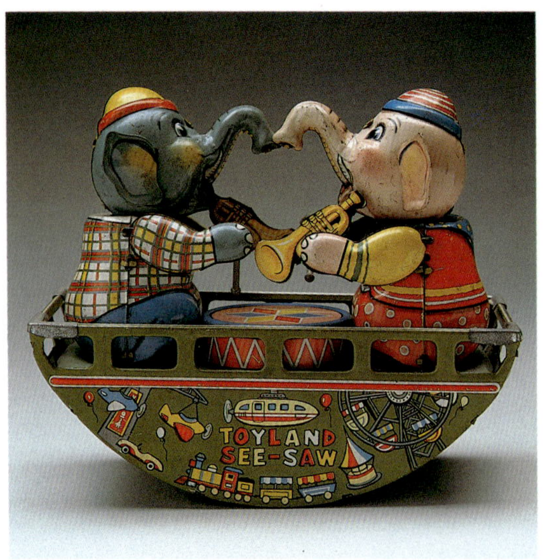

(175) 1950'S／ELEPHANTS AND SEESAW／HISIMO SANGYO／180 ×

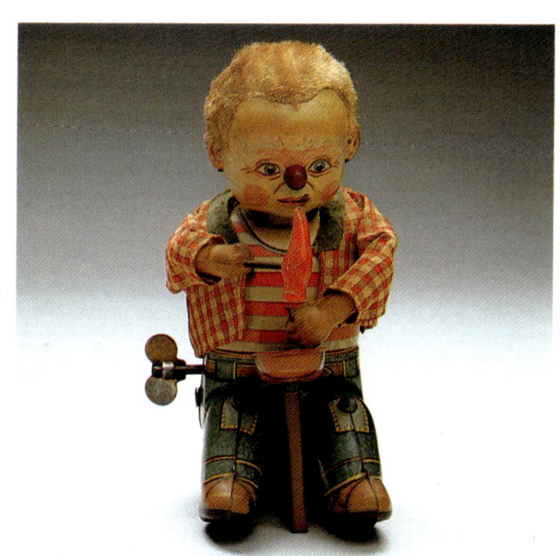

⑰⑥1950'S／SHOEMAKER／UNKNOWN／100×80×160

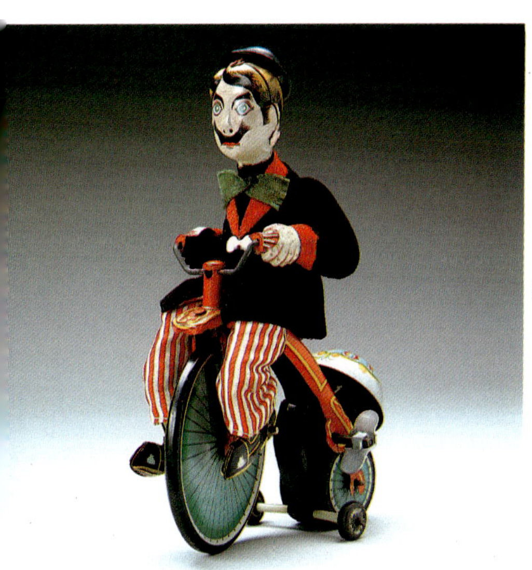

⑰⑦1950'S／OLD MAN AND BICYCLE／TOPLY／115×55×165

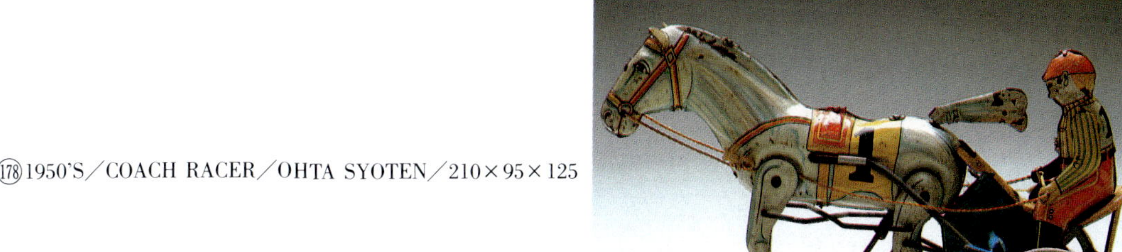

⑰⑧1950'S／COACH RACER／OHTA SYOTEN／210×95×125

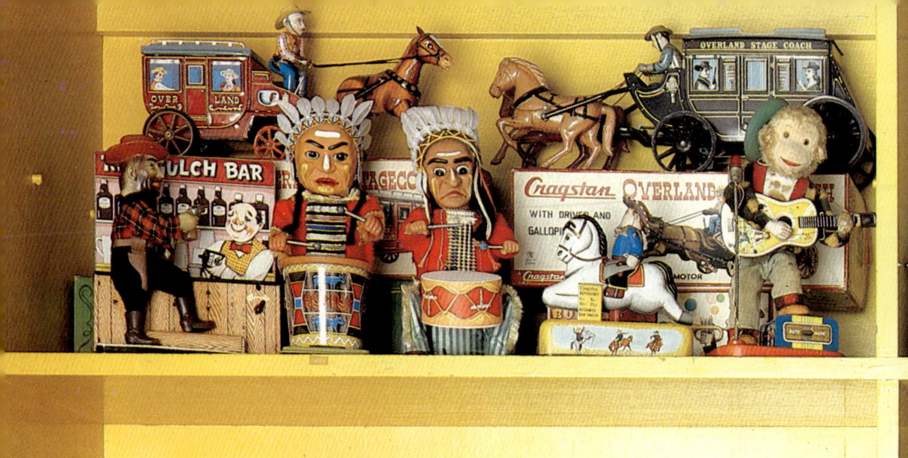
OVERLAND STAGE COACH
Cragstan OVERLAND
WITH DRIVER AND
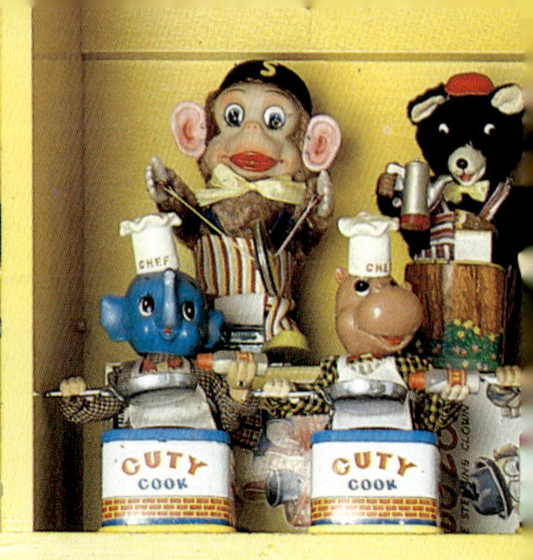
CUTY COOK
CUTY COOK
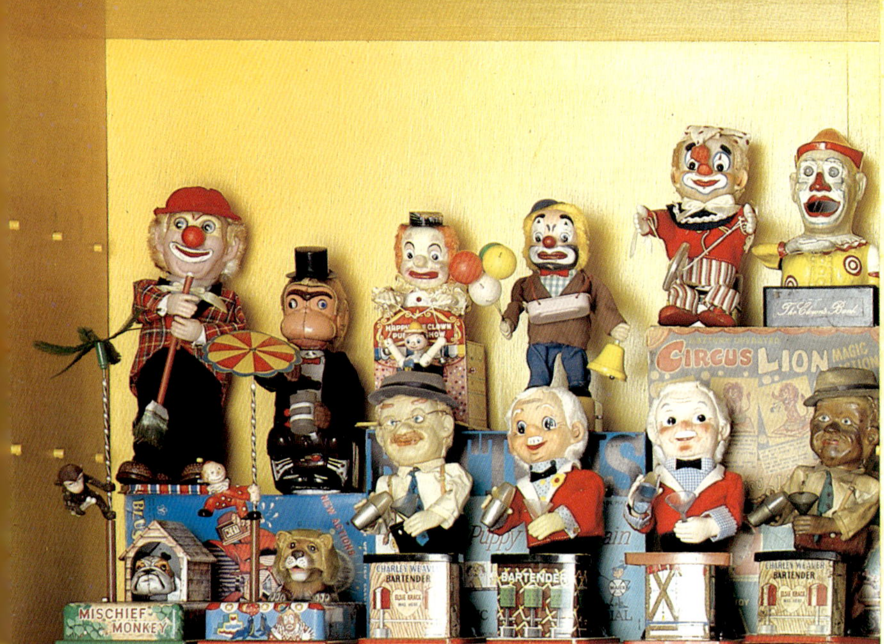
HAPPY THE CLOWN PUPPET SHOW
CIRCUS LION
MISCHIEF MONKEY
CHARLEY WEAVER BARTENDER
BARTENDER
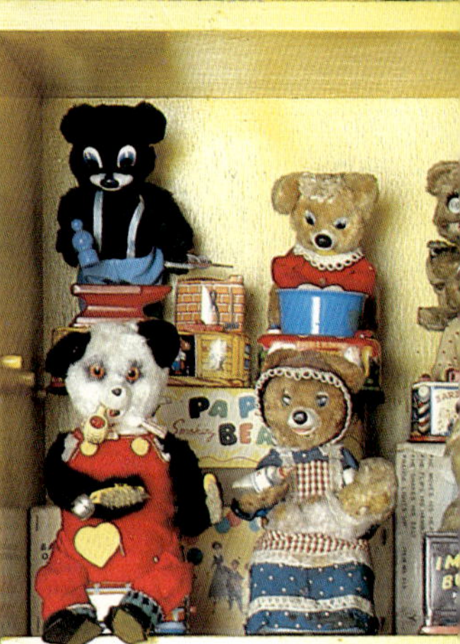
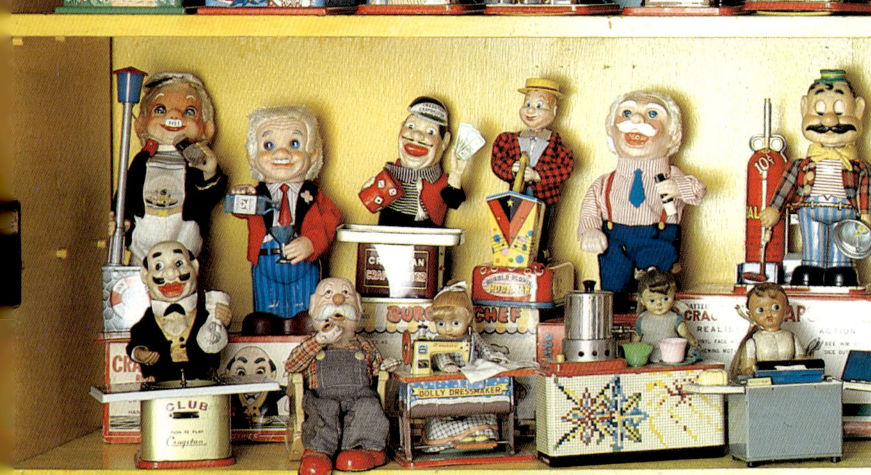
CLUB
Cragstan
DOLLY DRESSMAKER
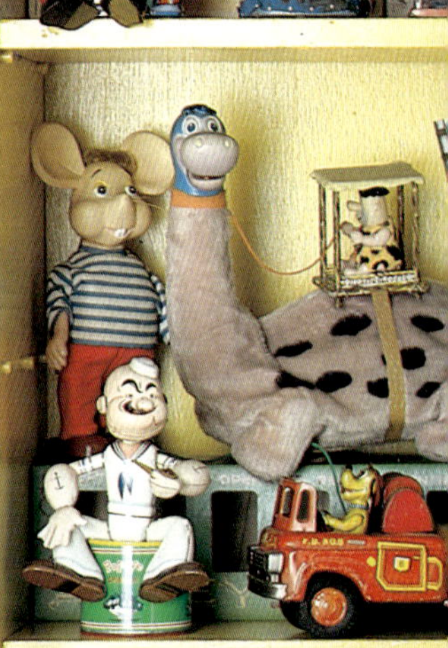
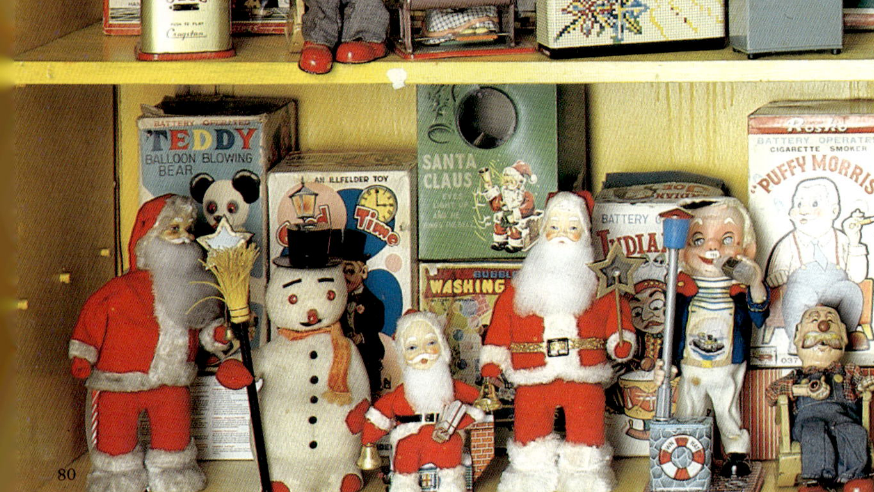
BATTERY OPERATED
TEDDY
BALLOON BLOWING BEAR
AN ILLFELDER TOY
SANTA CLAUS
WASHING
BATTERY OPERATED CIGARETTE SMOKER
"PUFFY MORRIS"
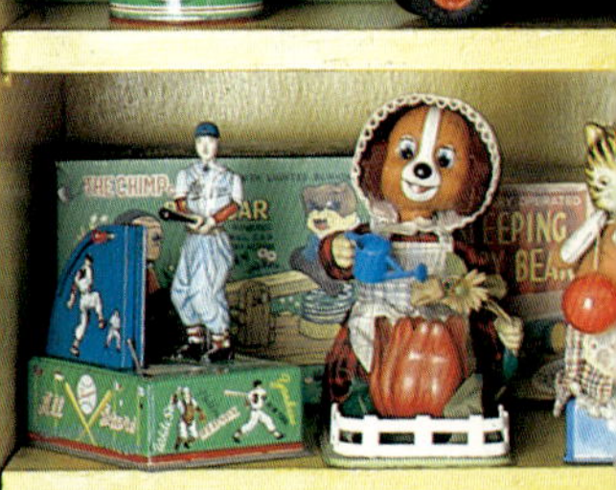
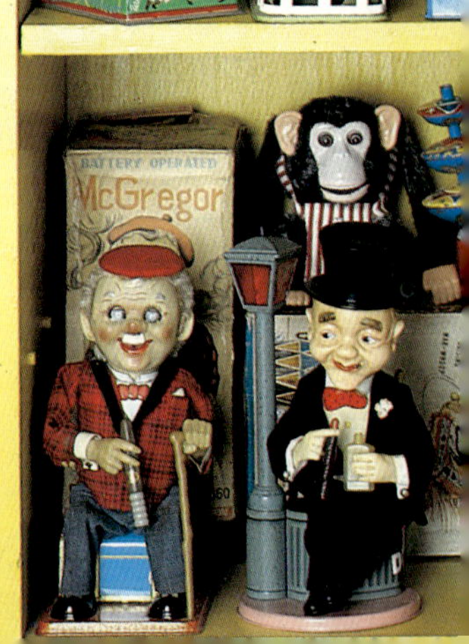
BATTERY OPERATED
McGregor

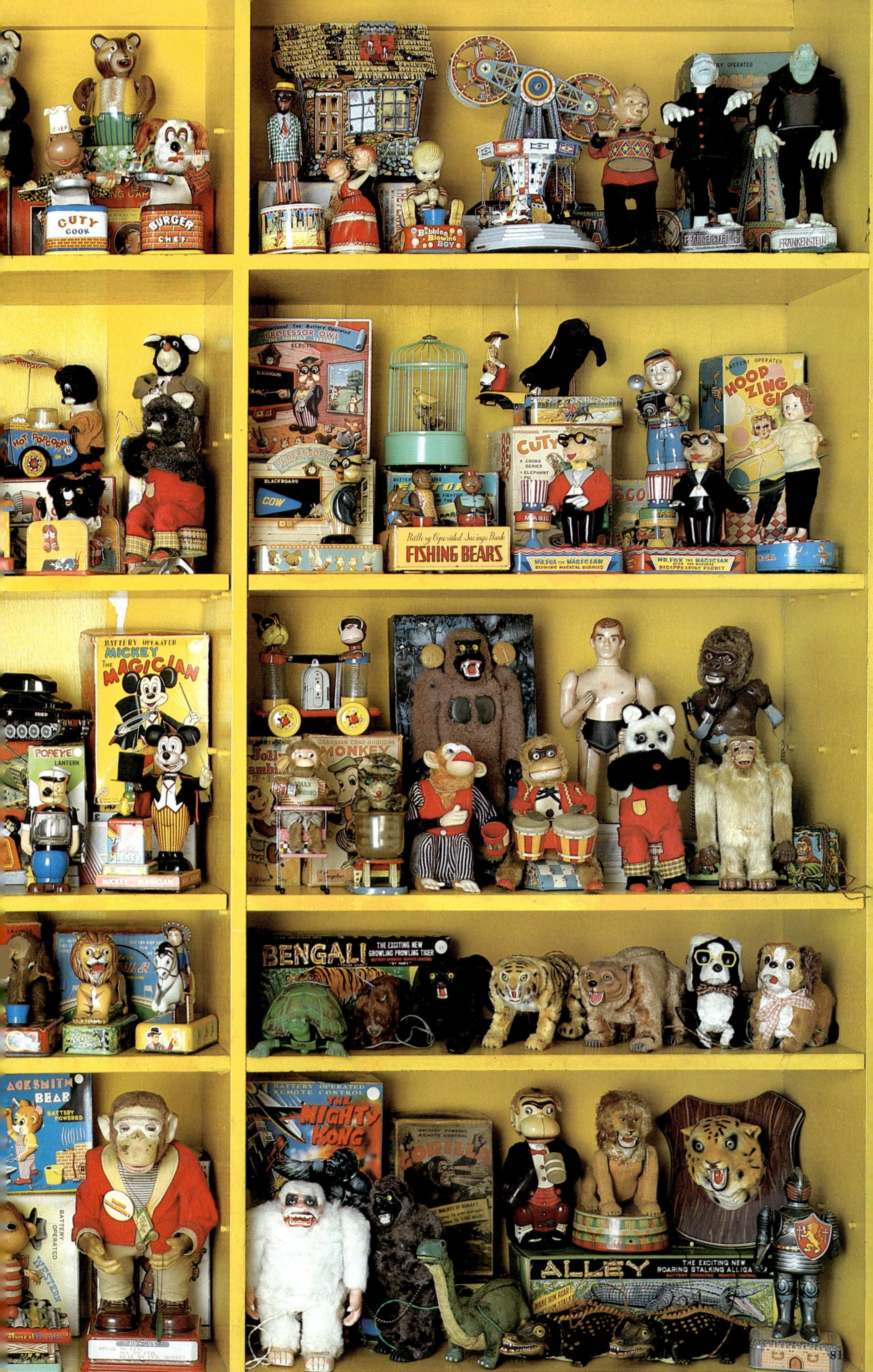
CUTY COOK
BURGER CHEF
Bubbles Blowing Boy
FRANKENSTEIN
FRANKENSTEIN
PROFESSOR OWL
HOT POPCORN
BLACKBOARD
COW
Battery Operated Savings Bank
FISHING BEARS
CUTY
HOOP ZING
BATTERY OPERATED
MICKEY THE MAGICIAN
POPEYE
LANTERN
MONKEY
BENGALI
THE EXCITING NEW GROWLING PROWLING TIGER
BATTERY OPERATED REMOTE CONTROL
THE MIGHTY KONG
ALLEY

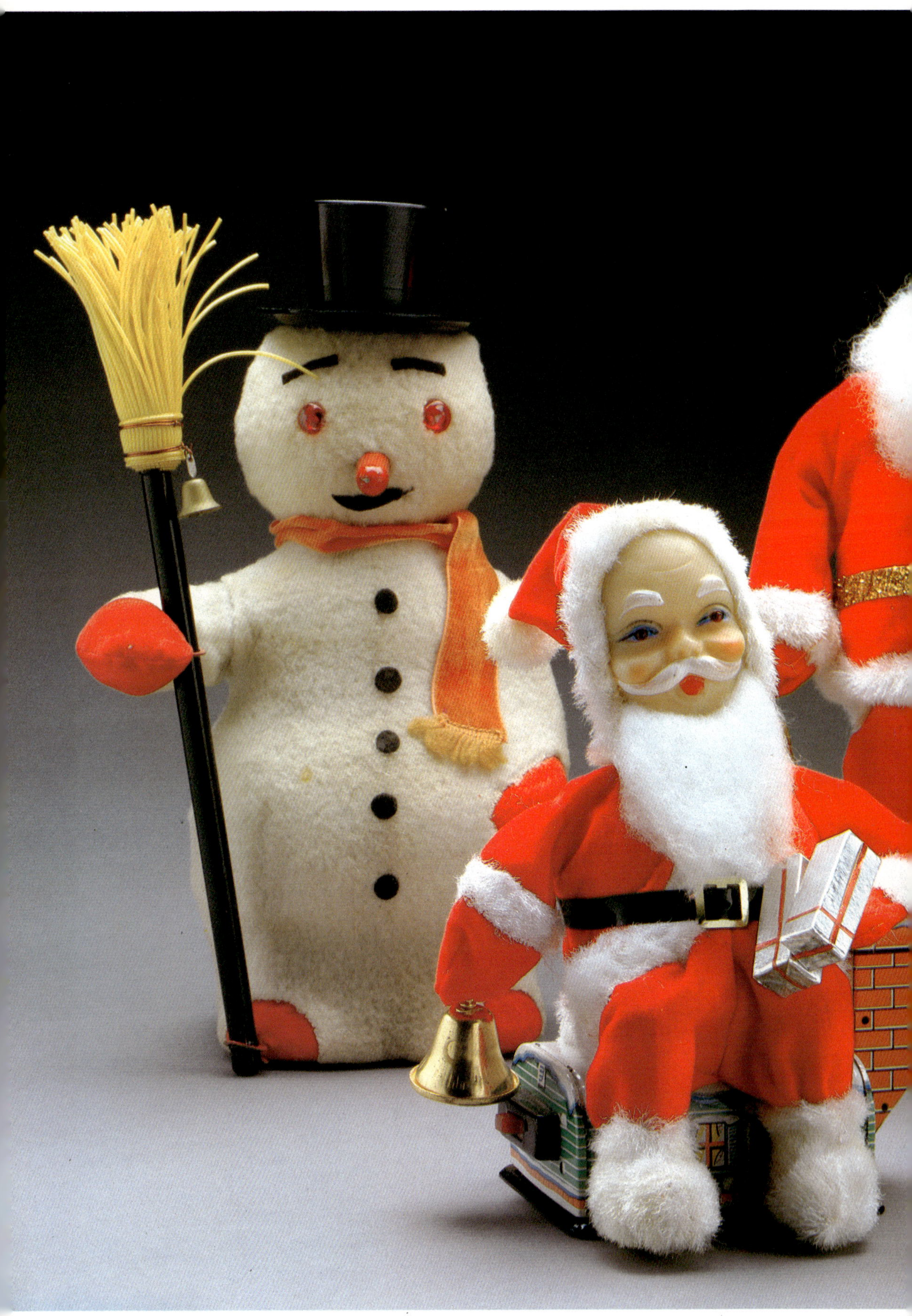

⑰⑱⑱ 1950'S／SNOWMAN, SANTA CLAUS AND CHIMNEY, SANTA CLAUS／MASUDAYA, SWALLOW／125 × 170 × 280, 140 × 1

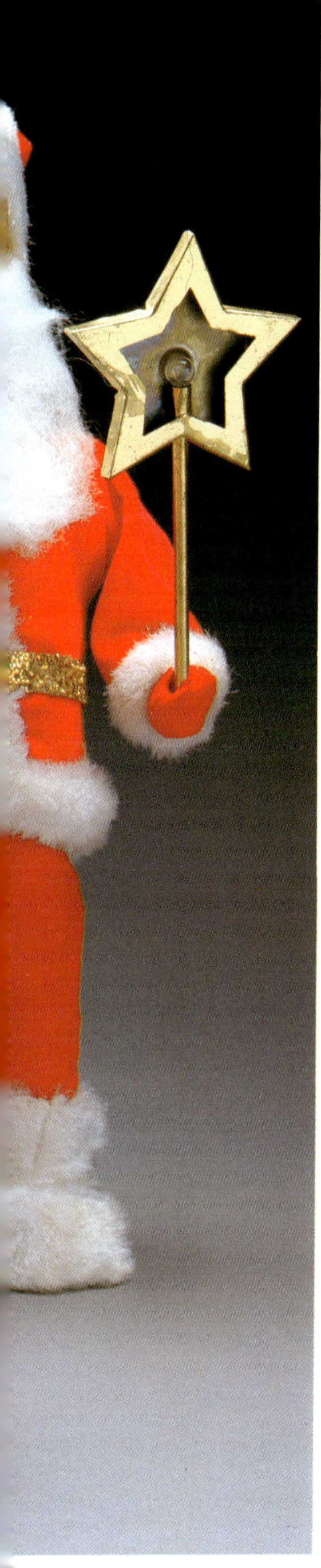

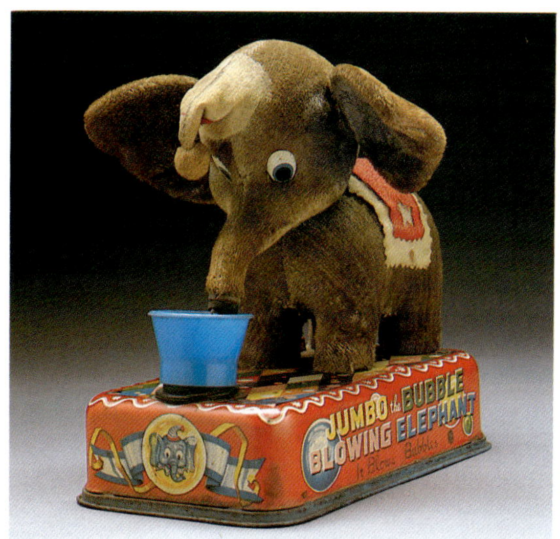

(182) 1950'S／ELEPHANT BLOWING BUBBLES／TOMIYAMA／180×105×180

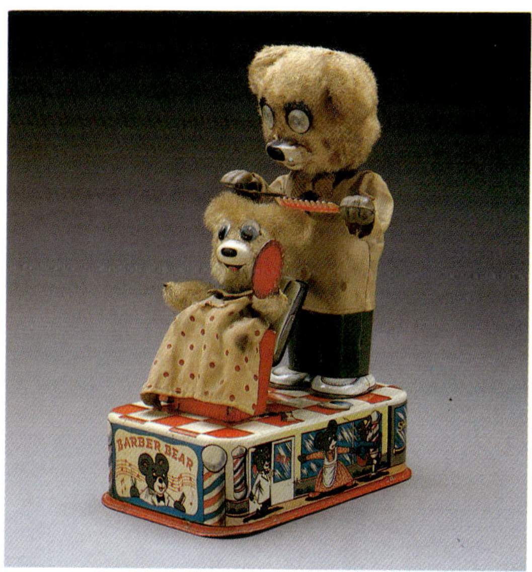

(183) 1950'S／BEAR BARBER／NOMURA／172×108×240

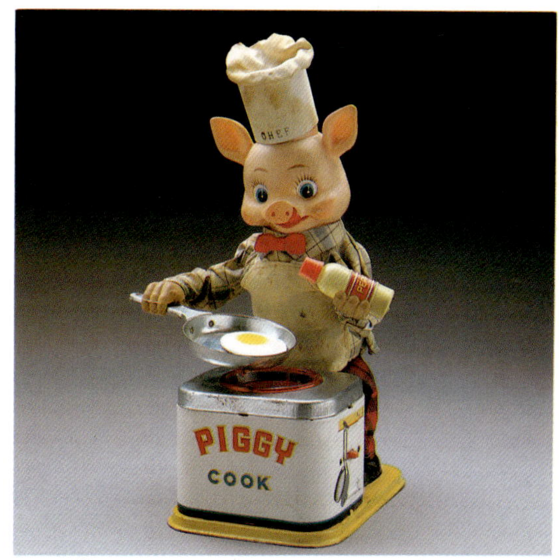

(184) 1960'S／PIG CHEF／YONEZAWA／150×170×265

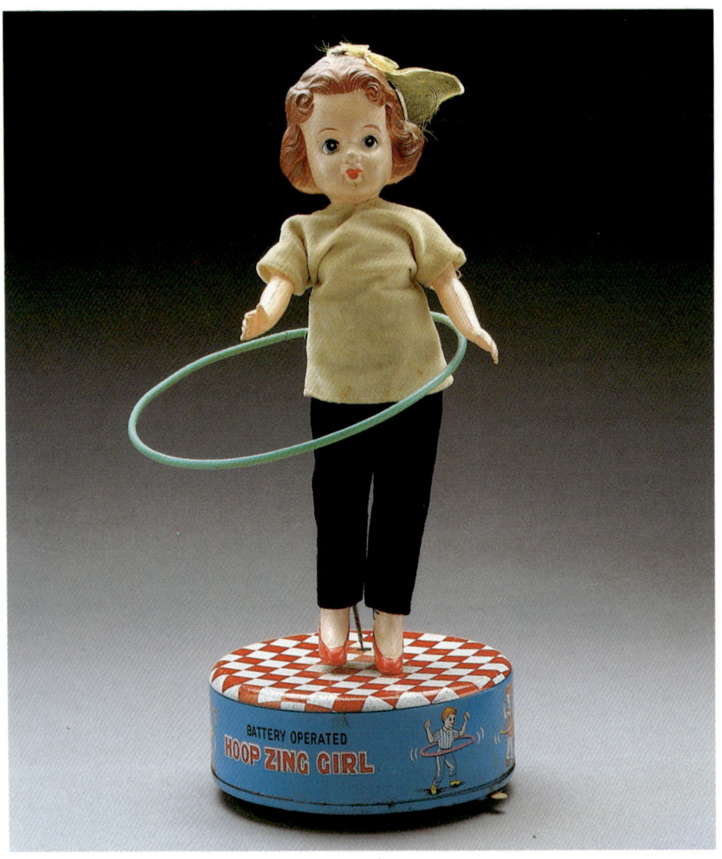

⑱ 1950'S／HULA HOOP／PLAYTHING／130×130×300

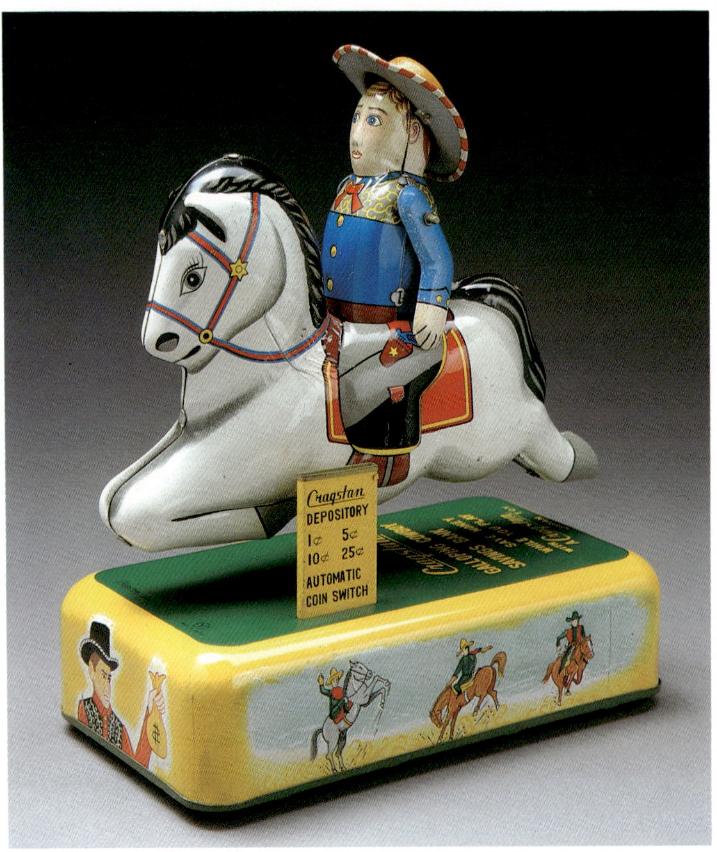

(186) 1950'S／COWBOY SAVINGS BANK／YONEZAWA／170 × 95 × 190

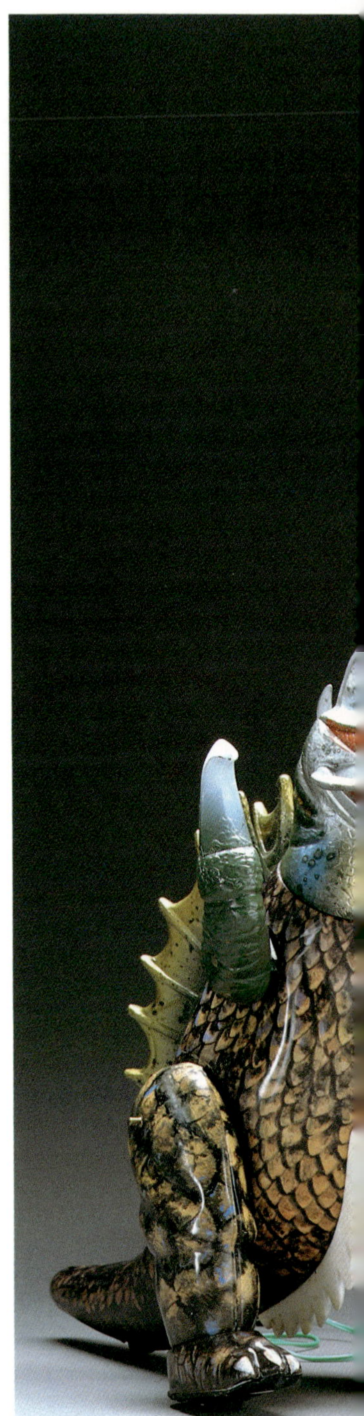

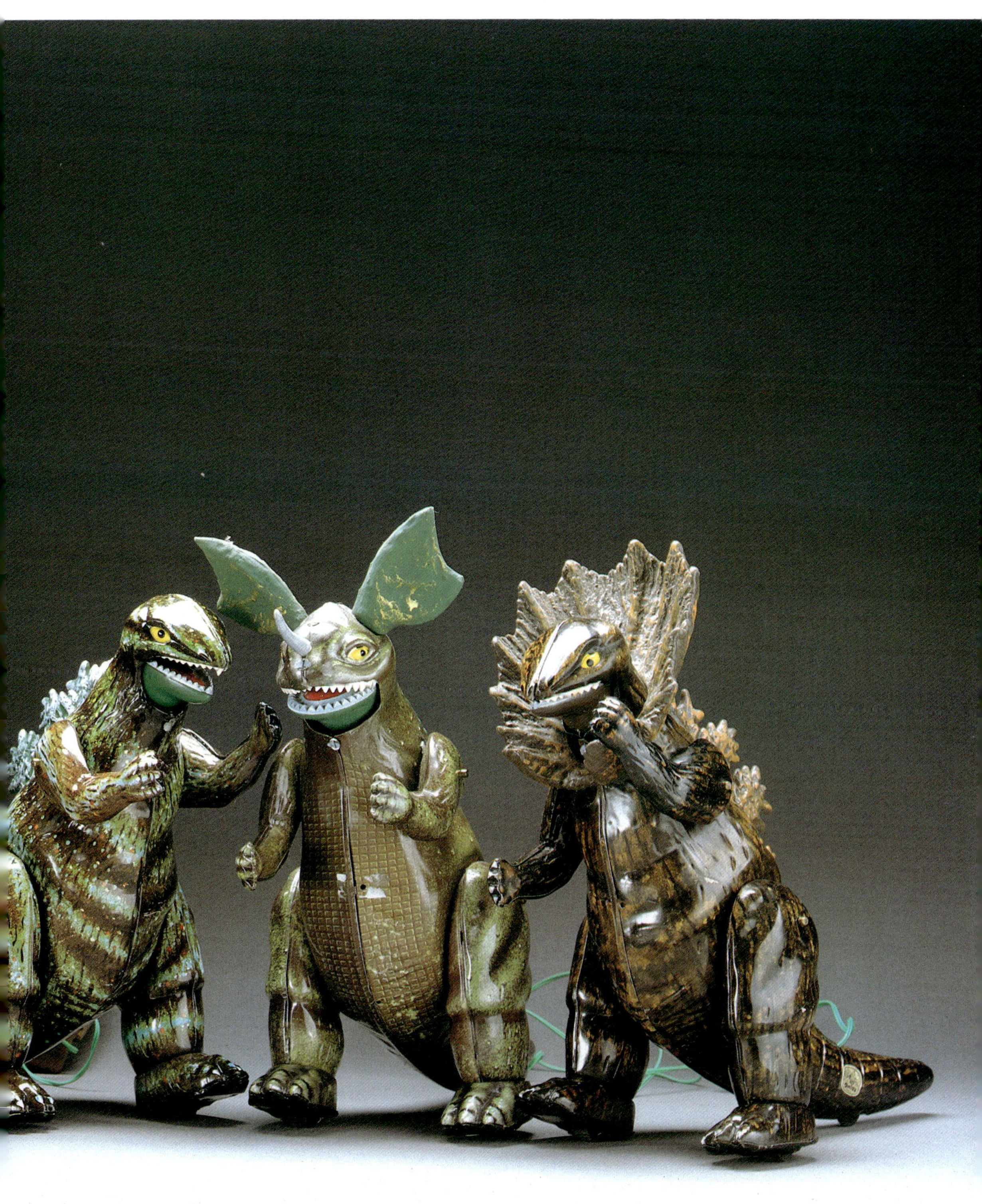

(187) (188) (189) (190) 1960'S／JAPANESE MONSTERS／BULL MARK／285×135×250, 300×130×295, 285×130×280, 285×135×280

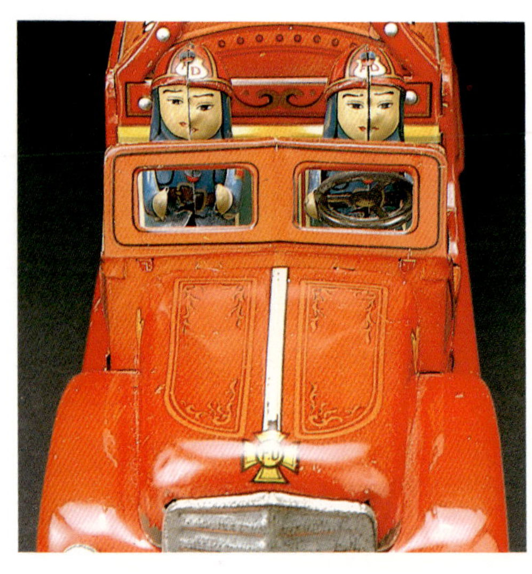

(191) 1950'S / FIRE ENGINE / YOSHIYA / 425×120×180

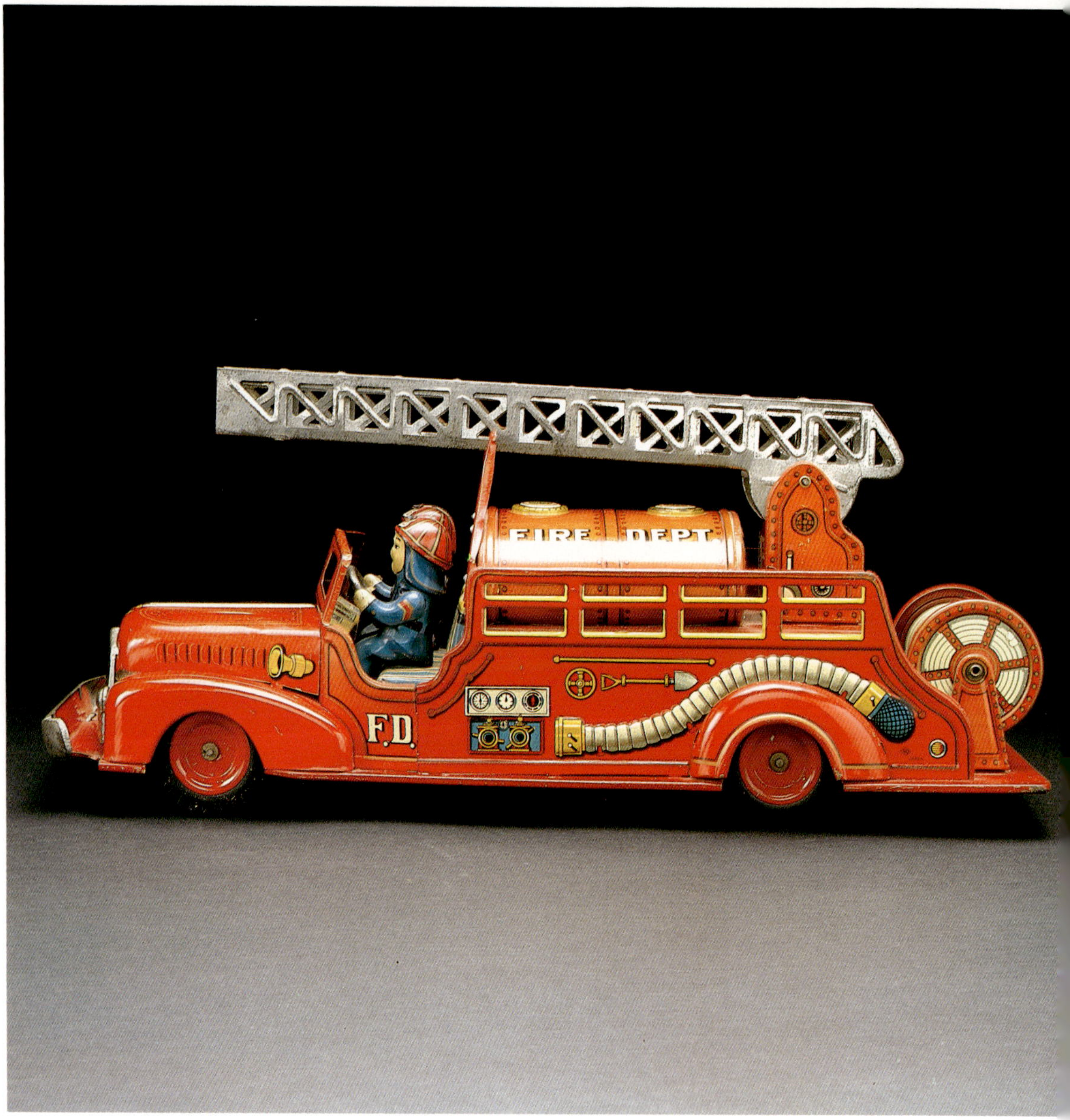

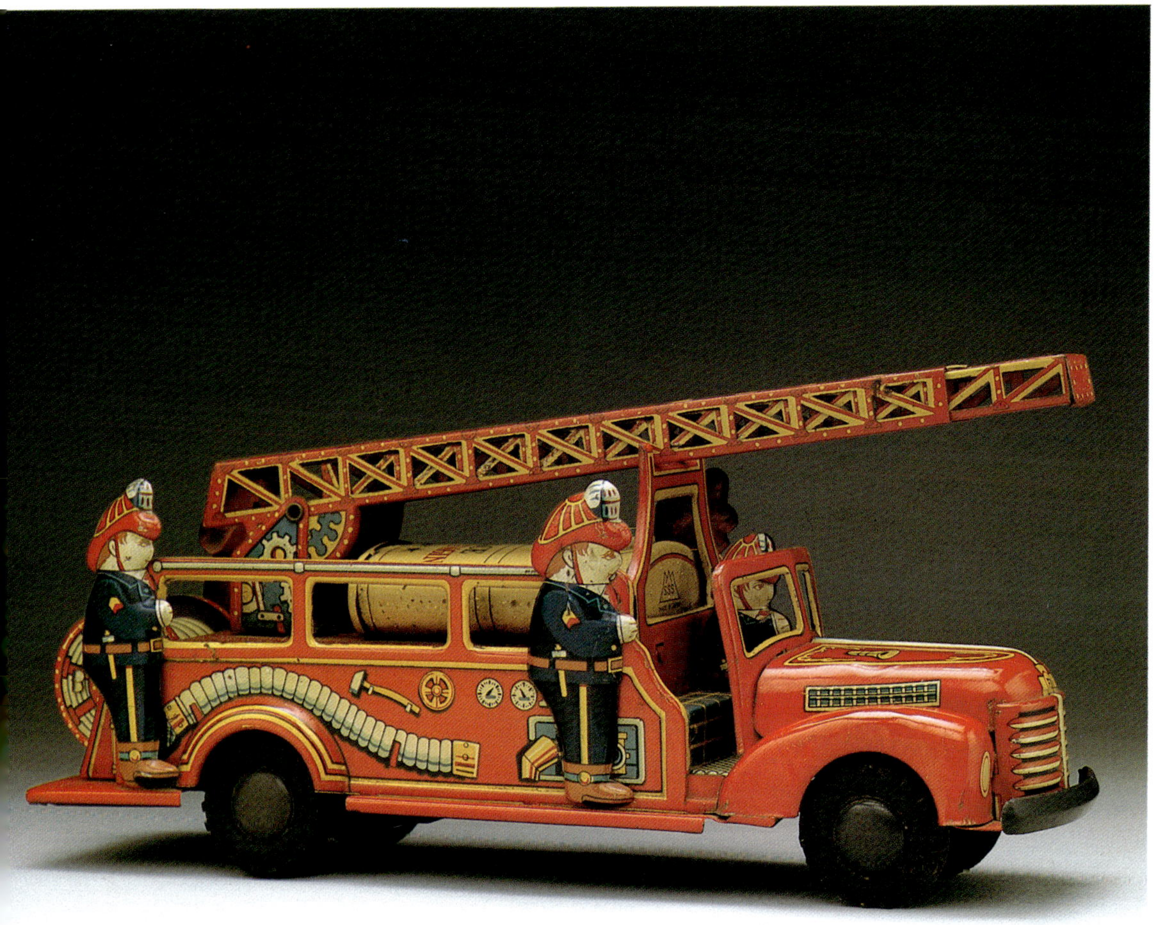

(192) 1950'S／FIRE ENGINE／SANESU／250×70×115

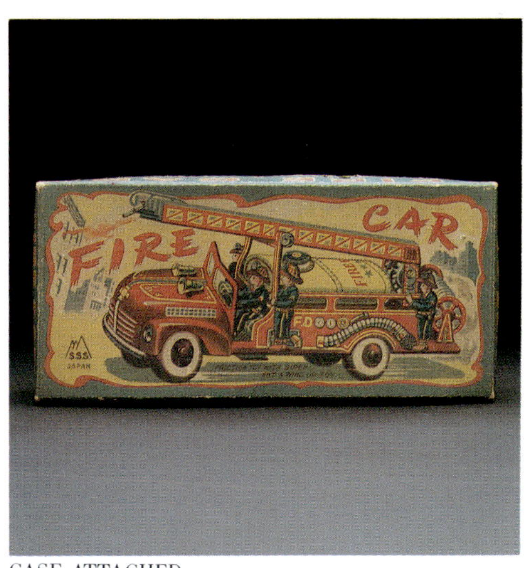

CASE ATTACHED

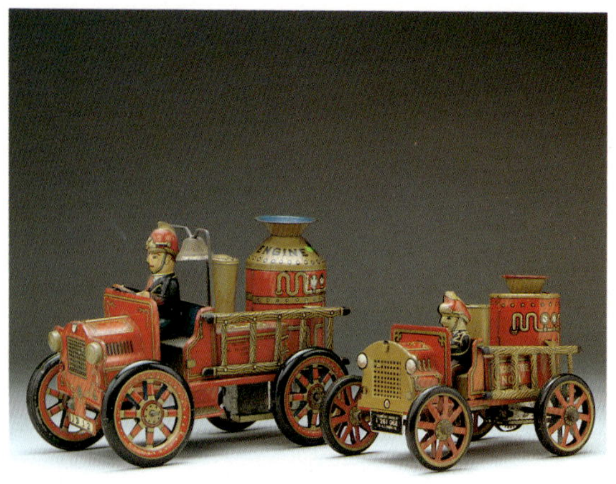

(193)(194) 1950'S/FIRE ENGINE/MASUDAYA, LINE MAR/
140×80×100, 108×70×75

(195) 1950'S/FIRE ENGINE/UNKNOWN/175×55×80

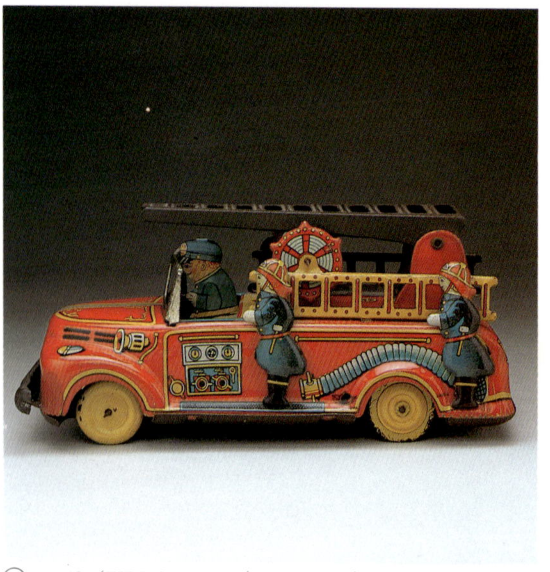

(196) 1950'S/FIRE ENGINE/MOMOYA/190×80×85

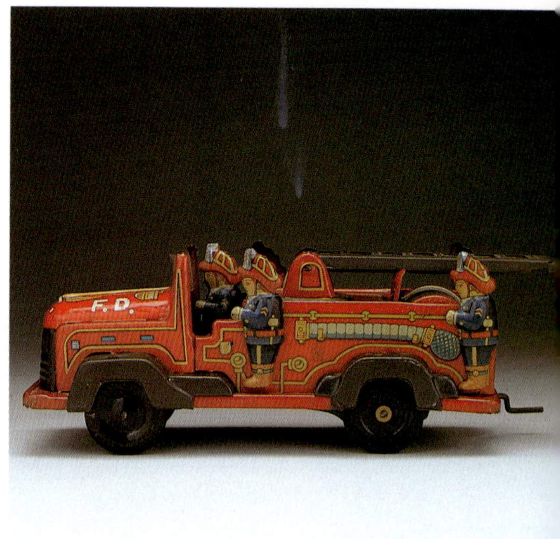

(197) 1950'S/FIRE ENGINE/KOKYU SHOKAI/180×60×

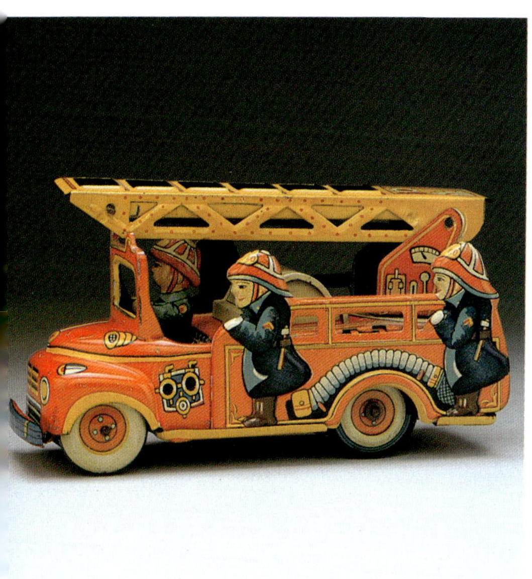

⑲⑧ 1950'S／FIRE ENGINE／YONEZAWA／135×50×70

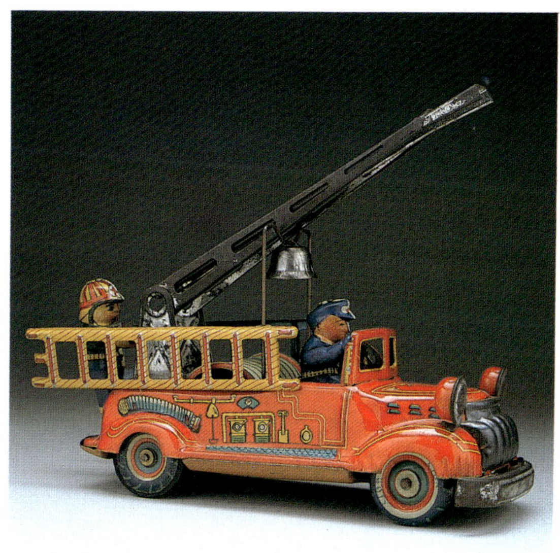

⑲⑨ 1950'S／FIRE ENGINE／MARUSAN／175×70×90

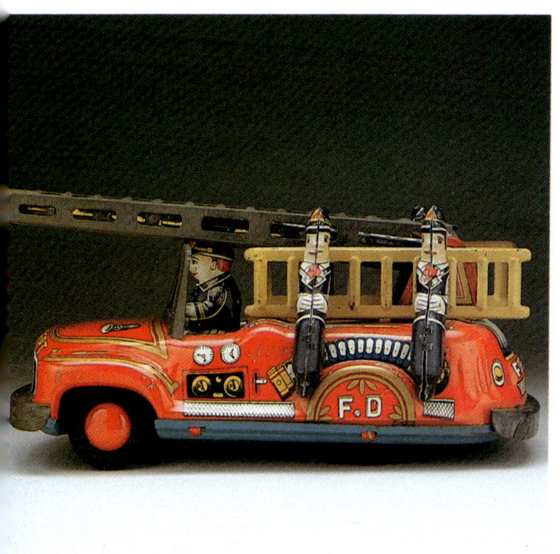

⑳⓪ 1950'S／FIRE ENGINE／KOSHIBE／195×105×105

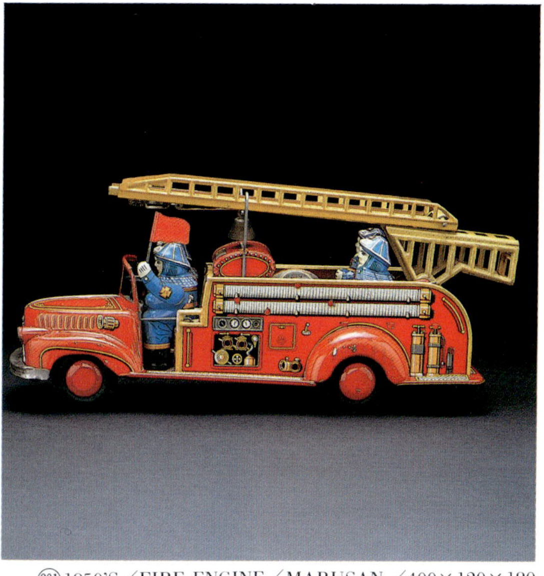

⑳① 1950'S／FIRE ENGINE／MARUSAN／400×120×180

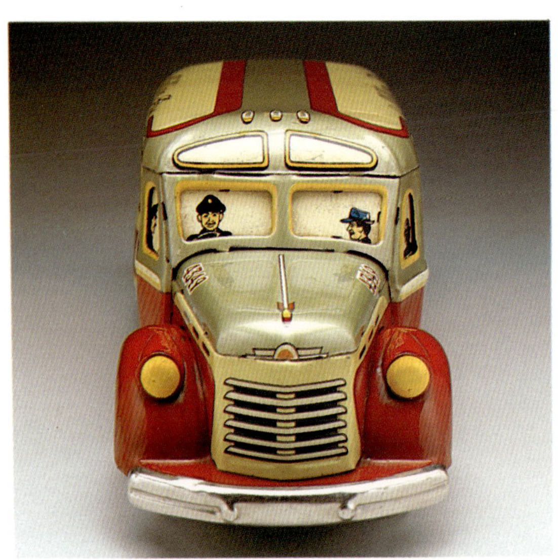

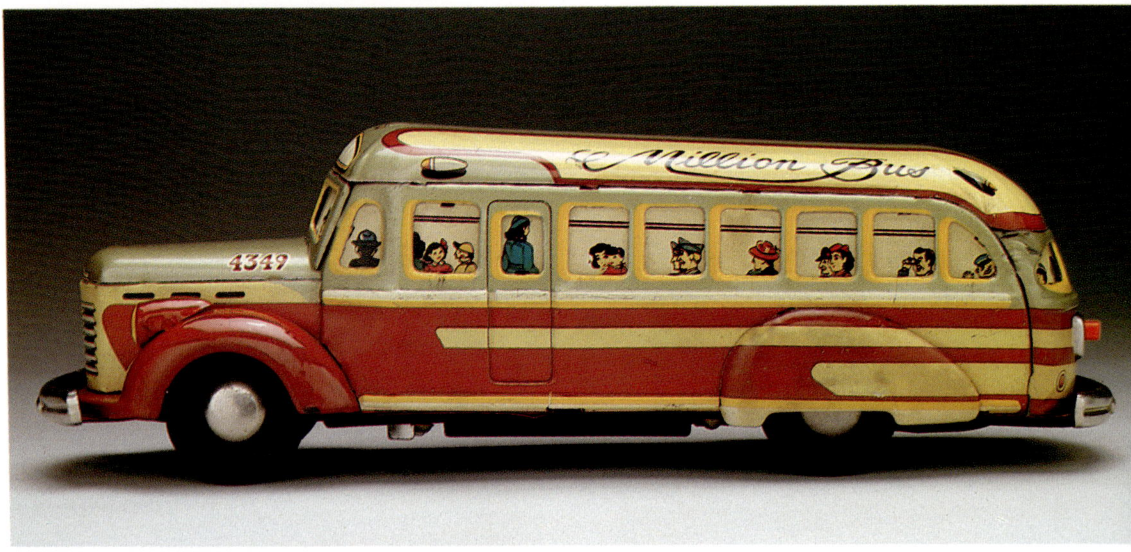

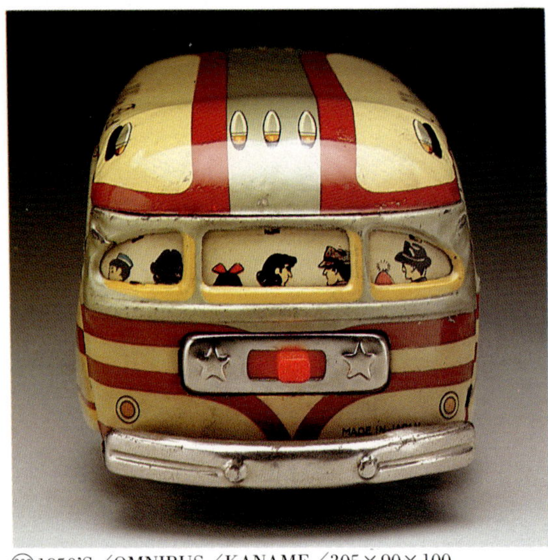

⑳1950'S／OMNIBUS／KANAME／305×90×100

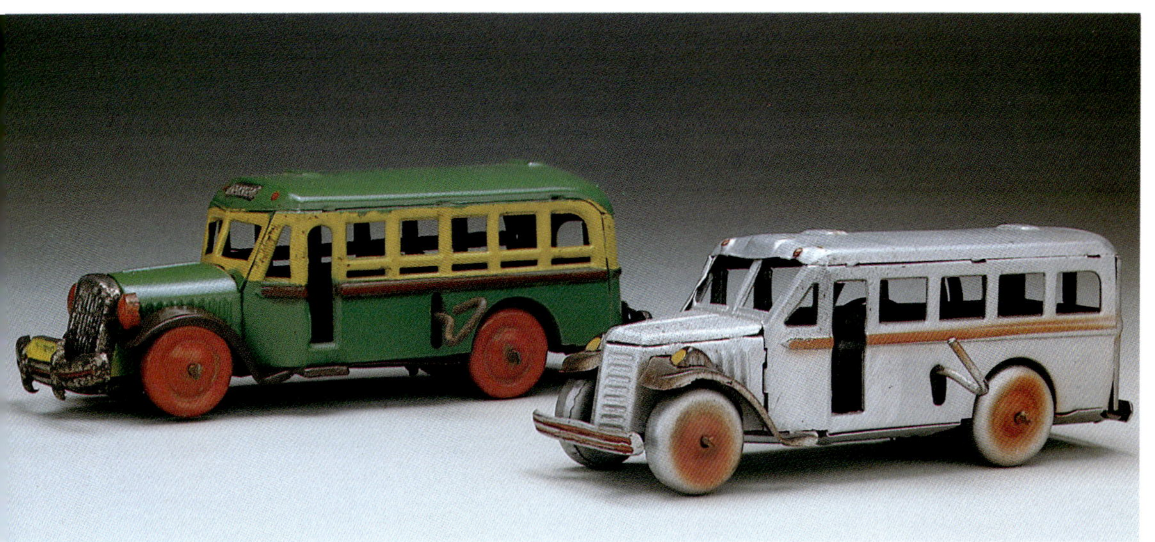

⑳③⑳④ 1950'S／OMNIBUS／UNKNOWN／140×45×40，160×45×34

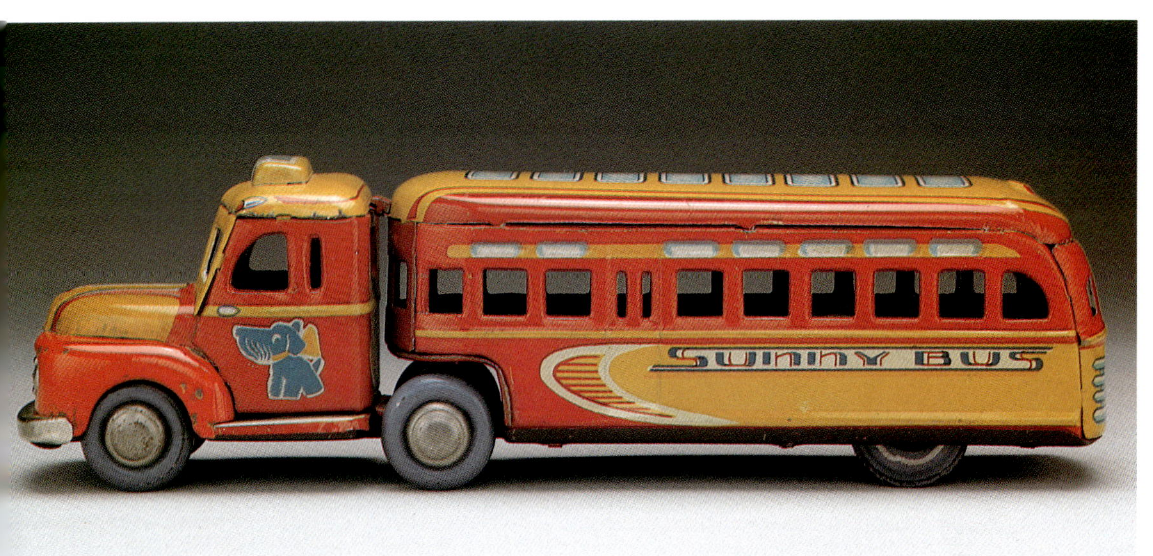

⑳⑤ 1950'S／OMNIBUS／NIHON BOEKI／245×55×75

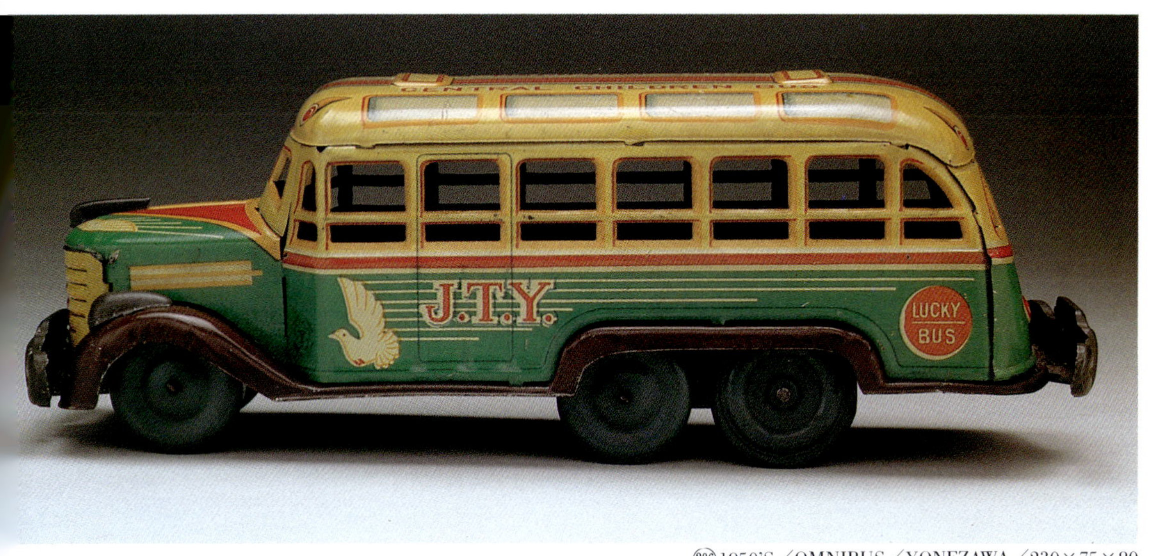

⑳⑥ 1950'S／OMNIBUS／YONEZAWA／230×75×80

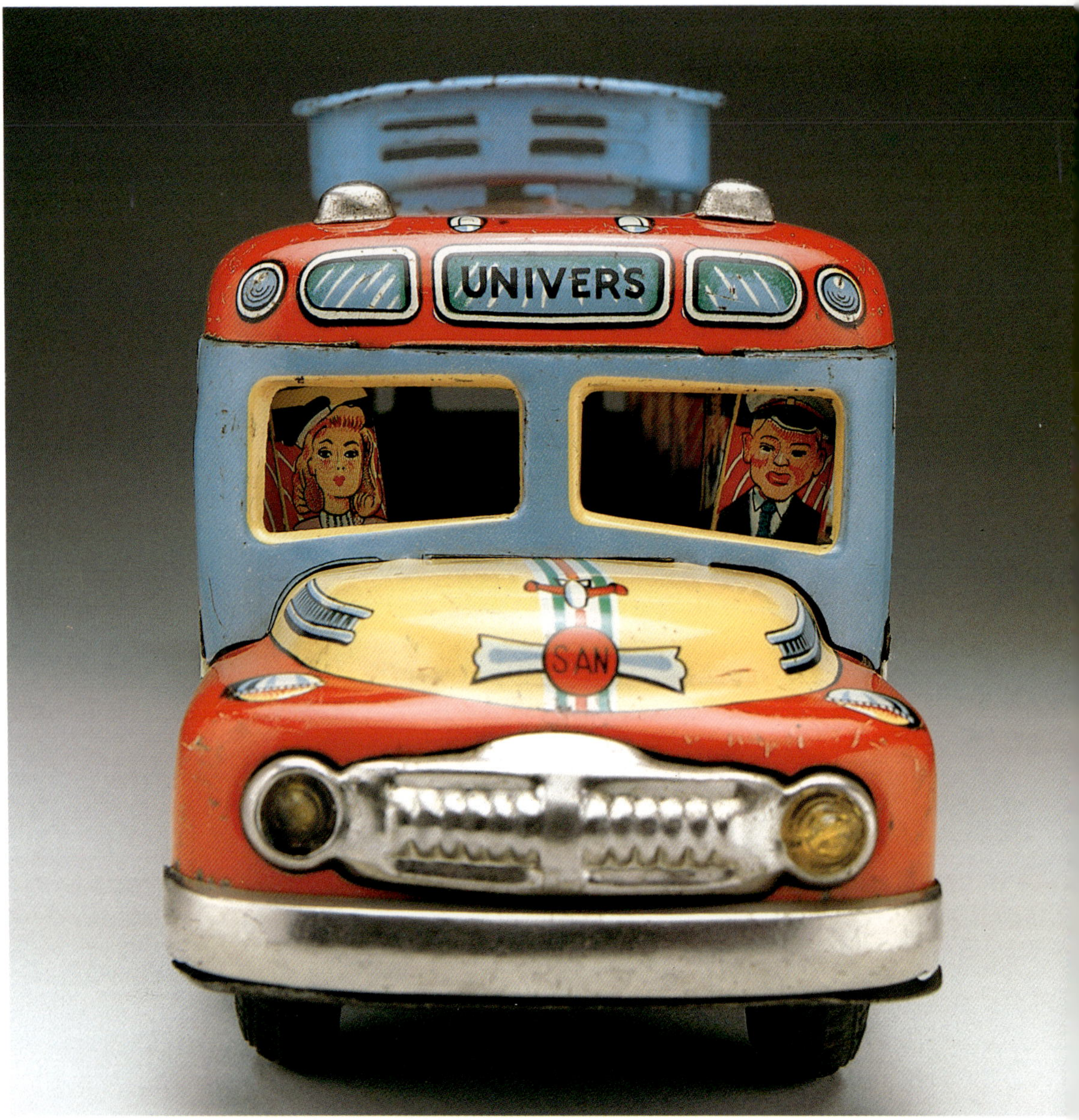

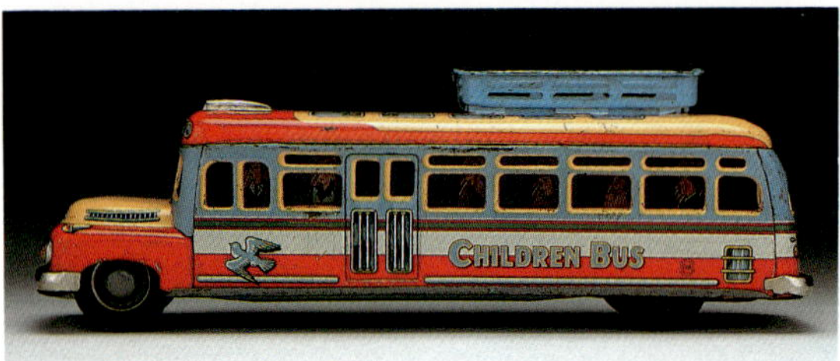

207 1950'S／OMNIBUS／MARUSAN／370×90×120

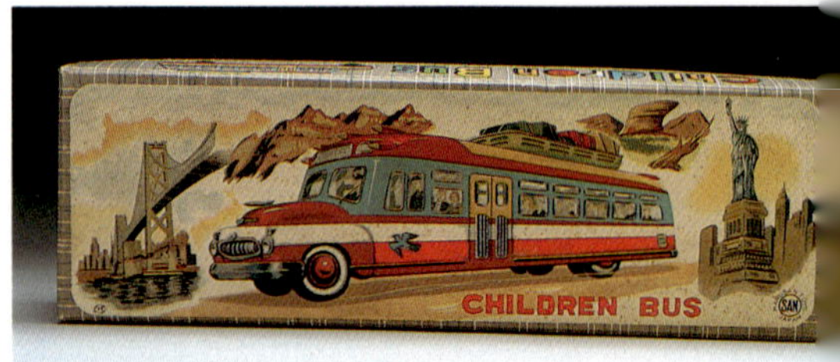

CASE ATTACHED

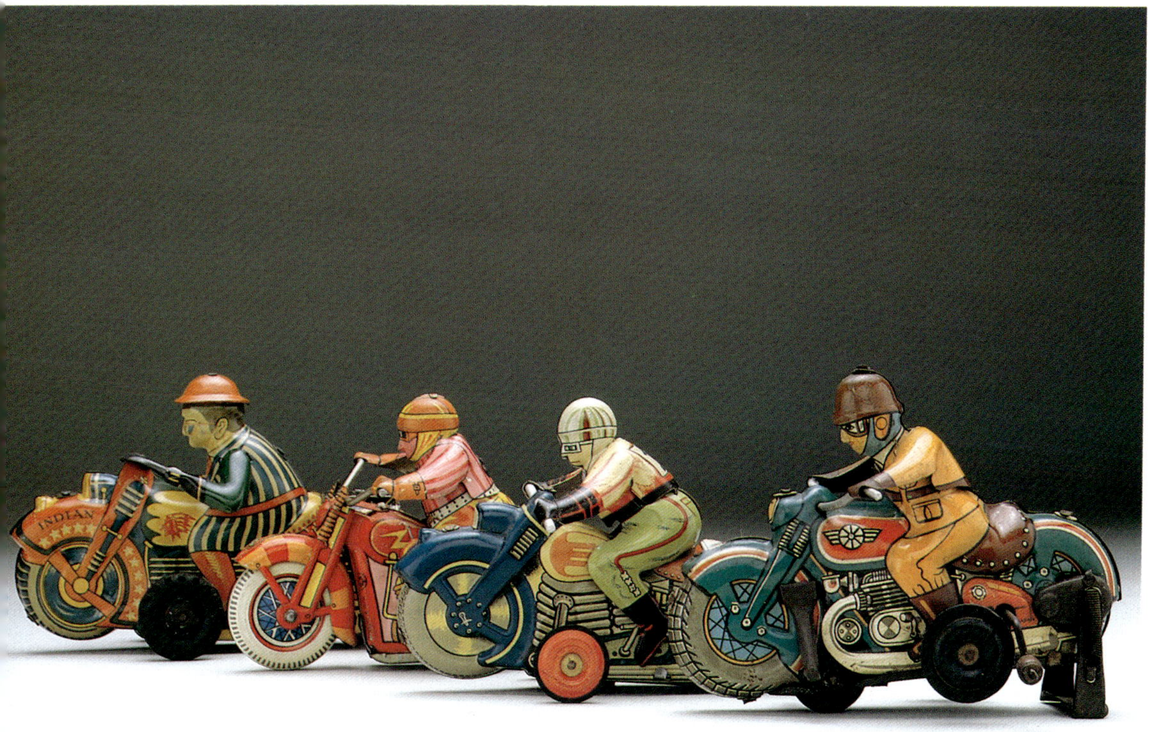

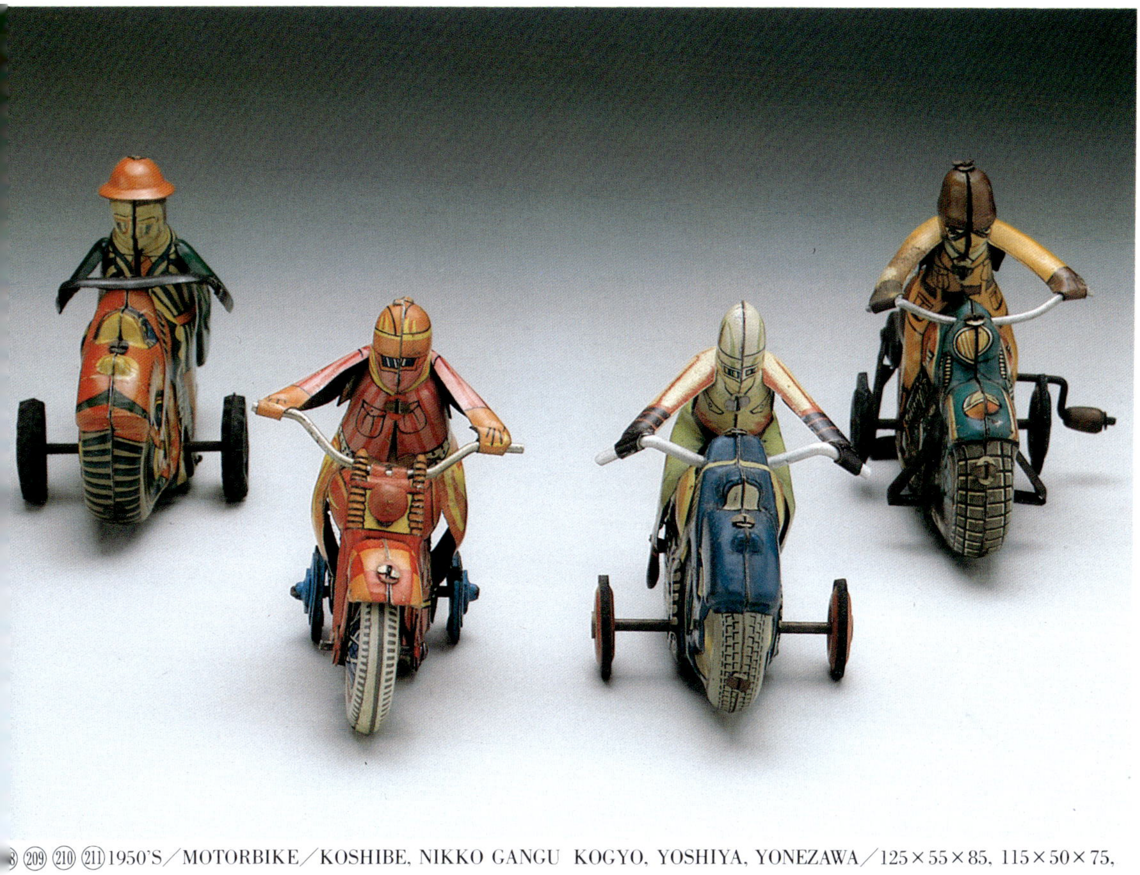

⑧ ⑳⑨ ㉑⓪ ㉑① 1950'S／MOTORBIKE／KOSHIBE, NIKKO GANGU KOGYO, YOSHIYA, YONEZAWA／125×55×85, 115×50×75, 115×55×75, 115×50×90

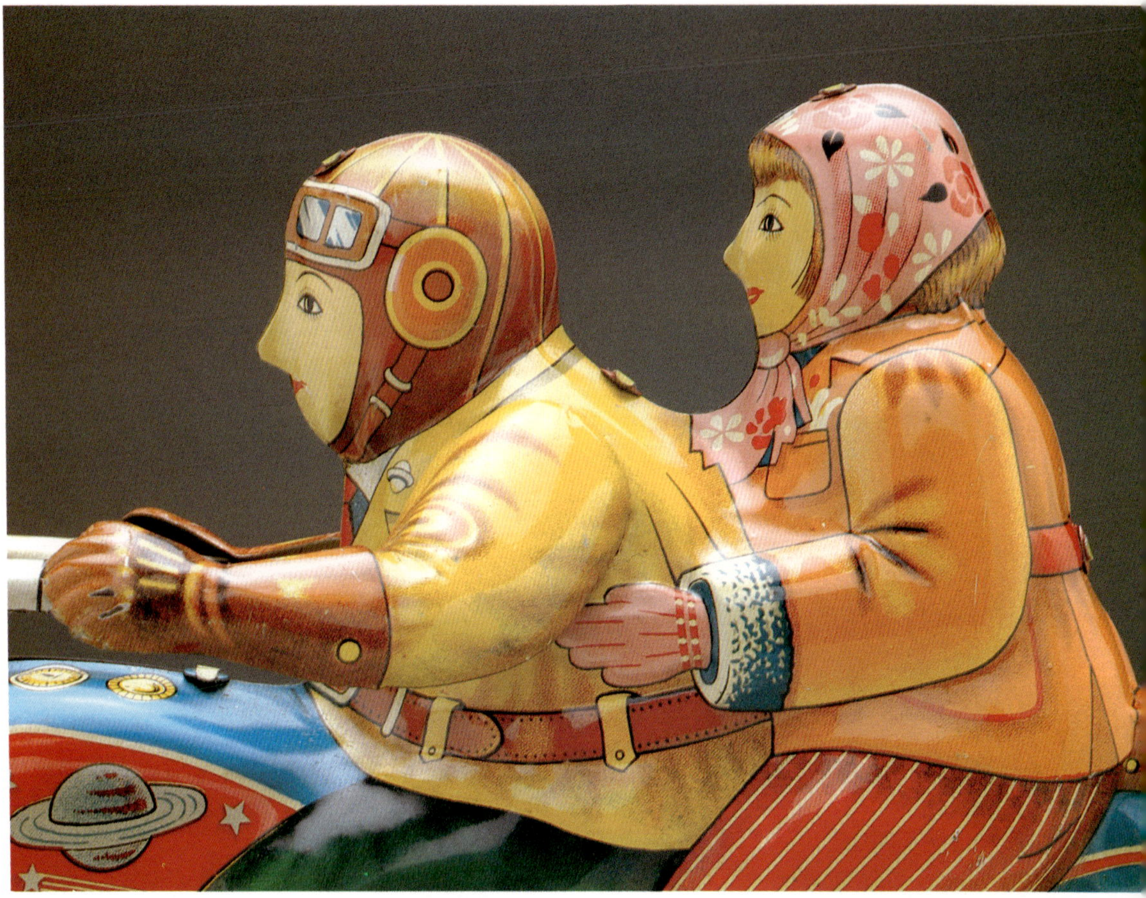

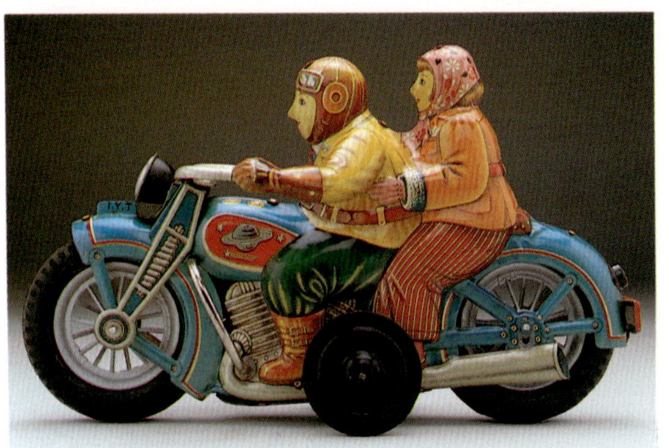

⑫ 1950'S／MOTORBIKE／I. Y. METAL TOYS／300×100×175

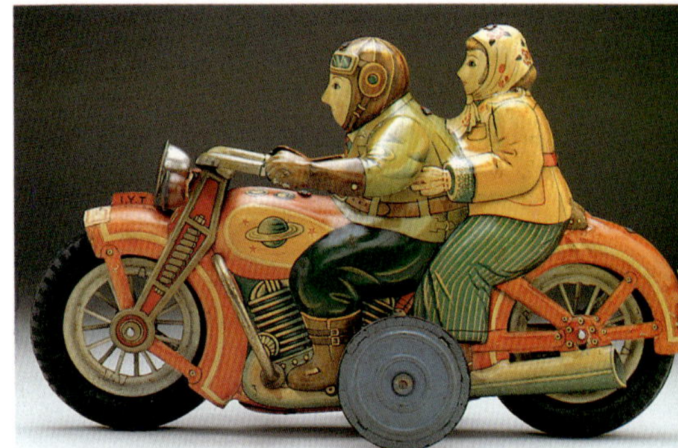

⑬ 1950'S／MOTORBIKE／I. Y. METAL TOYS／300×100×

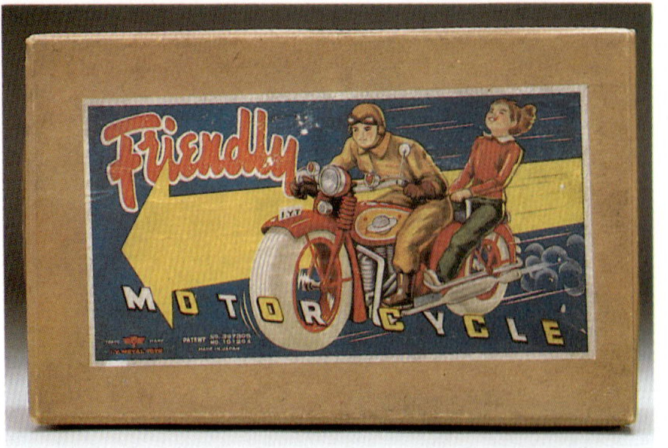

CASE ATTACHED

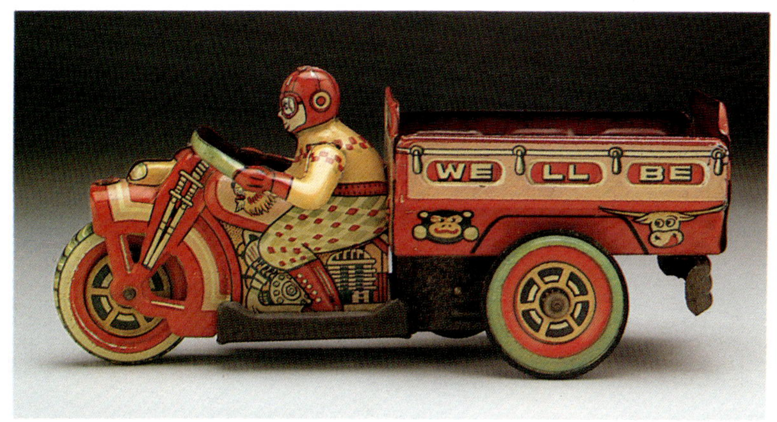

214 1950'S／TRICYCLE／SANKEI ／145×50×65

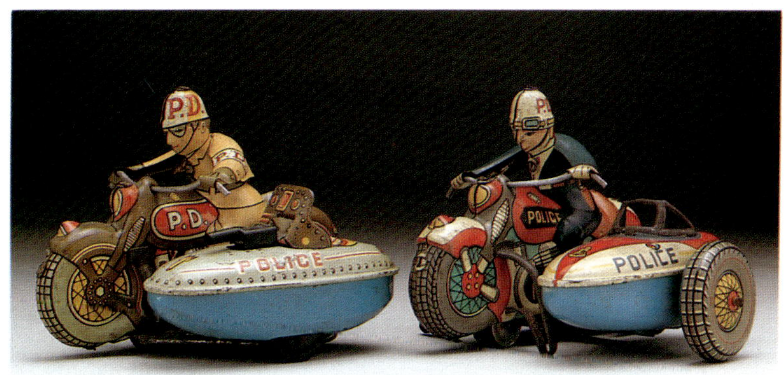

215 216 1950'S／SIDECAR／YONEZAWA ／120×75×80, 120×110×85

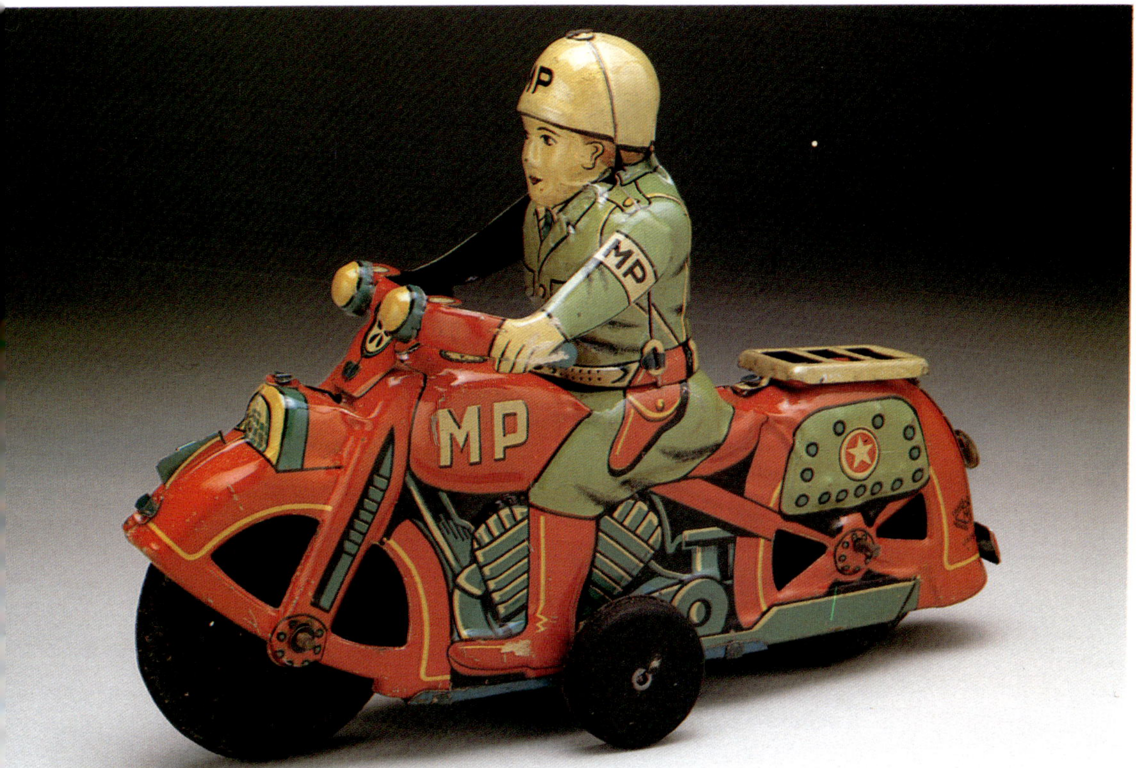

217 1950'S／MILITARY POLICE MOTORBIKE／MASUDAYA／170×50×120

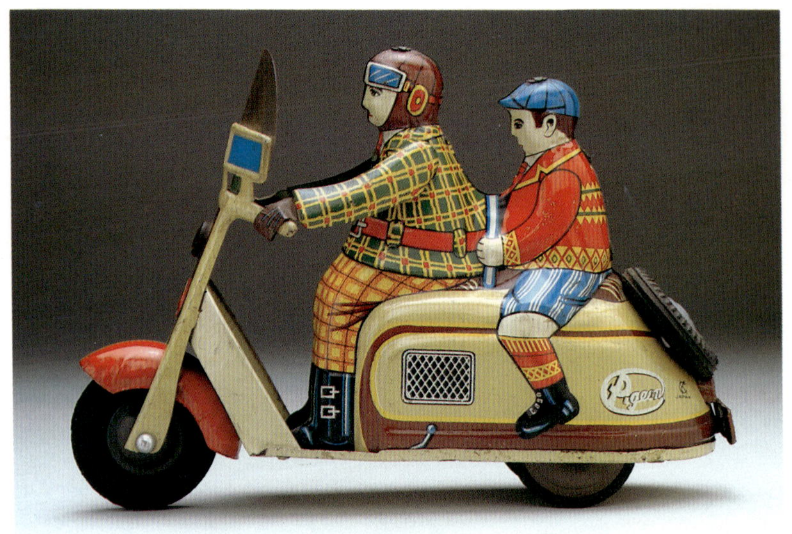

(218) 1950'S／SCOOTER／KOSHIBE／
200×55×130

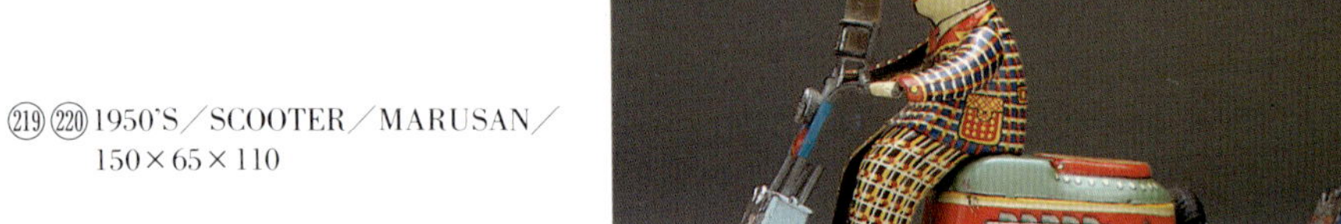

(219) (220) 1950'S／SCOOTER／MARUSAN／
150×65×110

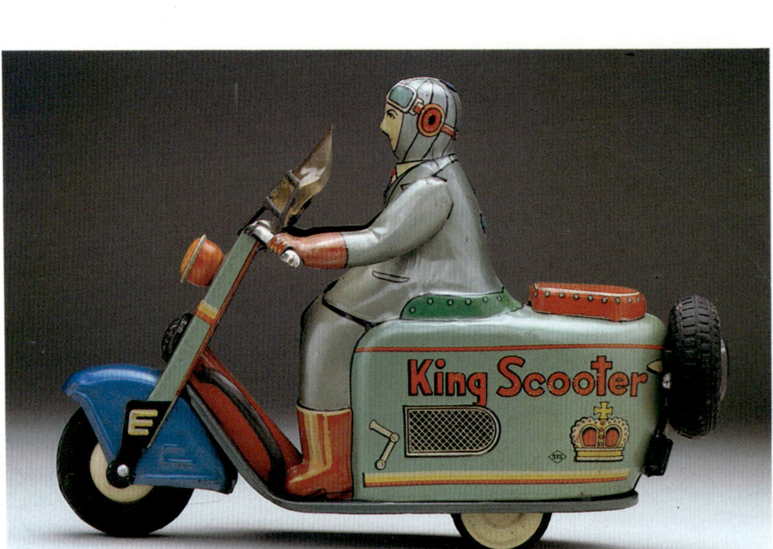

(221) 1950'S／SCOOTER／YONEZAWA
225×55×155

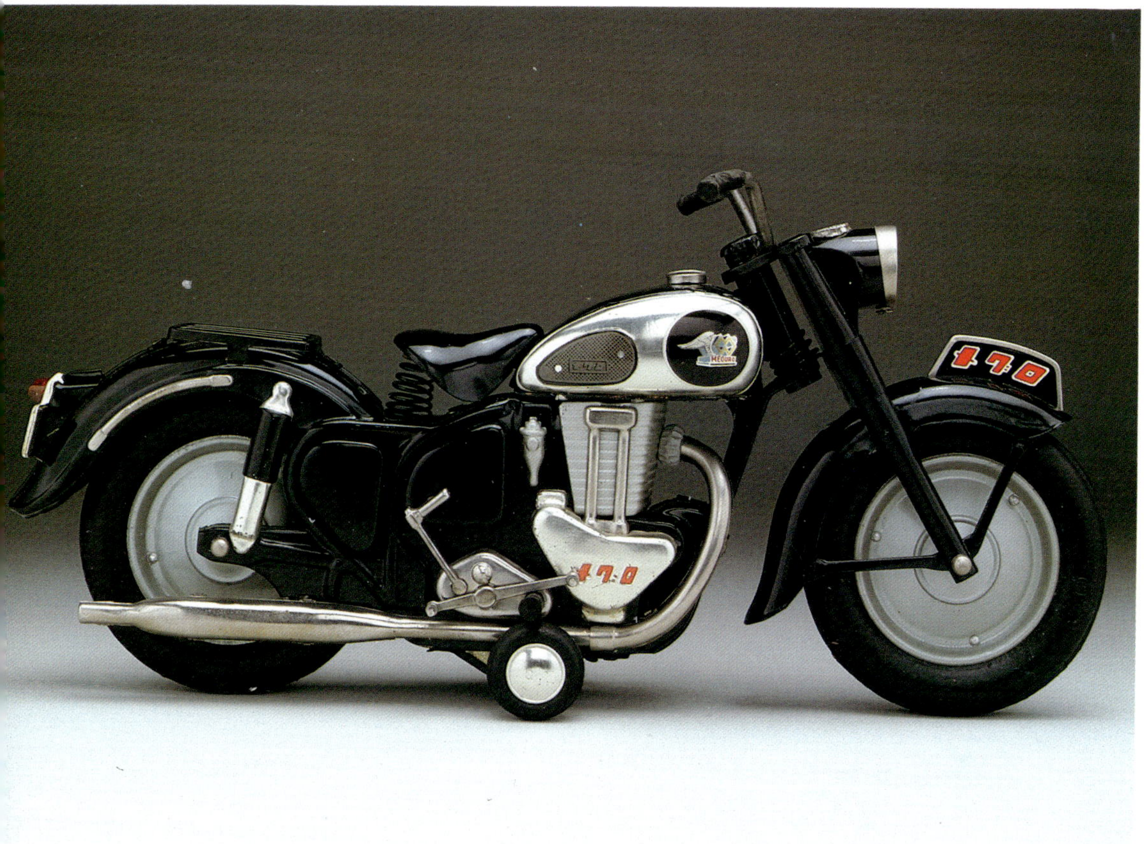

㉒ 1950'S／MOTORBIKE MODEL:MEGURO／BANDAI／300×130×147

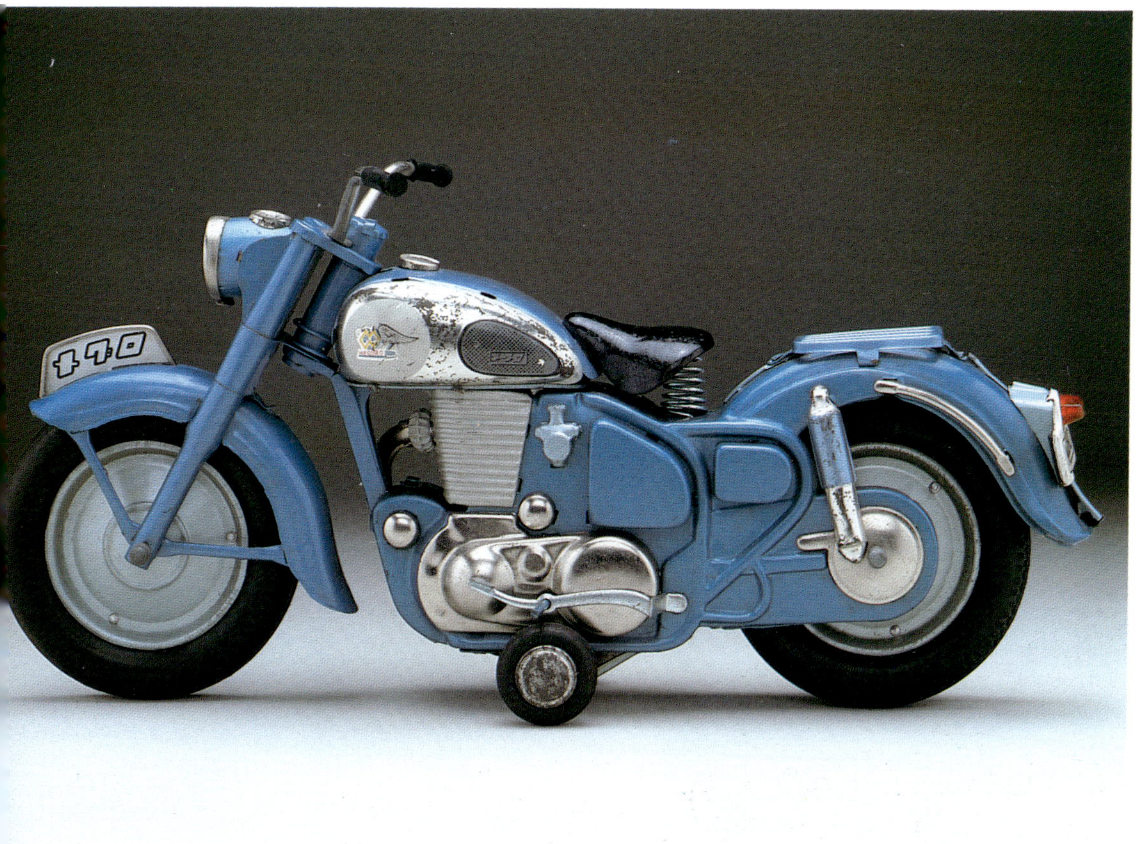

㉓ 1950'S／MOTORBIKE MODEL:MEGURO／BANDAI／300×130×147

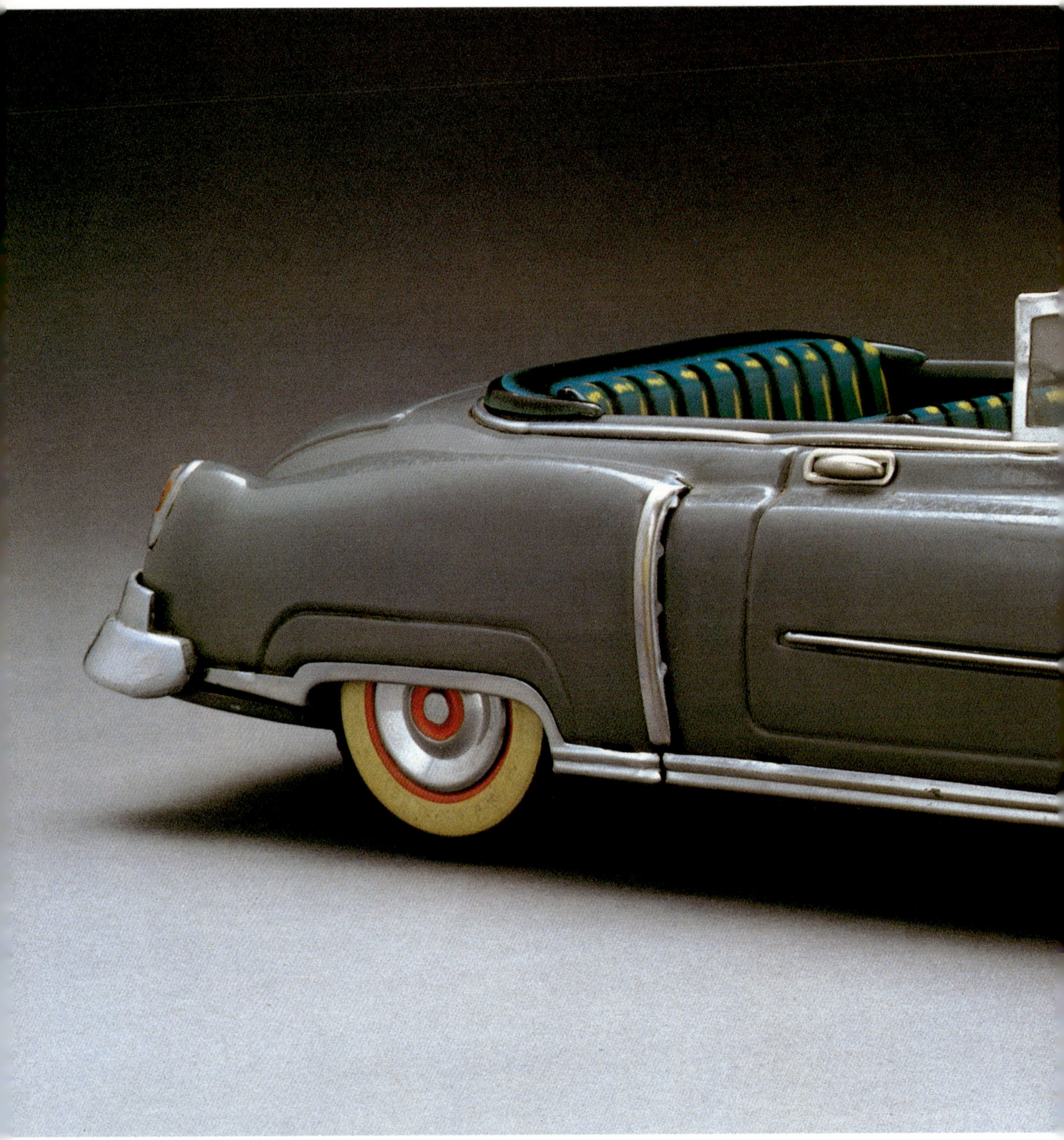

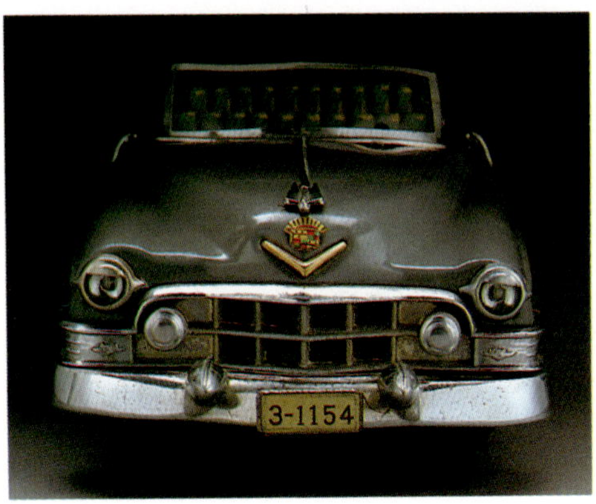

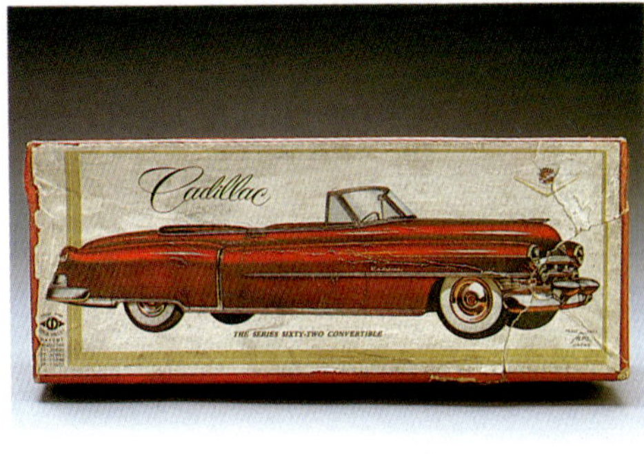

CASE ATTACHED

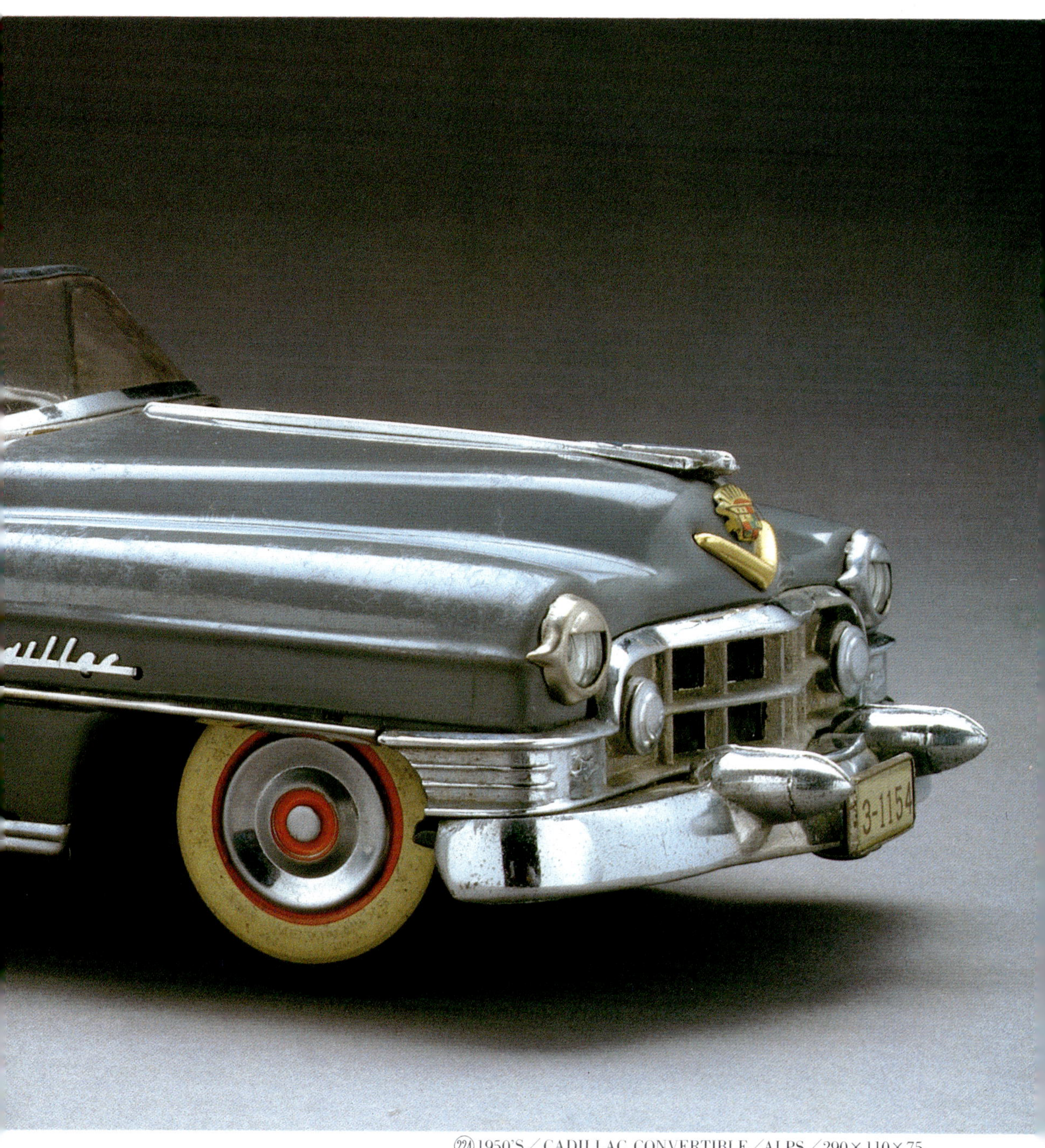

(224) 1950'S／CADILLAC CONVERTIBLE／ALPS／290×110×75

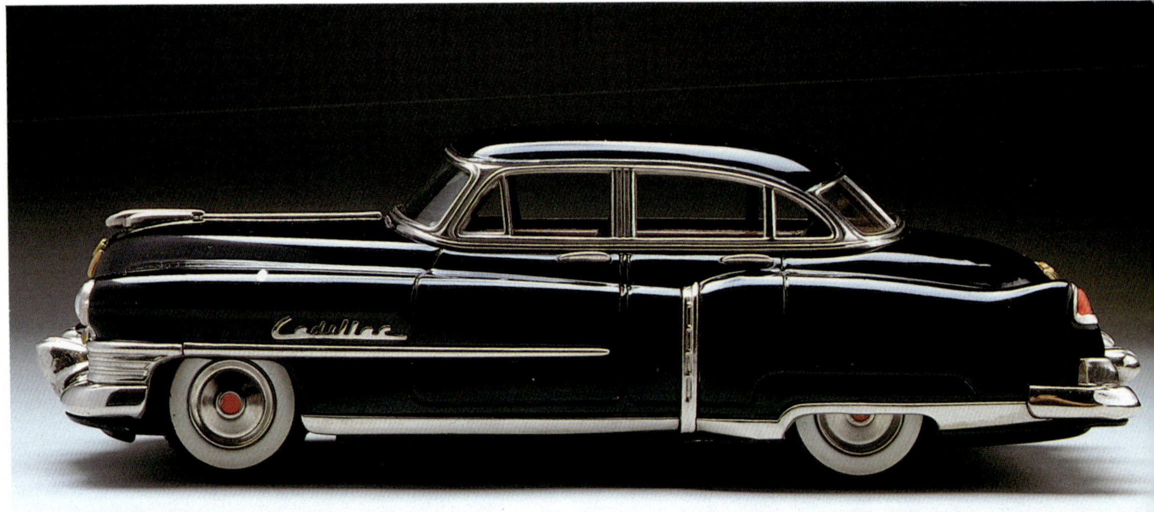

㉒⑤ 1950'S／CADILLAC／MARUSAN／310×125×95

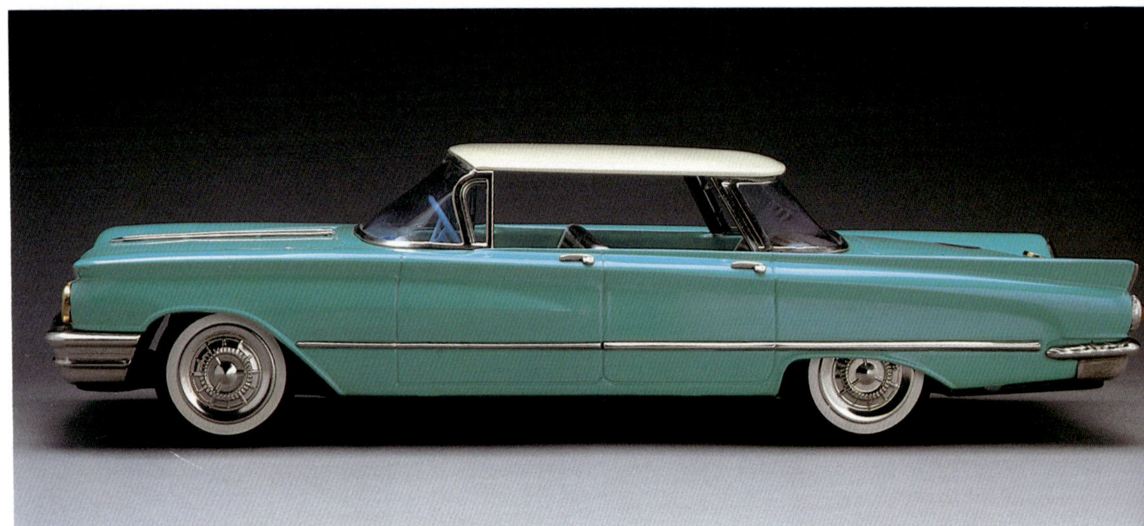

㉒⑥ 1960'S／BUICK／ICHIKO／455×165×110

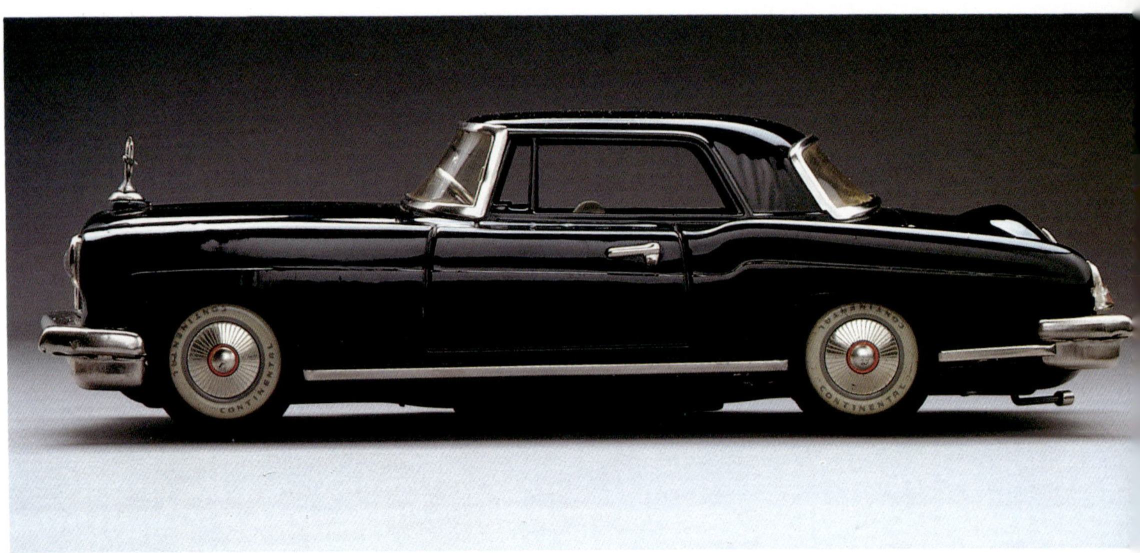

㉒⑦ 1950'S／LINCOLN CONTINENTAL／LINE MAR／290×105×80

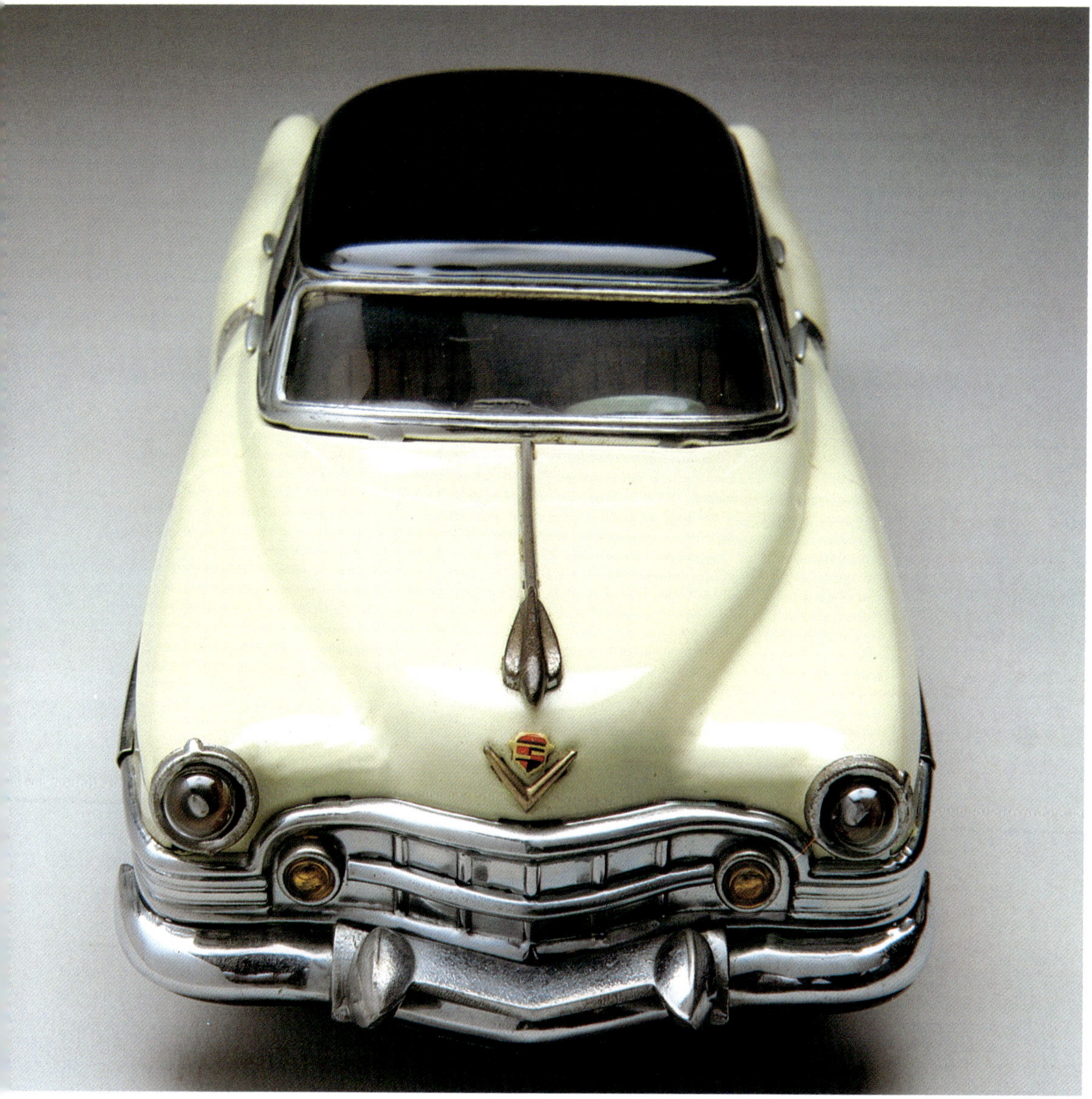

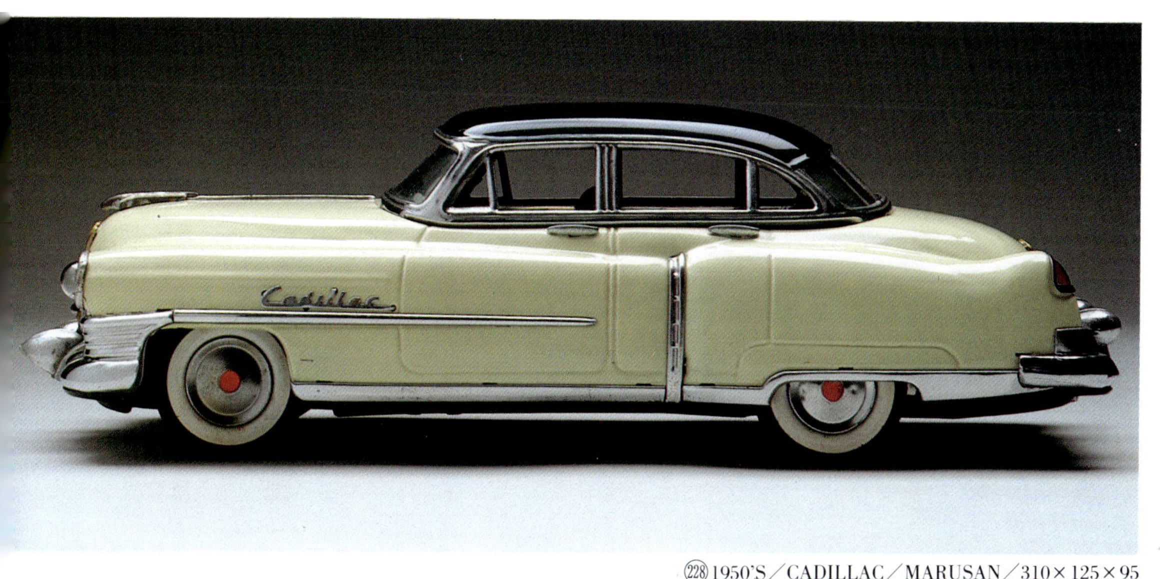

(228) 1950'S／CADILLAC／MARUSAN／310×125×95

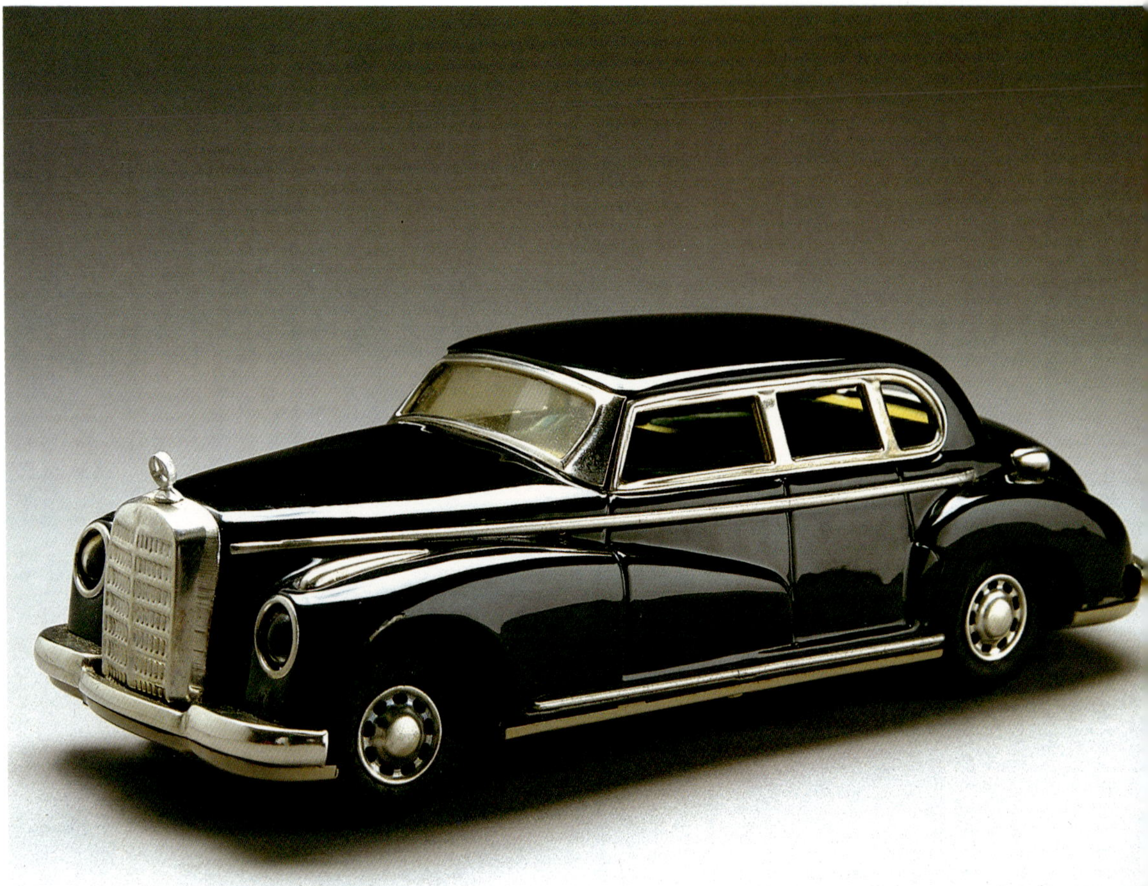

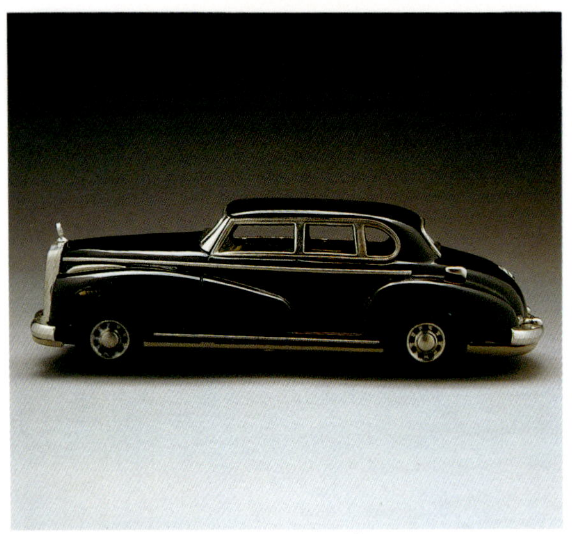

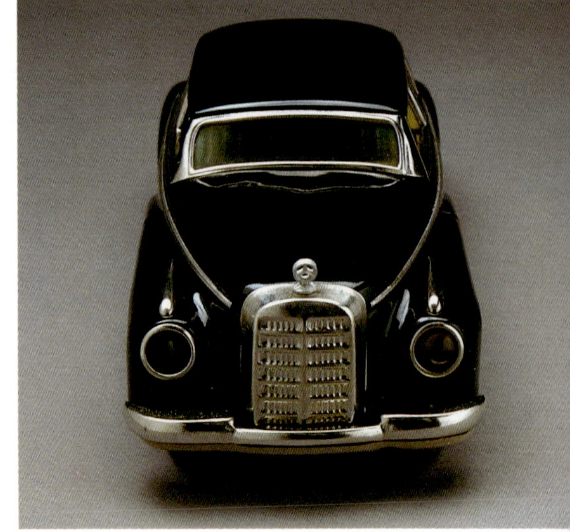

(229) 1950'S／MERCEDES BENZ／ALPS／240×95×75

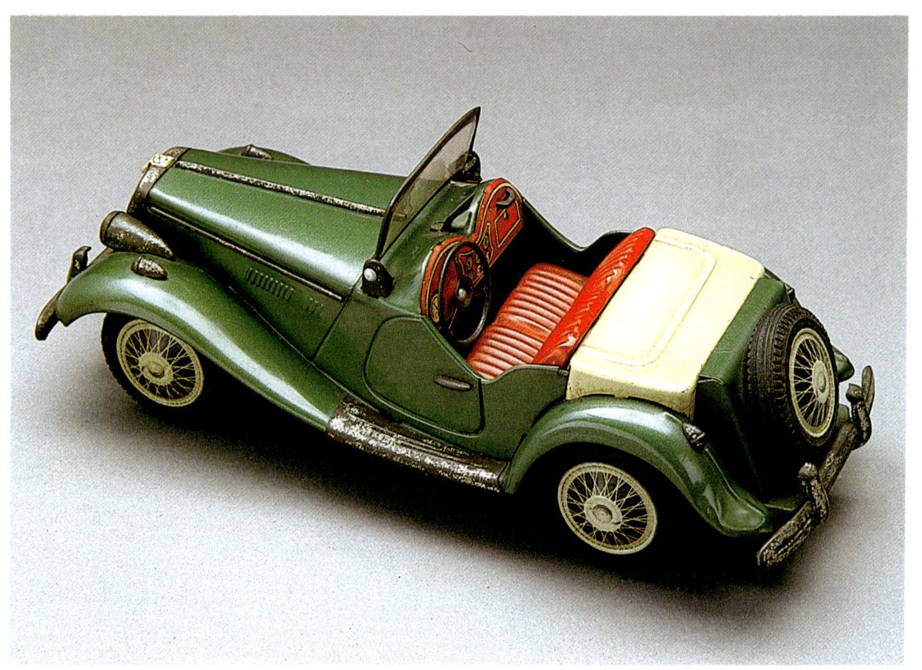

(230) 1950'S／M. G.／BANDAI／210×85×80

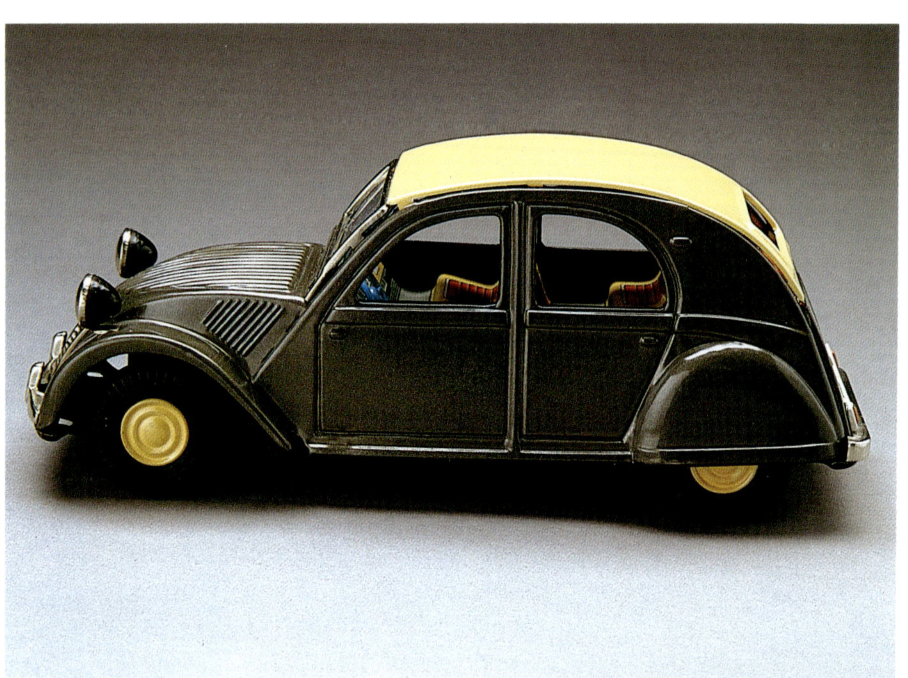

(231) 1950'S／CITROEN 2CV／DAIYA／210×75×80

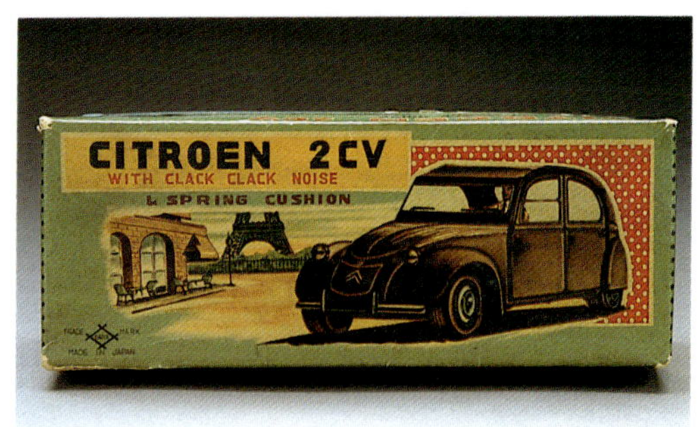

CASE ATTACHED

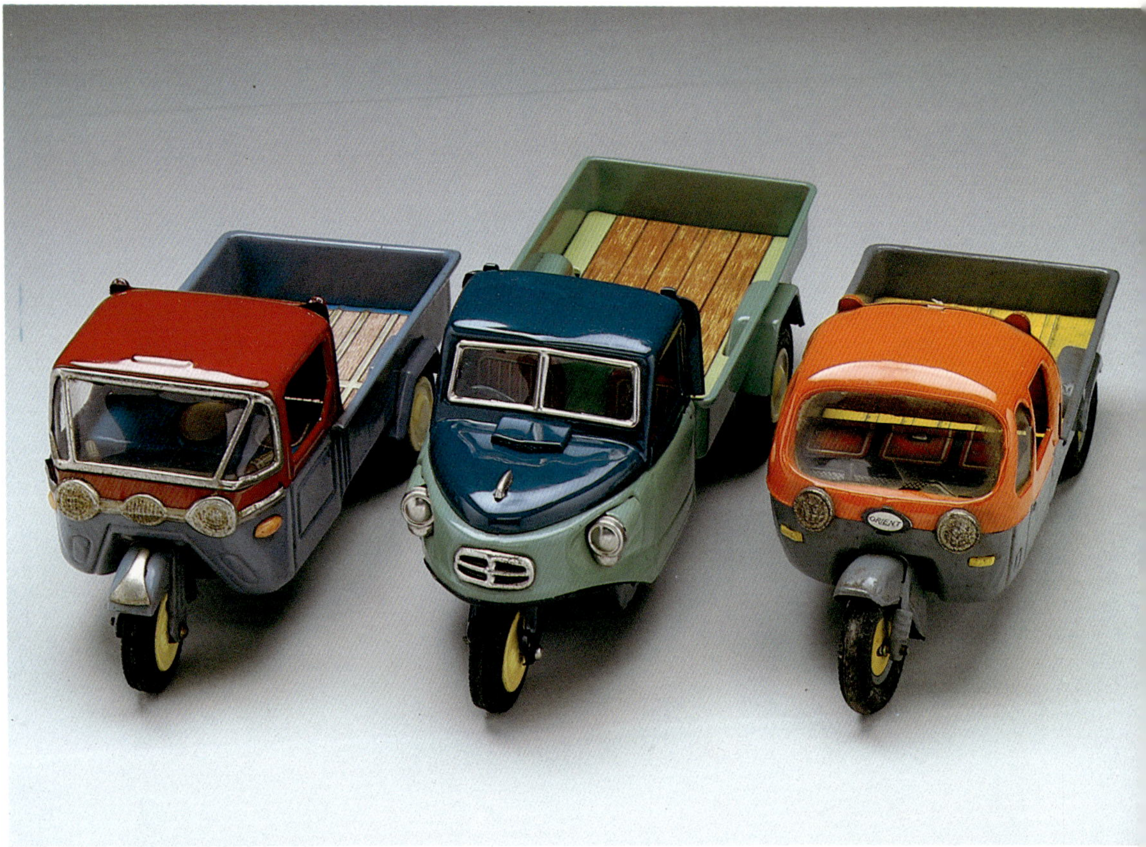

(232)(233)(234) 1950'S／AUTO TRICYCLE／BANDAI, BANDAI, YONEZAWA／210×95×90, 260×95×100, 225×85×90

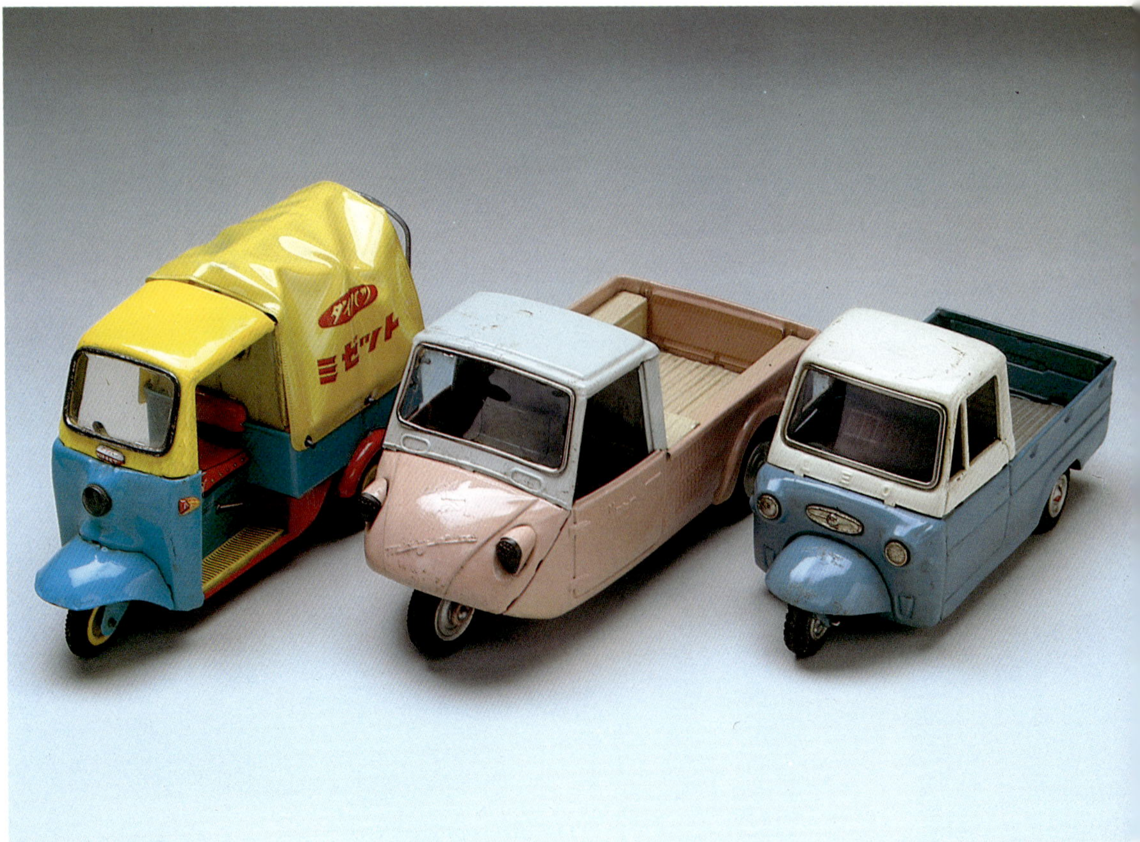

(235)(236)(237) 1950'S／AUTO TRICYCLE／KOKYU SHOKAI, BANDAI, BANDAI／165×70×95, 190×85×88, 155×70×85

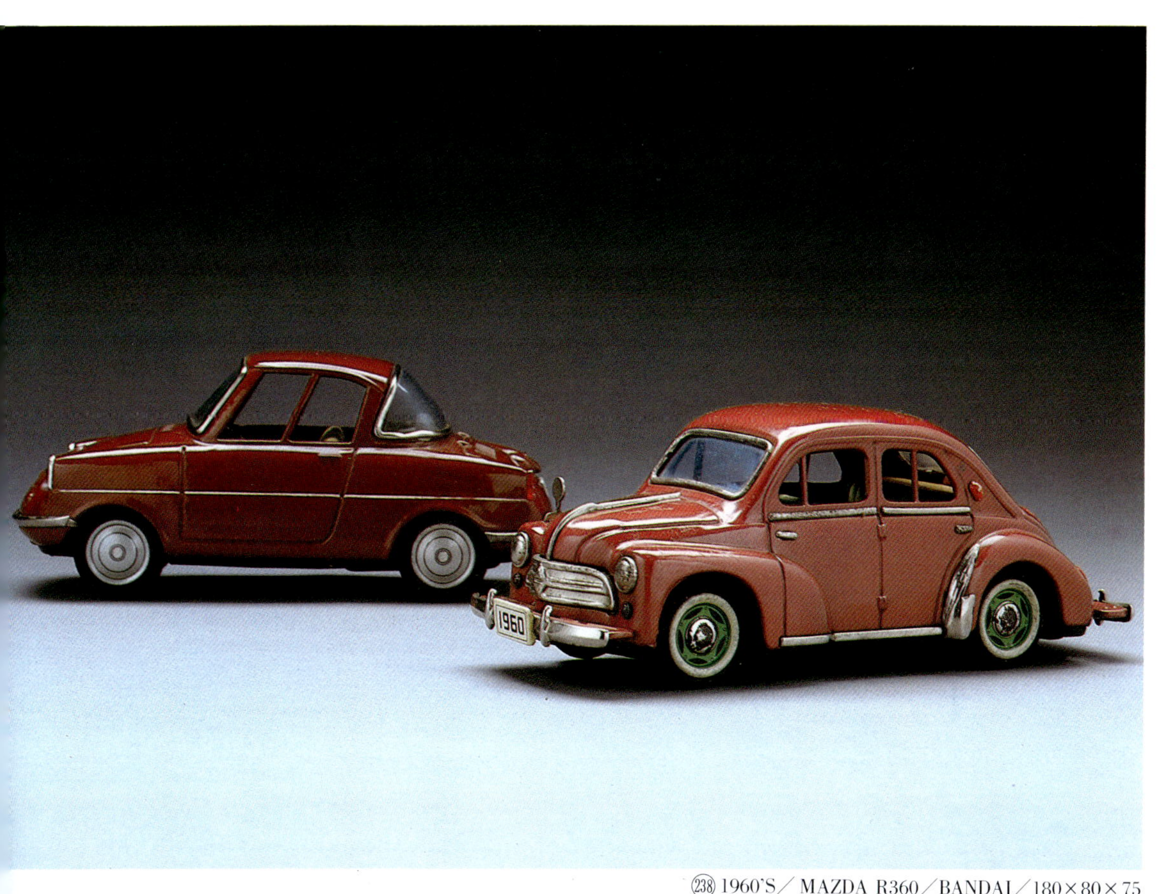

(238) 1960'S／MAZDA R360／BANDAI／180×80×75
(239) 1950'S／RENAULT／YONEZAWA／195×75×70

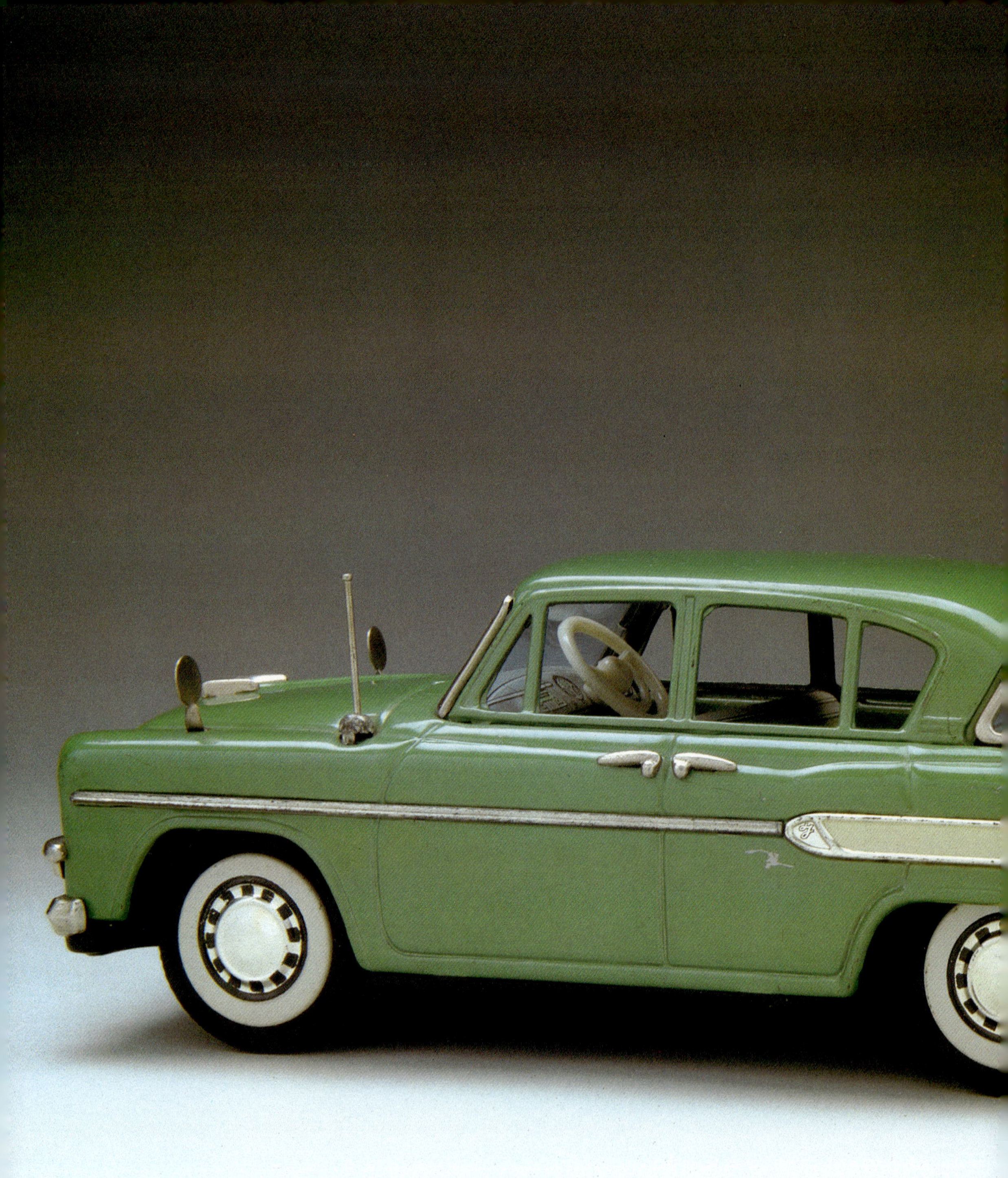

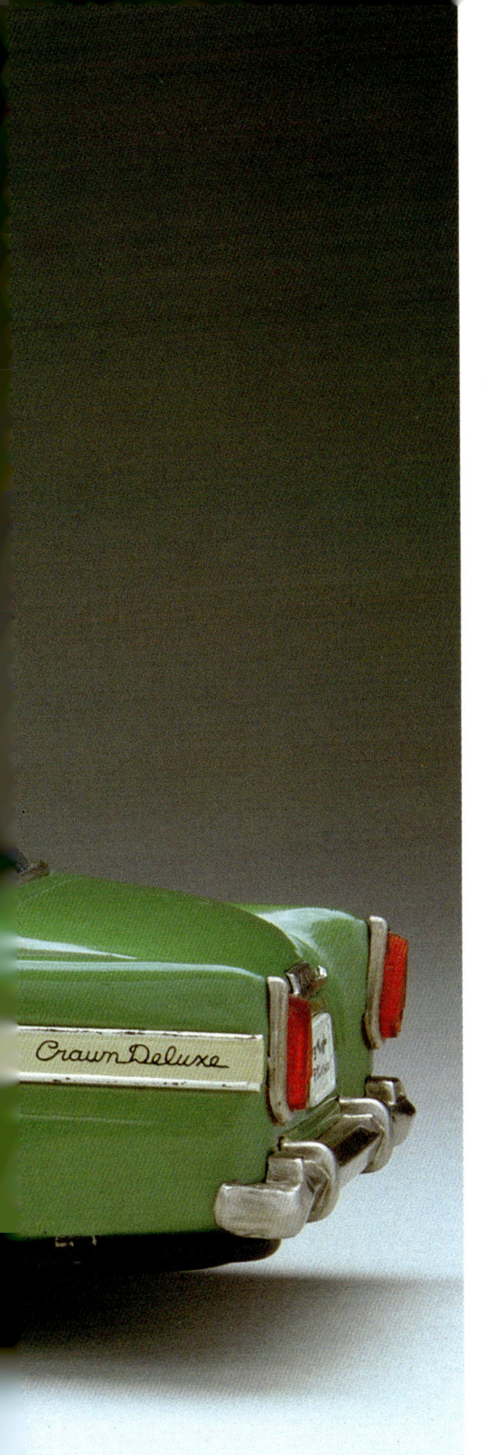

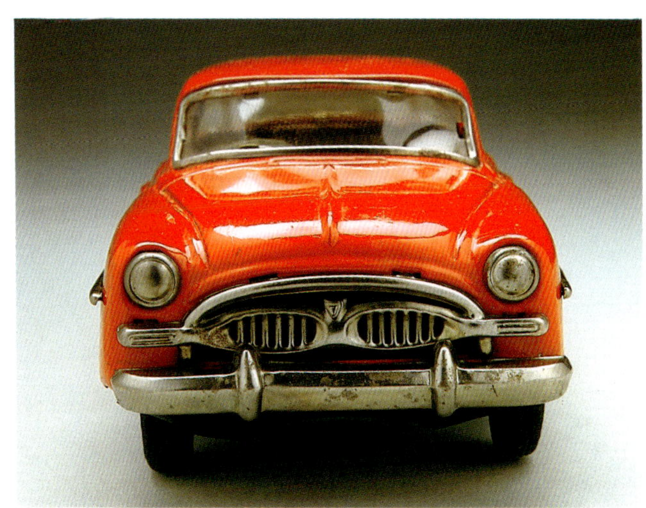

(241) 1950'S／TOYOTA CROWN／BANDAI／207×75×69

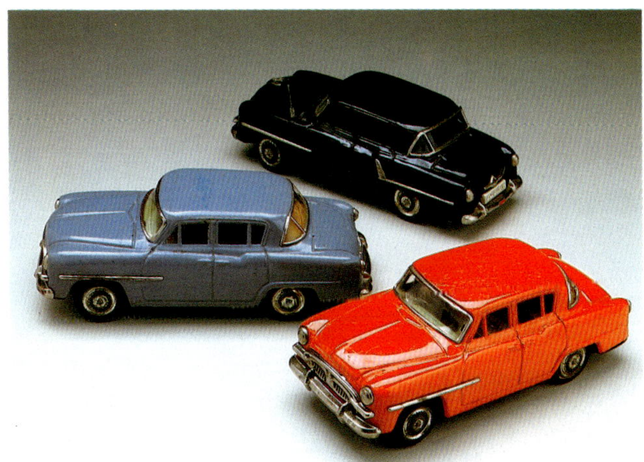

(242) 1950'S／TOYOTA CROWN／BANDAI／207×75×69
(243) 1950'S／TOYOTA CROWN／ASAHI／206×80×70

(240) 1950'S／TOYOTA CROWN／BANDAI／230×90×78

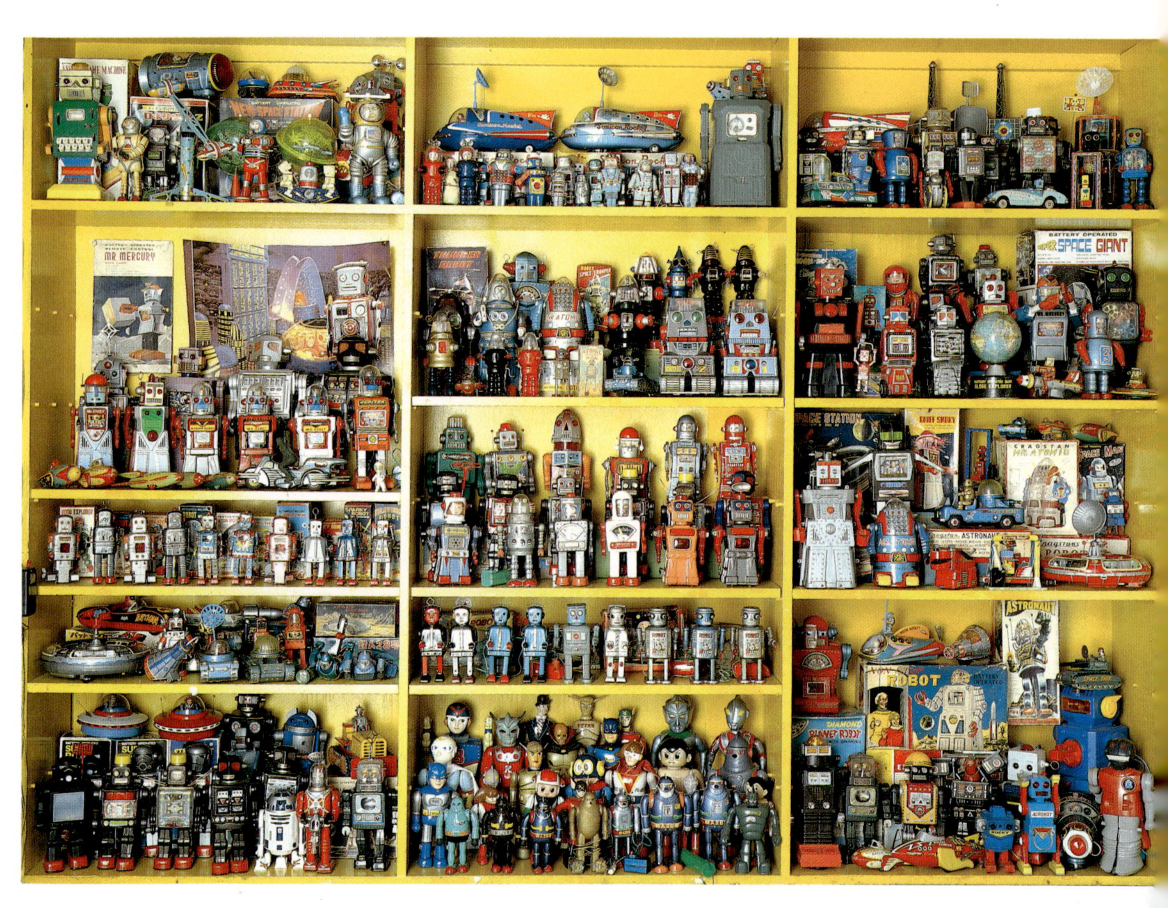

(244) OCCUPIED JAPAN ／ROBOT AND ITS CASE／UNKNOWN／40×60×12

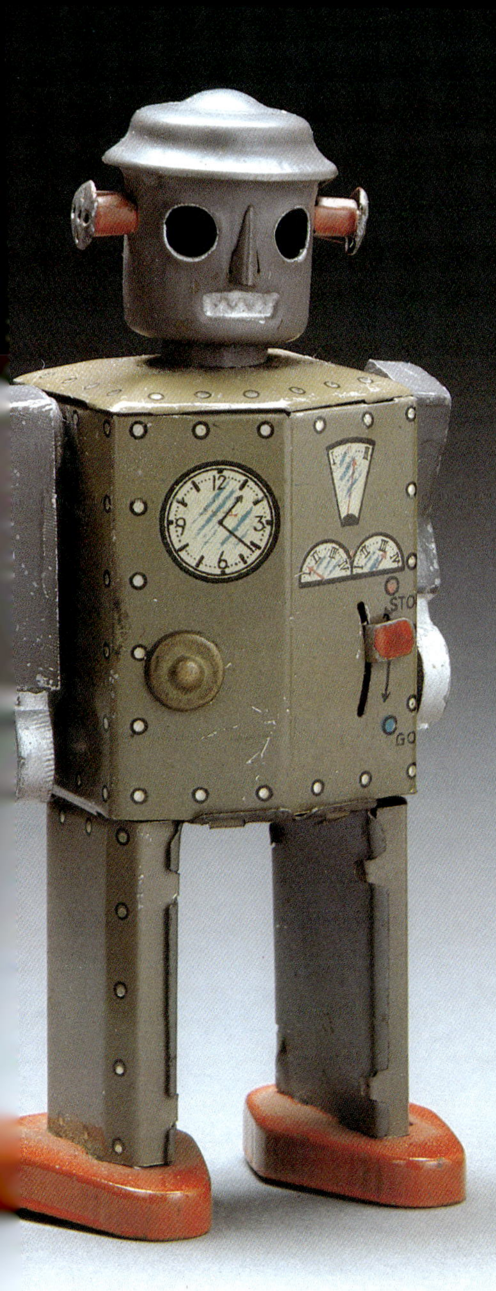
GO
ATOMIC
ROBOT
MAN

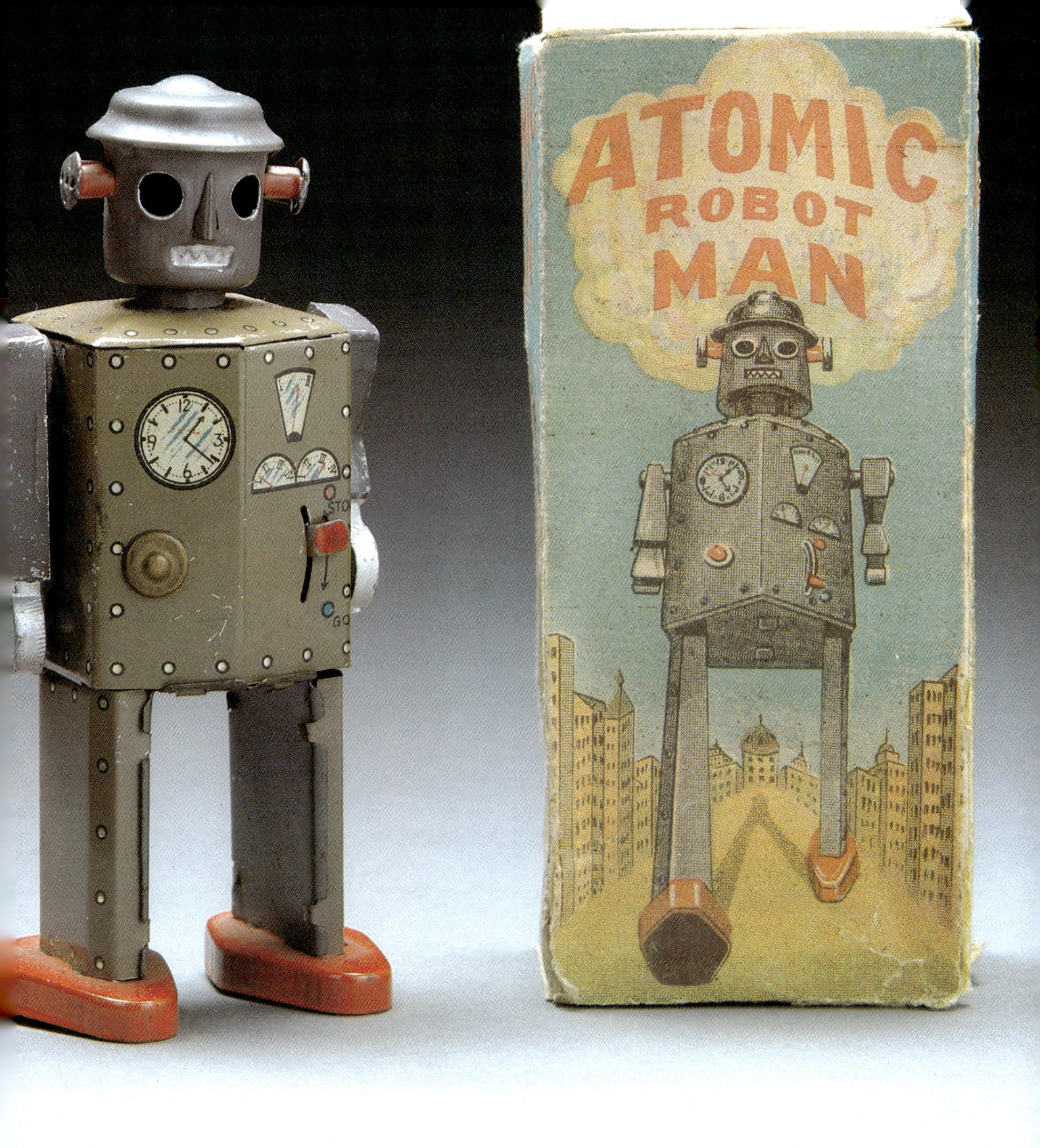

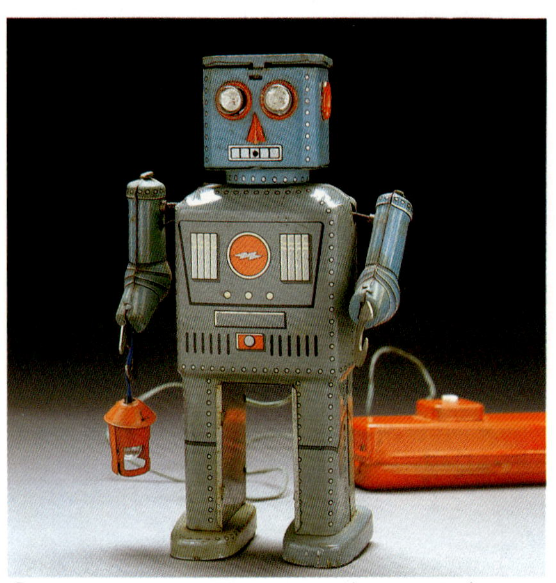

(245) 1950'S／ROBOT WITH LANTERN／LINE MAR／90×115×200

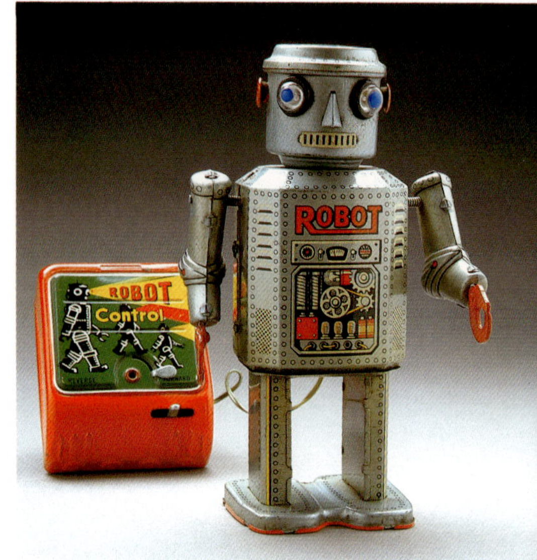

(246) 1950'S／ROBOT／MASUDAYA／80×115×190

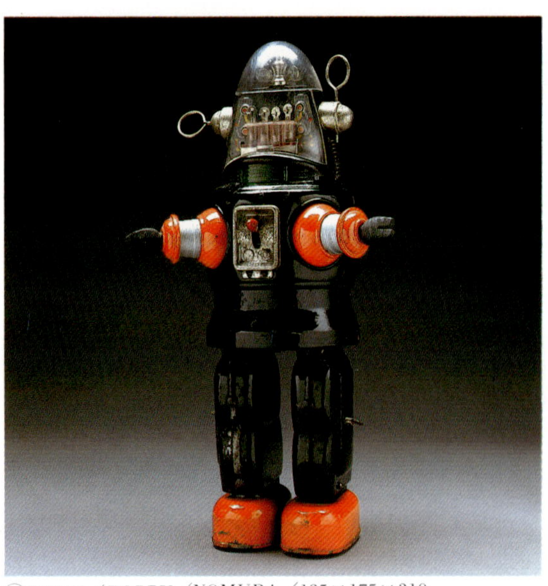

(247) 1950'S／ROBBY／NOMURA／135×175×310

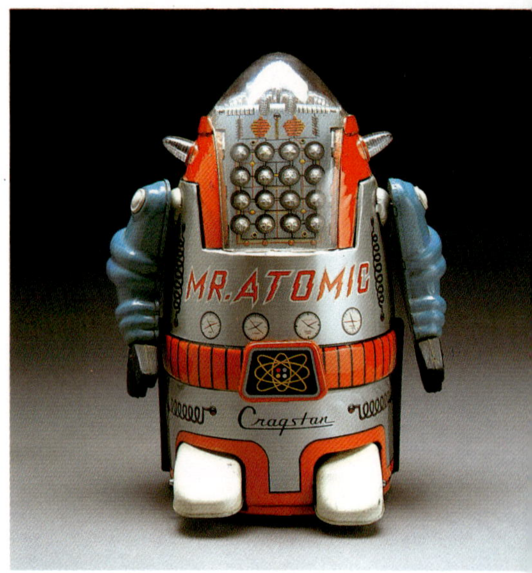

(248) 1950'S／MR. ATOMIC／YONEZAWA／160×160×225

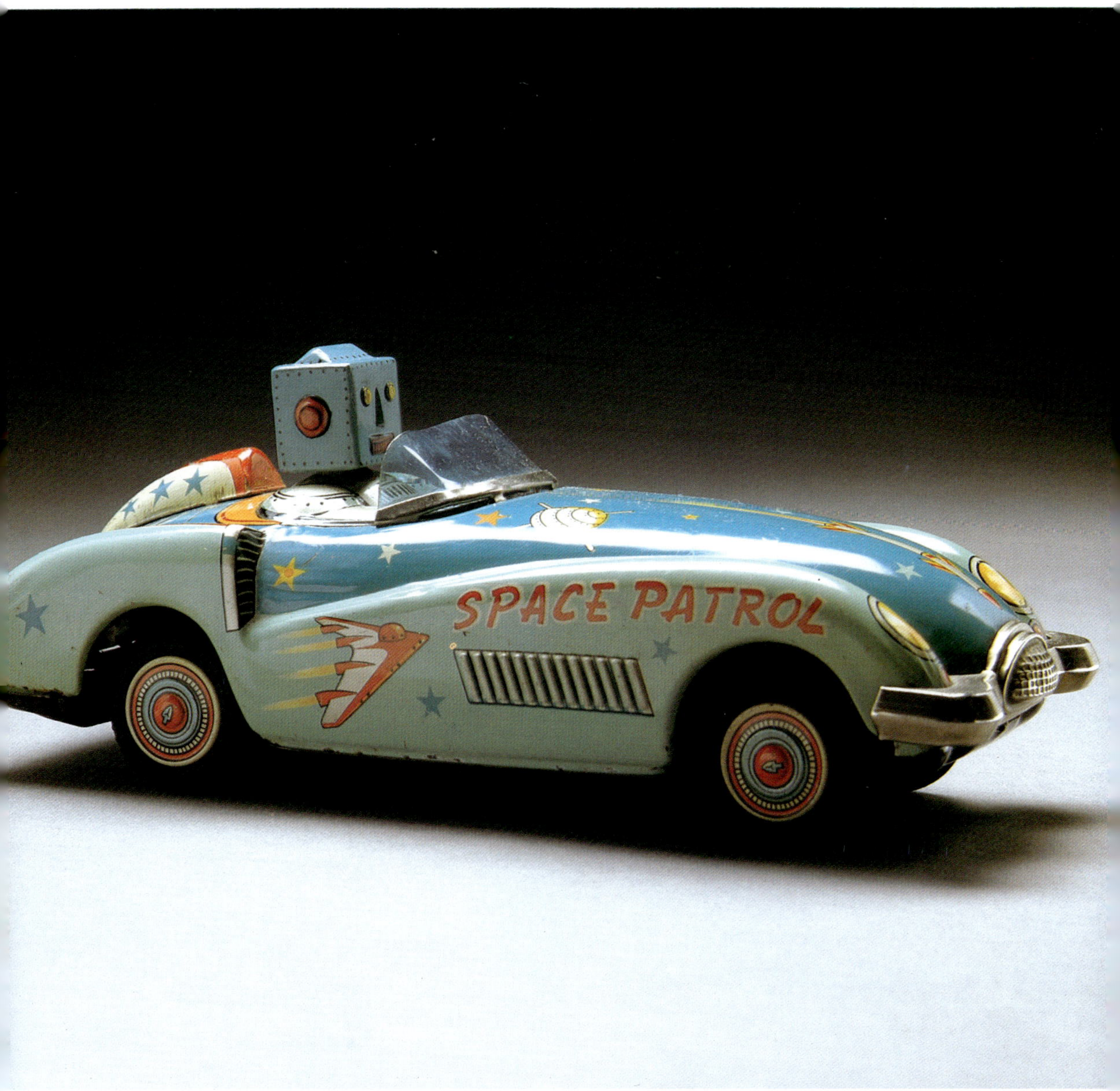

(249) 1950'S／ROBOT AND HIS CAR／ICHIKO／217×85×82

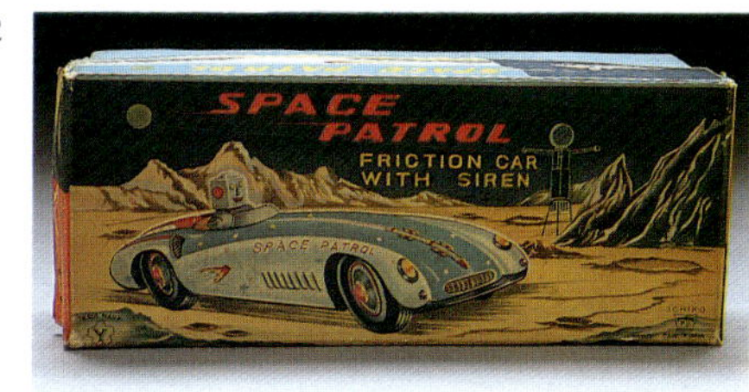

CASE ATTACHED

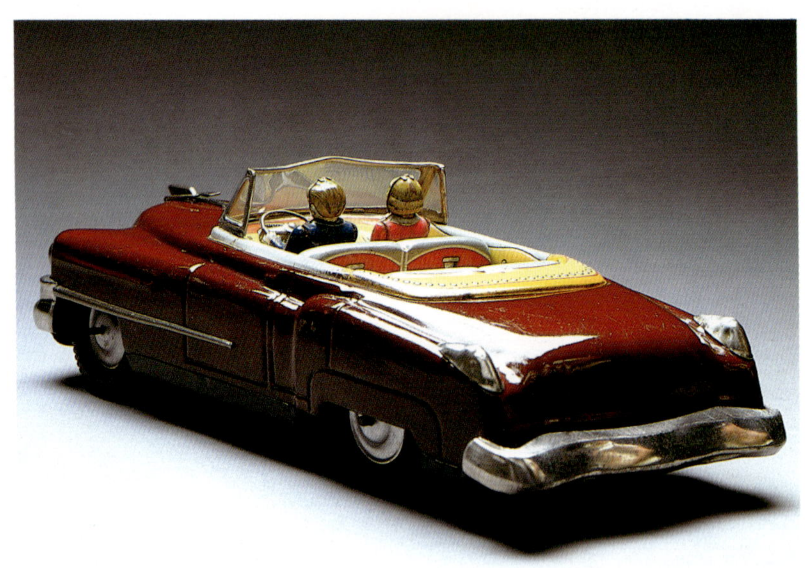

(250) 1950'S／CADILLAC CONVERTIBLE／NOMURA／340×150×105

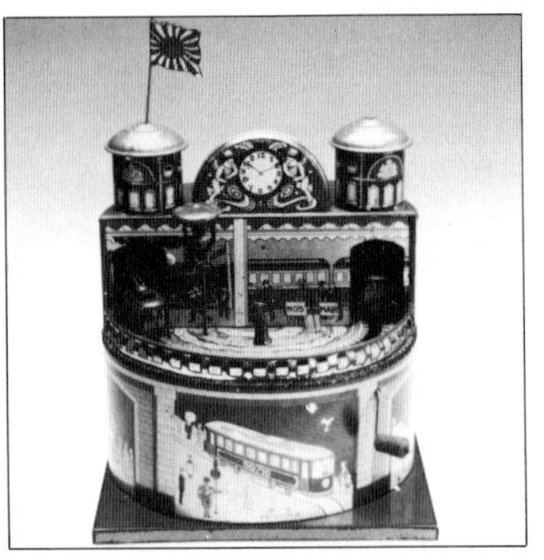

1. **Street Cars** (Unknown) page 3
Manual. A tinplate chronicle of a rapidly changing Japan: the crank turns and moves the trolleys through a tunnel and past scenes of the early 1900s, including a laborer carrying a sack of rice and a policeman on horseback.

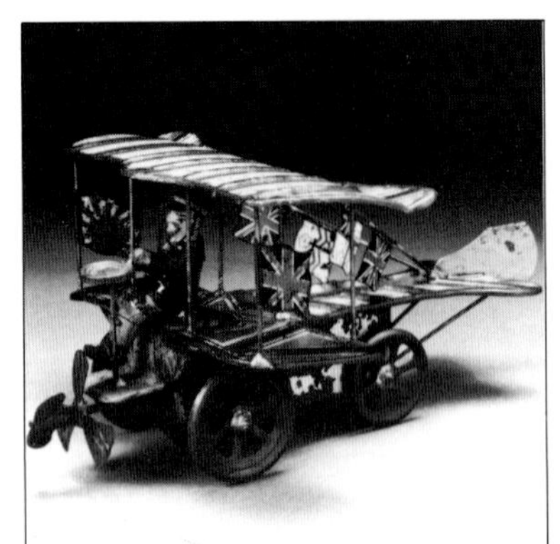

2. **Biplane** (Unknown) page 4
Spring mechanism. Metal tabs and slots for assembly had yet to be invented when this toy was made; all parts are soldered together. Note the wire spring, the absence of a cockpit, and the Union Jacks flying from the wings.

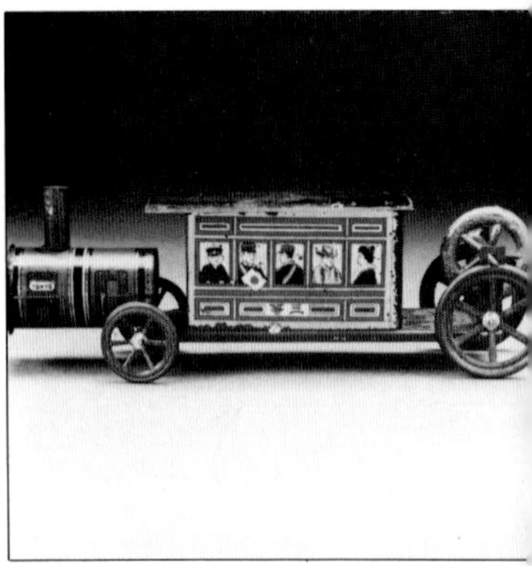

3. **Steam Locomotive** (Unknown) page 5
Friction. This is the oldest toy in the book and predates clockwork toys. It is simply constructed but captures the feeling of the mid-and late 1800s in Japan: the traditional hairstyles and dress of passengers in a third-class coach; little boys waving two versions of the national flag.

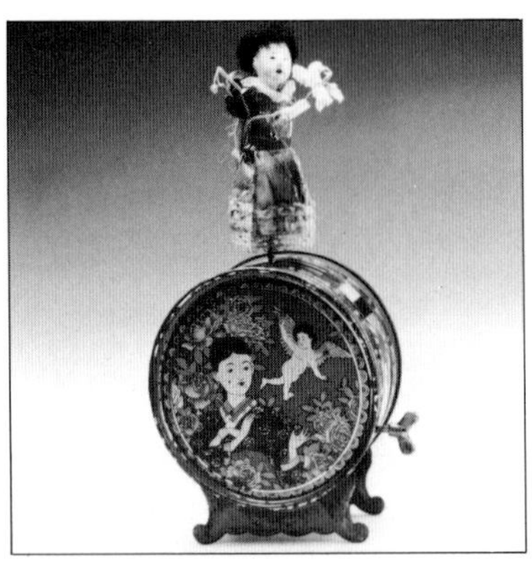

9. **Doll upon Drum** (Namiki) page 8
Spring mechanism. The little doll twirls while the drum beats. Her face and hands are made of paste and sawdust, but the rest of the toy is tinplate. Flags, including those of Great Britain and Germany, decorate the side of the drum.

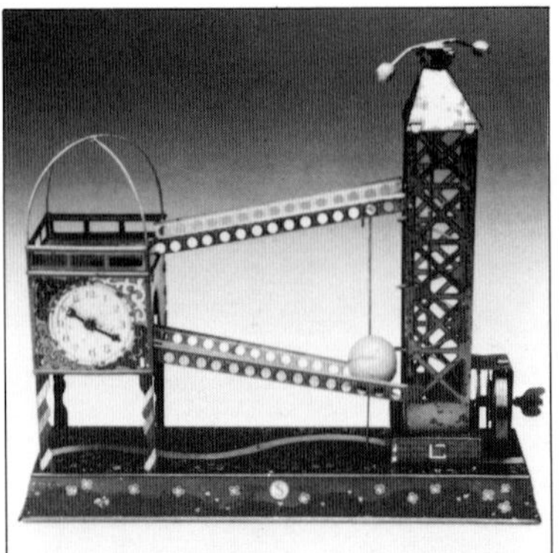

15. **Ball Escalator** (Unknown) page 10
Spring mechanism. In the 1920s this toy was in big demand. The ball climbs the tower by means of a rotating wire spiral. Once at the top it rolls down the chute, falling into a clock tower midway and moving the hands of the clock.

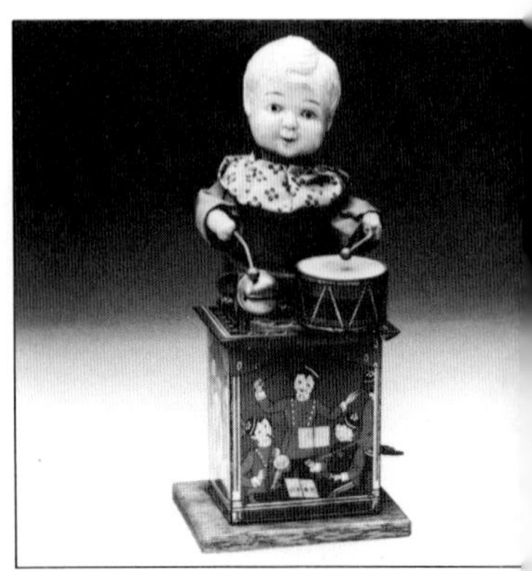

18. **Drummer** (Unknown) page 11
Spring mechanism. The bell and drum are struck rhythmically, if not melodically. This celluloid, wood, and tinplate toy was acquired through persistence, passing through three collections before the author acquired it.